1496/02

W9-CJF-596

How is theology liberating? In the context of a post-Gorbachev world, where many demand freedom, but which the Western powers seem ill-equipped to deliver, is it even possible to envisage a liberative theology? Taking as his starting point the Marxist complaint that Christianity is ideological, Peter Scott argues that it is not enough for Christian theology to talk about liberation: it must *be* liberative. Stressing with feminist and liberation theologies the embodied, contextual nature of theology, the constructive proposal made here locates God's liberating abundance towards society in an interpretation of resurrection as social. Only in this way, in the author's view, can a trinitarian Christian account of liberation be adequately grounded. This book will be of interest to all those who wish to know if theology may speak truthfully about the transformation of society: it offers the shape of a liberative theology which points towards social freedom.

CAMBRIDGE STUDIES IN
IDEOLOGY AND RELIGION 6

THEOLOGY, IDEOLOGY AND LIBERATION

CAMBRIDGE STUDIES IN IDEOLOGY AND RELIGION

General Editors: DUNCAN FORRESTER *and* ALISTAIR KEE

Editorial Board: JOSÉ MÍGUEZ BONINO, REBECCA S. CHOPP, JOHN DE GRUCHY, GRAHAM HOWES, YEOW CHOO LAK, DAVID MCLELLAN, KENNETH MEDHURST, RAYMOND PLANT, CHRISTOPHER ROWLAND, ELISABETH SCHÜSSLER-FIORENZA, CHARLES VILLA-VICENCIO, HADDON WILLMER

Religion increasingly is seen as a renewed force, and is recognised as an important factor in the modern world in all aspects of life – cultural, economic, and political. It is no longer a matter of surprise to find religious factors at work in areas and situations of political tension. However, our information about these situations has tended to come from two main sources. The news-gathering agencies are well placed to convey information, but are hampered by the fact that their representatives are not equipped to provide analysis of the religious forces involved. Alternatively, the movements generate their own accounts, which understandably seem less than objective to outside observers. There is no lack of information or factual material, but a real need for sound academic analysis. Cambridge Studies in Ideology and Religion will meet this need. It will give an objective, balanced, and programmatic coverage to issues which – while of wide potential interest – have been largely neglected by analytical investigation, apart from the appearance of sporadic individual studies. Intended to enable debate to proceed at a higher level, the series should lead to a new phase in our understanding of the relationship between ideology and religion.

A list of titles in the series is given at the end of the book.

THEOLOGY, IDEOLOGY AND LIBERATION

Towards a liberative theology

PETER SCOTT

Lecturer in Theology,
Cheltenham and Gloucester College of Higher Education

Published by the Press Syndicate of the University of Cambridge
The Pitt Building, Trumpington Street, Cambridge CB2 1RP
40 West 20th Street, New York, NY 10011–4211, USA
10 Stamford Road, Oakleigh, Melbourne 3166, Australia

© Cambridge University Press 1994

First published 1994

Printed in Great Britain at the University Press, Cambridge

A catalogue record for this book is available from the British Library

Library of Congress cataloguing in publication data

Scott, Peter, 1961–
Theology, ideology and liberation: towards a liberative theology
/ Peter Scott.
p.   cm. – (Cambridge studies in ideology and religion)
Includes bibliographical references and index.
ISBN 0 521 46476 5 (hardback)
1. Sociology, Christian. 2. Idolatry. 3. Ideology – Religious
aspects – Christianity. 4. Liberation theology. I. Title.
II. Series.
BT738.S394   1995
230′.046 – dc20 93–51059 CIP

ISBN 0 521 46476 5 hardback

CE

For Amanda,
with thanks for so much

Contents

General editors' preface

In the early 1970s it was widely assumed that religion had lost its previous place in Western culture and that this pattern would spread throughout the world. Since then religion has become a renewed force, recognised as an important factor in the modern world in all aspects of life, cultural, economic and political. This is true not only of the Third World, but in Europe East and West, and in North America. It is no longer a surprise to find a religious factor at work in areas of political tension.

Religion and ideology form a mixture which can be of interest to the observer, but in practice dangerous and explosive. Our information about such matters comes for the most part from three types of sources. The first is the media which understandably tend to concentrate on newsworthy events, without taking the time to deal with the underlying issues of which they are but symptoms. The second source comprises studies by social scientists who often adopt a functionalist and reductionist view of the faith and beliefs which motivate those directly involved in such situations. Finally, there are the statements and writings of those committed to the religious or ideological movements themselves. We seldom lack information, but there is a need – often an urgent need – for sound objective analysis which can make use of the best contemporary approaches to both politics and religion. Cambridge Studies in Ideology and Religion is designed to meet this need.

The subject matter is global and this will be reflected in the choice both of topics and authors. The initial volumes will be concerned primarily with movements involving the Christian religion, but as the series becomes established movements involving other world religions will be subjected to the same objective critical analysis. In all cases it is our intention that an accurate and sensitive account of religion should be informed by an objective and sophisticated application of perspectives from the social sciences.

In this book Dr Scott addresses the question whether Christian theology can be other than alienating and oppressive. This leads into a sustained debate with the Marxist critique of ideology, and with varying theological responses. But the main thrust of the argument is forward-looking, examining carefully and critically the possible shape of a Christian theology that is liberative. The argument is controversial, and will be a significant contribution to a contemporary debate.

DUNCAN FORRESTER AND ALISTAIR KEE

New College, University of Edinburgh

Preface

I first became interested in the relation between theology and
society more than ten years ago. But that is merely to mark the
chronology, and not the investment. In the writing of this
book, I have been seeking to show for myself the liberative
character of Christian theology. Such is the personal nature of
the investment. The argument has taken me in unexpected
directions. (Indeed, this version is very different from a previous attempt.) During this process, I have often had my
expectations disconfirmed and connections, previously taken
for granted, put into question. That perhaps is how it should
be: if the basic dynamic of this book is a critique of idolatry,
there is no reason why its author should be free from its
criticism.

In developing this interest I have accrued many debts.
Indeed, it is difficult cheerfully to write a book on theology and
ideology without realising the very particular nature of such
debts: as a guard, in my own writing, against ideology. In the
first instance, I am grateful to Rex Ambler for helping me to
see, just as I was about to set out in a very different (ideological!) direction, the theological importance of the issues
raised here. Denys Turner supervised my initial research in
theology and ideology; his influence can be traced throughout
the text. I am grateful for his support and encouragement
through many conversations. He has also read parts of the text
– as has David McLellan, who has also encouraged me in my
writing. I am grateful to both of them for their comments.
They have tried to get me to write a better book; I hope that
they will not be too disappointed. Alistair McFadyen has

responded to the rehearsal of the themes of this book more times than can have been good for him. Such conversations have been important in the development of my thinking, and his willingness to engage with my concerns marks him as a friend as well as a partner in conversation.

I owe a rather different sort of debt to my colleague, Stanley Rudman, who has, in many practical ways, enabled me to complete this book. I am grateful also to Alex Wright of Cambridge University Press for pursuing this book with calm efficiency through its trials and tribulations.

Lastly, I wish to acknowledge a special debt to Amanda Pitt, my wife. She, in times that were busy enough for her, has encouraged me both to start and finish this book. Through this, she has put up with many things: my absences, on occasions (I regret to say) my presence, and my cooking. To her this book is dedicated.

PETER SCOTT
Bristol

Introduction

This book is about the liberation of theology from ideology. It seeks to discern whether theology is the critic of the eclipse of God or an unwitting contributor to that very eclipse. My main concern is with the question: how might theology be non-ideological? This is no academic matter. Ideological strategies are those which effectively obscure, mis-speak or misrecognise the social history of which they are a part. If we cannot be sure that theology may speak non-ideologically, then we cannot be sure that theology is the critic, rather than the apologist, of society.

But who comprises this 'society'? 'We' are those who inhabit the dominant 'centre' of this global society, and whose activities, as Enrique Dussel (1985) suggests, shape the activities of those on the periphery (whether intentionally or not). My question then is asked from the centre, and is directed to the centre. But what theological word should be spoken from the centre?

The urgency of this matter lies in the problems currently facing Western society and that Christianity claims to speak a message of hope. On the one hand, this society is undergoing its own profound difficulties regarding its relations with external nature, its relations with the periphery, and the attempt to secure over again its global economic dominance. The 'subjective' outworking of this is a suspicion regarding our institutions and democratic processes, even our immediate relationships, and a concern as to whether the complexities of our situation can be addressed.

On the other hand, Christianity speaks a message of hope.

Yet here lies the rub for it is not clear, both to Christian communities and beyond, whether this message is relevant. Christianity speaks of freedom, but is it an account of freedom that engages with social freedom? Can Christianity speak so that it might be heard? Can the message of hope, of the Word enfleshed, be received, or is there too much static on the line? Or indeed, is Christianity, as some report, concerned rather with 'religious subjectivity', with support for the individual amid the contingencies of life? (Christianity does seem, on too many occasions, to have chosen the side of reaction rather than liberation.)

At stake here is whether we may trust our constructive theological work, or whether theology is already 'placed' as an unwitting contributor to processes of legitimation. I think that this is the central issue facing Christian communities both in themselves and in their witness to wider society. Do we speak of a God of freedom who engages with human beings in the demand to extend social freedom? Or something else? The issue is not really the survival of Christianity in this modern, or, indeed, postmodern world. The issue is rather: can Christianity speak to this world?

For the task of theological discernment even to begin, we need some confidence that theology is not ideological. What it might mean for theology to be non-ideological, and how the task of theological discernment might be possible, is the argument of the following chapters. I wish to stress that this is not a matter simply of investing theology with some political interests, but of rethinking theology against the epistemological critique of ideology, of exploring theological protocols against the eclipse of God in ideology.

The dominant concern of this book is to set out one response to this set of questions. The only way that Christianity's message of hope and freedom can be heard is, I argue, through a sustained engagement with the critique of ideology. This is ironic indeed. In a post-Gorbachev world, I am suggesting that we need to employ Marxist materials in order to secure the relevance of Christianity.

Although Marxism is important to my argument, this is not

a revival of the Christian–Marxist dialogue. In some ways, the following has affinities with Latin American liberation theology and the political side of feminist theology, although I concentrate on one issue – ideology – and develop a somewhat different methodology and structure. I also hope to offer a theological response that is systematic in scope if not in execution. It is this thoroughly theological response, whether persuasive or not, which will, I hope, be of some interest. This response is, I contend, a matter of engaging at the centre of theological construction with the critique of ideology. Indeed, crucial to the later stages of my argument is an engagement with resurrection: what appears to be the most unlikely feature of a liberative theology turns out to be central. As such, my argument may interest those who are concerned to develop a theological response to this post-Gorbachev era. The expectations raised by the 'revolutions' in Europe in 1989 have hardly been met; and despite the enthusiasms of some American theorists we are certainly not enjoying the 'end of history'.

Implicitly, I am suggesting that a retreat into the Christian heartlands is not an option, as it fails to engage with the complexity of our current situation. As such, it is to deny the relevance of Christian hope. Instead, in the face of such complexity, we do need to be sure that our theological interpretations are truthful, and that our theology is contextual.

And yet, for the Christian, the task of discernment remains *theological*. In order for theology to be engaged with the current situation it needs to be contextual; and in order for the engagement to be Christian, it needs to be thoroughly theological. Theology and context, context and theology: only here lies the possibility of securing the 'identity and relevance' (Jürgen Moltmann) of Christianity. It seems to me that the only way of doing this is by the critique of ideology because it is this critique which insists that theology is already thoroughly contextualised. If theology wishes to bear contextual witness to the liberating power of the Word, then this can only be shown through a serious engagement with the critique of ideology.

I have learned much about these issues from Latin American liberation theology, in two respects especially: a methodologi-

cal insistence on the social context of theological work and on
the political interests that inform the task of theological
discernment; a constructive commitment to holding together,
although in rather different ways, the theological categories of
creation and redemption (compare Gutiérrez, 1974 and
Assmann, 1975 with Míguez Bonino, 1975 and Rubem Alves,
1975). Here lies, as I interpret their work, the persistent connection made between salvation and liberation.

A commitment to an account of embodiment, which I shall
call 'materiality', also marks a connection between my argument and some feminist theologies. In this area of theological
work, there is a stress on social context (often construed in
terms of pluralism: see Rebecca Chopp, 1978: 245–6) as the
basis for a methodological programme incorporating women's
experience which seeks to affirm human embodiment. Such an
insistence on the incorporation of women's experience (see
Pamela Young, 1990: 11–17) might be understood as the
oppositional strategy against the absence of women's 'bodies'
in theological work up until now. This affirmation of embodiment, including rootedness in nature, is at the centre of the
critical assessment of body-denying, world-denying motifs in
'theology proper' (Chopp).

Such a commitment to embodiment, to seeing things whole
and in relation, does often lead to the avoidance of such
terminology as creation and redemption because these categories, it is claimed, carry overtones of human beings being
saved from their bodies and from this world. (For a forceful
presentation of this point of view, see Ruether, 1981: 57–70.)
Yet, in common with liberation theology, an eschatological
horizon persists in the insistence on the theological contribution to the transcendence of unjust, restrictive social structures. Theological construction does shape and guide our commitments and our energies, and inform our attitudes and
attention. The task of theological reconstruction is then to offer
fresh interpretations of its practical task that will nerve oppositional (that is, world affirming), liberative practices.

The argument of this book also insists on theology as practical, on an eschatological horizon toward the transformation of

social relations, and the holding together of creation and redemption. But its basic dynamic is to offer an outline of a theology that is not ideological (it is not silenced by the static on the line!), and yet is genuinely theological. If the argument is right, a theology that is not ideological is liberative: it speaks of a triune God governed by relations of freedom whose presence is the enactment of and demand for social freedom. In this way, I argue, Christianity speaks a theological word to the world: addressing the fundamental questions of this social world in theological categories of freedom.

PART I

The shape of the argument

CHAPTER I

Theology and the Marxist critique of ideology

I   THE SOCIAL LOCATION OF THEOLOGY

It is perhaps somewhat ironic that there is now a need for European theology to catch up with the concerns of theologies coming out of Latin America, Africa and Asia. As I read them, these theologies are asking the profound question as to what it is that we, as social animals, might trust. I am speaking here of a specific account of trust: a concern with the trustworthiness of our social structures and relations. More precisely, it is to ask whether there may be (liberative) theological insights into the question of the restrictive or emancipatory character of social relations and structures.

At the back of this for Christians is the difficult matter of whether theological interpretations may be trusted. How might Christians think theologically about social matters? Is a theological contribution possible that will not be assimilated into the post-Cold War 'order' and which does not retreat into 'religious subjectivity'? Against such a background, the intention of this book is to offer a constructive proposal for a liberative theology. I plan to do this by joining the debate on the relation between theology and Marxism. It is out of this engagement, I shall be suggesting, that a genuinely liberative theology may emerge. So this book is a theological enquiry from the 'centre': an economic and military 'centre' which structures the space-time of this para-national society. As will become clear, a theology of the powerful 'centre' is above all required to pay attention to the dangers of ideology.

The theological proposal developed here may be linked with many other styles of theology in insisting upon the importance of context: all theology with pretensions to be liberative must be contextual. Theology must reflect upon and be directed to determinate situations. Theology is concerned with the particular and not the general, the ambiguities of the real history of people in struggle, with commitment to the struggle for liberation. In particular, the commitment to theological thinking in a specific context raises the issue of the social location of theology: what is the 'place' of theology? To what pressures is it exposed?

My argument is concerned with the social location of theology. But this is a theological inquiry, not an essay in the sociology of religion. This inquiry is concerned with the status of theology as liberative: what is it that allows us to grasp a theology as liberative? As Segundo has argued, from his particular context: 'It is my feeling that the most progressive theology in Latin America is more interested in *being liberative* than in *talking about liberation*. In other words, liberation deals not so much with content as with the method used to theologize in the face of our real-life situation' (Segundo, 1976: 9). Taking a cue from Segundo's remark, my argument is thus an argument in epistemology (and, implicitly, in the ontology presupposed by such epistemological considerations). Indeed, it is only at the epistemological level that the issue of the liberative status of theology can be addressed.

Framing the issue of liberative status in such fashion does perhaps sound strange enough. To make matters stranger still, the epistemology promoted is Marxist. In other words, I try to establish what it is that Marxism claims for itself in terms of epistemological status – often referred to by Marxists as the 'scientificity' or the 'scientific' character of Marxism. I argue that the Marxist claim to be a non-ideological 'science' raises serious questions for theology. I then suggest ways that theology might interpret and respond to Marxist epistemological strictures through the construction of an outline of a liberative theology.

Such an odd way of doing theology requires some explanation. As I hope will be clear by the end of the book, an
explanation must turn upon the location of theology as the
theory of the practice of the Christian religion, of the practices,
religious and social, of Christians. So an explanation of an
argument concerned with the social location of theology must
ask the question: what is the context of the practice of Christianity?

Some comments by Jürgen Habermas might be considered
here. Habermas has argued that:

> In the industrially advanced societies we observe for the first time as a
> mass phenomenon the loss of the hope in redemption and the expec-
> tation of grace, which, even if no longer within an ecclesiastical
> framework, are still supported by interiorized faith traditions. For the
> first time the mass of the population has been shaken in the basic
> levels of securing its identity; in limit situations it cannot get away
> from a fully secularized everyday awareness and have recourse
> to institutionalized or at least deeply internalized certainties.
> (Habermas, 1983: 18)

The Judaeo-Christian tradition, according to Habermas, is
losing its capacity to secure identity and meaning. And this loss
of capacity has serious consequences because there seems to be
no obvious and immediate substitute. Certainly not the
'rational' society for which Marx and Engels hoped and
worked. Habermas also adds that there seems to be no substitute for religion that has shown itself 'capable of mastering by
means of consolation and trust the *de facto* meaninglessness of
death in its contingency, that of individual suffering, or that of
the private loss of happiness – in general, the meaninglessness
of the negativity of the risks built into life' (Habermas, 1983:
17–18). And yet, what Habermas seems to miss – perhaps
because he welcomes the end of the availability of the certain-
ties of the Judaeo-Christian tradition[1] – is the very persistence
of religion. The growth of Green Spirituality and the New Age

---

[1] This impression is reinforced by Habermas' paper 'Transcendence from Within,
Transcendence in this World', in Don S. Browning and Francis F. Fiorenza (eds.),
1992: 226–50.

movement (not entirely separate phenomena) are two good examples of this persistence.

If this does characterise our period – the rise of 'religiosity' and the reduction in the 'reach' of the Judaeo-Christian tradition – then these may be understood as dangerous times for Christianity and Christian theology. Why dangerous? Because, if there is something in Habermas' argument, Christianity needs to avoid being appropriated as a 'myth' of identity and meaning.[2] As David Harvey has noted, following Simmel, it is during 'times of fragmentation and economic insecurity that the desire for stable values leads to a heightened emphasis upon the authority of basic institutions – the family, religion, the state. And there is abundant evidence of a revival of support for such institutions and the values they represent throughout the Western world since about 1970' (Harvey, 1989: 171). In order not to become a new 'myth' of stability Christian theology needs to have some sense of itself, to avoid being coopted. It needs to be critical of false forms of stability and exploitative accounts of identity, and of the danger of being employed as a guarantor of meaning and stability: '... in moments of despair or exaltation, who among us can refrain from invoking the time of fate, of myth, of the Gods?' (Harvey, 1989: 202).[3] It needs some sense of its own epistemological location within the class divisions of capitalist society so that it might discipline Chris-

---

2 For more detail, see Scott, 1993.
3 A key attempt to found and fund false forms of identity in Europe has, of course, been fascism, or what Paul Tillich termed the 'revolutionary' form of 'political romanticism' (see Tillich, 1977). There are plainly dialectical connections between the aestheticisation of space in fascism and the acceleration of time within the capitalist dynamics of modernity. It is here, under the conditions of 'space-time compression', that a renewed emphasis upon place, tradition, race, culture and gendered patterns of work may find the community-forming and tradition-oriented aspects of Christianity to be important. (Indeed, somewhat speculatively, it may be that Christianity provides precisely a kind of predisposition toward myth which, as Jameson notes, following the work of Norman Holland, 'enables' remythologisation: 'only if we have been told the work is mythic ahead of time, the unquestionable "resonance" of the mythic rewriting presupposing not the operation of some mythic unconscious but rather our own preliminary conscious "set" toward the reading in question' (Jameson, 1989: 67).) The only extended theological critique of fascism known to me is Tillich, 1977; I have tried to offer some account of the importance of Tillich's critique in Scott, 1994. For an account of the cultural search for myths in this century, see Harvey, 1989: part 1.

tian praise and practice (cf. 2 Cor. 4.4). As Nicholas Lash has noted: 'The function of theology ... is to facilitate acquaintance [of us by God] by checking our propensity to go whoring after false gods' (Lash, 1986b: 187). But how might it do this?

Paul Tillich recognised this problem of idolatry. James Luther Adams reports on Tillich's awareness of the fact that difficult times sometimes lead to a 'return to religion', and that such an identification of Christianity with forms of cultural longing are to be resisted by the Christian theologian. Adams reports Tillich's comments written out of the depths of Germany's serious economic difficulties in 1922:

It would be an annihilating judgment about our time ... if a future historian would write about it: 'At that time people turned again to religion; ... in spite of the increase in non-spiritual forces through the economic situation, it was a religious epoch.' Such a judgment could be annihilating, for it could be saying, 'That time lacked God; in His place, however, it had religion. After having tried technology and world politics, after having tried idolizing the nation, or the class, and having failed in these attempts, it tried religion.' (Tillich, cited by James Luther Adams, 1985: 2)

Adams then proceeds to draw out the implications of Tillich's argument. Underscored here is the way in which Tillich's position is, in part at least, a critique of idolatry: religion is not a sphere separate from or 'alongside' the world. The effect of such 'spatializing serves to produce and protect idolatry and complacency, that is, to protect the culture from radical criticism ... and also to "cabin" the creative, renewing power of the really real' (Adams, 1985: 3). The two themes identified here – criticism and creativity – will be important to my argument.

Two separate but closely related points are being made here. 'Myths' of stability are required to counter the sense of meaninglessness left by the loss of power of the Judaeo-Christian tradition (Habermas); Christians are sometimes implicated in the complicity between social forces and the common human quest for meaning, in which theological insights are articulated in response to the demands and pressures of a cultural situation (Tillich), rather than in response to the actions and demands of God. Indeed, with some prescience, Adams reports Tillich as suggesting that the danger lies precisely in a *religious* epoch. Strangely, it may be easier for Christian theology to respond to periods of 'indifference and hostility', to retain some critical detachment from pressures that seek the appropriation of Christianity as a 'myth' of identity, stability and meaning, in an irreligious or non-religious time. Indeed, Habermas seems to be suggesting that there is perhaps for the first time a profound need for such a myth of stability.

The difficult question here, bearing in mind liberation theology's 'theological demonstration that, for the Christian, *ideology* and *idolatry* are synonyms' (Turner, 1983: 227), is: how is Christianity to avoid the charge of idolatry? How is it to avoid becoming a new 'myth'? Centrally, is it possible for theology consistently to speak of God through attentiveness to its own discourse and engage in a theological interpretation of social forms? And might this attentive interpretation be understood as non-ideological and as counter-hegemonic? This is the issue of trust again. If there needs to be a wide-ranging theological engagement in the interpretation of social forms, how may we be sure (trust) that such an engagement yields liberative interpretations? (Christianity's own history is not so helpful here as it has often chosen the 'wrong' side in matters of freedom and emancipation (cf. Moltmann, 1990: 4–6).) How may we be sure that theological engagement is not simply another ideological contribution that serves to buttress the dominant hegemony?

II   IDEAS AND IDEOLOGY

Responding to this question depends, first, on getting some sense of the social location of theology. This is not, in the first instance, a matter of constructing a 'better' theology: 'Let's do a more liberatory theology! Fresh paper! More pencils!' The first concern here is not with better theological materials: arguments and concepts. Instead, a liberative theology is one which builds into its construction an account of 'the effects upon it of the objective constraints and pressures generated by the class character of that society' (Turner, 1984: 72). Let me try, in what will appear to be a somewhat roundabout way, to set out the implications of this for Christian theology.

A central Marxist point is that ideas are not innocent. Recent reflections on the centrality of language to human life make this point more rather than less pertinent. Indeed, the centrality of language was noted by Marx and Engels: 'From the start the "spirit" is afflicted with the curse of being "burdened" with matter, which here makes its appearance in the form of agitated layers of air, sounds, in short of language.' There is also the insistence that language is to be understood only in relation to consciousness: indeed, 'language *is* practical consciousness ... ' And Marx and Engels conclude by making a point that will become important later in the argument: language is itself a structure which pre-exists particular individuals. It is thereby one of the conditions into which we enter. Indeed, it is a *social* condition: language is 'practical consciousness that exists also for other men, and for that reason alone it really exists for me personally as well ... ' (Marx and Engels, 1970: 51).

We are here invited to go beyond the claim that ideas, arguments and theories have their particular social place so that, for instance, 'we cannot understand the history of ideas if we do not consider them as manifestations of the lives of the communities in which they arose ... ' (Kolakowski, 1978: 370). Rather it is that such ideas have a particular function: either as a contribution to the explanation of our situation and so to overcoming or transcending this situation or as a contribution to the mystification or misconstrual of our situation.

As Roy Bhaskar has noted of social theory, from the perspective of his own Marxist 'critical realist' position: ' ... social theory is practically conditioned by, and potentially has practical consequences in society ... It always consists in a practical intervention in social life and sometimes (other things being equal) it logically entails values and actions' (Bhaskar, 1989: 5). This applies to theology, the theory of Christianity, as it does to social theory, the theory of society. Theology is con-

ditioned by society, and it has practical consequences. Yet may
it also be practically efficacious toward liberation? May it be a
liberatory intervention in social life? Theology needs to
demonstrate that it is so, and that it is not 'illusory' or 'false
consciousness' – the latter of course enjoying a rather different
sense of 'efficacious'!

The central point of this epistemological claim is that ideas,
contained in language, function either to liberate or oppress.
The problem here for Christian theology is that Marx (and
Engels) considered that, paradigmatically, it was the Christian
religion as a praxis which demonstrated par excellence the
depth of mystification. It follows always by implication, and
sometimes explicitly, that theology, the theoretical outworking
of the Christian religion, would also be mystificatory.

Laying bare this tendency to mystification is a complex
matter. For Marx, it was important to begin with the concrete
reality as it was presented in bourgeois theory, and to try to
explain the explanation: to locate its social status (see Marx,
1954, part I). This explanation of course began with an assessment of bourgeois theory in its own terms, but soon moves
beyond these terms when such terms prove to be inadequate or
misleading. Here, Marxism's interpretative power likewise
resides in its grasp of social and economic realities (which is
different from that of bourgeois theories), and its understanding of how to change those realities.[4] Critique, for the Marxist,
is thereby always, in a limited sense, constructive. Critique
here refers to a 'process of simultaneous criticism and explanation, rejection and comprehension' in which 'the appear-
ances of reality' are gone beyond, in that 'science both comprehends and rejects as inadequate the ordinary language and
concepts of the spontaneous understanding' (Edgley, 1983:
283). Both aspects of this process (a point which Edgley's
account somewhat obscures) are important: the self-
understanding of agents, spontaneous and ordinary or more

---

[4] Jameson, for instance, insists on the unsurpassability of Marxism on the grounds that
Marxism articulates the 'universal' horizon of History: '. . . History itself becomes the
ultimate ground as well as the untranscendable limit of our understanding in general
and our textual interpretation in particular' (Jameson, 1989: 100).

theoretical, is both criticised and explained – searched for ideology and located in its social position.

In this connection between criticism and explanation the dialectic between theory and praxis is located. A critical explanation not only reveals underlying social structures, but also reveals them to be inimical to full human development. Indeed, Marx employs aesthetic terminology to make his case here (see William Adams, 1991). Therefore explanation moves into the *practical* rejection of these structures, that is, the transformation in the conditions of labour – the changing, rather than the mere interpretation, of the conditions of human work. (Effectively, this is the denial of a sharp distinction between fact and value.)

This begins to hint at the difficulties that a theology enters into when it engages with Marxism. It is clear that these are problems very different from simply maintaining that Marxism is the best theory available for ensuring that theology is properly contextual – as sometimes seems to be the case in liberation theology (see Gutiérrez, 1974: 9–10; Míguez Bonino, 1975: 96–7).

What then is the argument of this book? I focus on how it is possible to do theology in the light of Marxist objections. I enquire into the epistemological grounds on which a theology might be developed which cannot be characterised by Marxism as against liberation. Put another way, what are the epistemological conditions that political theology must meet in order to be considered liberative by Marxism? Marxism, it must be understood, makes claims as to its own epistemological basis: it argues that its understanding of capitalism is true, that it is true theory and true practice, and that no theory comes to liberation except through it. These are, in effect, epistemological conditions which Marxism demands that other theories respond to *and meet*. If these conditions can be established, and theology can show that it meets them, then theology's own constructive proposals may be part of a liberative inquiry. And this is nothing other than suggesting that theology must reflect critically on its own social location: in the appropriate 'self-knowledge' of its social location resides its capacity to be liberative and not mystificatory.

If then it is epistemological conditions that a political theology must meet in order to establish its liberative status as genuine, what are these conditions?

III   BEYOND MARX'S CRITIQUE OF RELIGION?

To begin to answer this question, we may consider what is perhaps the most popular and well known area of analysis and dialogue between Marxism and Christianity: theological responses to the Marxian critique of religion. (For instance, this critique is addressed by some of the liberation theologians.) Analysing the critique may help in gaining some sense of the way that my argument seeks to move beyond this critique, narrowly interpreted.

Marx's account of religion, according to Alisdair MacIntyre, suggests a 'dual role' for religion. This duality refers to a negative and a positive aspect. As negative, religion 'buttresses the established order by sanctifying it and by suggesting that the political order is somehow ordained by divine authority, and it consoles the oppressed exploited [sic] by offering them in heaven what they are denied upon earth'. Of the positive, MacIntyre writes: 'At the same time, by holding before them a vision of what they are denied, religion plays at least partly a progressive role in that it gives the common people some idea of what a better order would be' (MacIntyre, 1968: 103). There are then two aspects of Marx's criticism of religion. One part relates to the use made of religion by the prevailing social order; the other to real, and yet mystificatory, hopes expressed in religion. It is important to keep these together if the full force of the Marxian criticism is not to be lost.

Both aspects are bound together in Marx's assessment of the origin of religion. Departing from the accounts given by Bruno Bauer and Feuerbach, he argued that religion arises out of contradictions in the present:

This state and this society produce religion, which is an *inverted consciousness of the world*, because they are an *inverted world* ... It [religion] is the *fantastic realization* of the human essence since the human essence has not acquired any true reality. The struggle against religion is therefore indirectly the struggle against *that world* whose spiritual *aroma* is religion. (Marx, 1975: 244)

Marx's objections to Bauer are set out in the article 'On the Jewish Question', in which Bauer is taken to task for suggesting that the question of religion should be transposed into a question about the secular state. According to Marx, Bauer argues that the secular state should abolish religion, and so dispense with the Jewish question. Marx objects by arguing that this has happened in the United States – religion is separate from the secular state – but this has not led to the end of religion; on the contrary, Marx draws attention to the religiosity prevalent there. Marx contends that this approach is insufficient: to abolish state support for religion is not to abolish religion, in that it neglects the fact that the source of religion is to be found in the area of civil society. The effect of this is to achieve only a limited, though welcome, *political* emancipation from religion (see Marx, 1975: 221).

What is required is not the 'privatisation' of religion, its confinement to the sphere of civil society which simply 'allows religion – but not privileged religion – to continue in existence' (Marx, 1975: 226; cf. 233). Instead, Marx calls for what he dubs 'human emancipation'. Human emancipation means the overcoming of political emancipation so that 'real, individual man resumes the abstract citizen into himself and as an individual man has become a *species being* in his empirical life, his individual work and his individual relationships ... only then will human emancipation be completed' (Marx, 1975: 234). Human emancipation is therefore not concerned with a form of political emancipation that all too faithfully reflects the split between the individual member of civil society and the citizen as moral agent. It is concerned with the overcoming of this dual conception of the individual in society and the establishment of forms of relationship appropriate to the species-being of humanity. To this extent, Marx is anticipating the argument of the 1844 *Economic and Philosophical Manuscripts* (in Marx, 1975: 279–400).

Marx's account of religion as rooted in social divisions and contradictions can also be seen in his interpretation of

Feuerbach. In the fourth of the 'Theses on Feuerbach', Marx argues (1975: 422): 'Feuerbach starts out from the fact of religious self-alienation, of the duplication of the world into a religious world and a secular one. His work consists in resolving the religious world into its secular basis.' Marx makes it clear that he has accepted Feuerbach's argument: the objectification of human attributes in religion is detrimental to the self-understanding of human beings.[5] But, in accordance with his dictum that 'man makes religion, religion does not make man', he contends that criticism must be directed not solely at religion, but also at the situation in which religion is found to be necessary. Marx wins an important insight here. What concerns him is the reasons for religion: 'the secular basis detaches itself from itself and establishes itself as an independent realm in the clouds'; but why? For Marx, this 'can only be explained by the cleavages and self-contradictions within this secular basis' (Marx, 1975: 422). We have here the process of criticism and explanation referred to earlier: the self-understanding of religious agents is (here) exposed as false, and its social 'place' identified.

If this brief account can be said to summarise the negative aspect of the Marxian account of religion, what form does the positive evaluation take? As I mentioned above, it refers to the capacity of religion to encapsulate forms of protest, best summarised in some of Marx's most famous words on religion from the *Critique of Hegel's Philosophy of Right. Introduction*: '*Religious* suffering is at one and the same time the *expression* of real suffering and a protest against real suffering. Religion is the sigh of the oppressed creature, the heart of a heartless world and the soul of soulless conditions. It is the *opium* of the people' (Marx, 1975: 244). Here again we find Marx developing the thought of Feuerbach: religion needs to be referred to material life if it is to be explained. Perhaps we might say that religion

---

[5] Perhaps this is not all of Feuerbach's criticism of religion: see Van A. Harvey, 'Ludwig Feuerbach and Karl Marx', Ninian Smart *et al.* (eds.), 1988: 291–328, esp. 292–301, 313–23. As Harvey points out, too often Feuerbach is interpreted by theologians simply as a precursor to Marx. For an example of just such an interpretation, see Mackey, 1983: 12–13.

has no genuine contribution to make in its own right: it can be understood as that area of life which best expressed the hopes and desires of people for their own emancipation, but it remains a substitute for a theory and a practice in which oppressed peoples understand their situation and change it. So if Marx does consider religion to have a positive significance it is, as David McLellan has noted, 'an extremely backhanded compliment' in that the role of religion is to 'represent humanity's feeble aspirations under adverse circumstances' (McLellan, 1987: 13). Religion is, in one sense, genuine: people have aspirations toward a better life. This is the material dimension of religion. But its religious expression is an illusory resolution of practical difficulties. Once this illusory character is grasped, the criticism of religion and theology gives way to the criticism of politics and economics.

What is the significance of this account of Marx's critique of religion for my argument? I concur with Nicholas Lash (1981: 153) that the most basic questions that Marxian theory puts to Christian theology are not those raised by the critique of religion. In asserting this, I am suggesting that theology needs to respond to *different* Marxist objections than to those raised by the Marxian critique of religion. Yet, it is to the critique of religion, selectively understood, that much theology, including liberation theology, is responding. Indeed, we may note that acceptance of the critique is a popular way forward chosen by those theologians who take Marxism seriously. In other words, they agree that Christianity has often been a buttress to the ruling forces in society. The second step is to take a cue from Marx's positive evaluation by arguing that Christianity does not need to be like this: Christianity can be politically progressive. In other words, if Christianity has so far served to legitimate the activities of the oppressor, it is now to be recast so as to reflect in its language the activities and hopes of the oppressed.

There is some evidence to suggest that this is how, for example, the liberation theologians have responded. David McLellan has identified three areas where liberation theology is indebted to Marxism: its criticism of 'the involvement of the Latin American Church in the social and political structures that have compounded the domination and oppression of the mass of the people'; next, its rereading of the Old and New Testaments: here a premium is placed on the 'earthy realism' of the former, in which, for example, the Exodus narrative is regarded as a 'paradigm for political liberation', and in the New Testament, evidence of 'Jesus's political messianism' is stressed; third, its insistence on the 'social and political dimension to traditional Christian concepts' (McLellan, 1987: 153–4). McLellan summarises the fresh understanding that liberation theology has secured from Marxism thus: ' ... of human beings as essentially social, of solidarity with the poor and outcast, of taking history seriously, and of looking towards the future' (McLellan, 1987: 156). In effect, if McLellan is right, liberation theology has responded in the way I suggested: by arguing that if there can be a theology of the right then there can also be a theology of the left. The appropriate terminological and methodological innovation follows in order to develop this new type of theology.

This type of response to the Marxian critique suggests, in turn, an emphasis on certain aspects of the critique: for instance, the complicity of much religion with the dominant social order and the capacity of religion to be 'the sigh of the oppressed creature'. What is not usually emphasised is Marx's contention that Christianity is inherently reactionary and is destined to wither away. When this last point is recognised, as in Segundo (1976: 13f.), the response is to show how holding such a position betrays a methodological inconsistency. If Marx was consistent about his method, Segundo argues, he would not have been able to reject religion in the way he did.[6] Of course, there are a number of possible responses to this issue. For example, McLellan suggests that it is not so strange for Marx to consider that, like the state, religion was destined to disappear under communism: 'the communist revolution

---

[6] Whether such an *a priori* rejection of religion is persuasive is discussed in chapters 2 and 3. Certainly, Turner sharply rejects the notion that an *a priori* evaluation of religion as *always* reactionary should be allowed to pass itself off as Marxist – see his assessment of Engels' *On the Peasant War in Germany* (Turner, 1983: 166ff., esp. 168).

implied "the most radical rupture with traditional ideas". The demise of religion was written in the laws of historical development and any attempt to combine communism with religion was simply evidence of ignorance of these laws' (McLellan, 1987: 24).[7]

Yet it is important to note that theological responses to the 'end of religion' question, along with those responses that accept a certain interpretation of the Marxian critique, obscure the most important argument. We can begin to grasp the significance of this by referring to a crucial quotation from *Capital*, volume I, which suggests an appropriate method for the assessment of religion. This method, although it is hardly a departure from Marx's earlier criticisms, displaces from the centre of attention such issues as the 'end of religion' and the liberatory, yet mystificatory, aspects of religion. Marx writes:

It is, in reality, much easier to discover by analysis the earthly core of the misty creations of religion than, conversely, it is, to develop from the actual relations of life the corresponding celestialised forms of those relations. The latter method is the only materialistic, and therefore the only scientific one. (Marx, 1954: 352)

In other words, it is easier to be a Feuerbachian than a Marxist, but the Marxist approach is the only scientific one. The proper method is thus not to investigate religion and see if it is possible to detect its anthropomorphisms. Instead, Marx suggests that certain types of economic and social relations will generate or determine the appropriate creations of religion. This passage is difficult and yet also catches the richness of Marx's mature criticism of religion. It is of course easy to interpret this profoundly spatial image too simply and so suggest, along the lines of the base/superstructure model, that religion is determined by another, more 'powerful', level of reality. I touch on this matter briefly in the next chapter. Here

[7] I am not persuaded (some comments by Marx to the contrary) that Marxism requires an account of the unfolding of historical laws: see, for other ways of construing the issue, the stress on 'guiding thread' in Carver (1982), the distinction between explanation and prediction in Bhaskar (1989), the discussion of necessity in Mészáros (1970) and the distinction between historical inevitability and political possibility in Ball (1991).

I only want to suggest that theoretical practices (including theology) cannot be understood fully without reference to interpretations of determining social and economic practices. Often, but with varying force, the latter may be seen as affecting the former; indeed, many theoretical practices are inscribed by such 'determining pressures'. In parts II and III we shall come across examples from theology which might be interpreted as evidence of such pressures. What is of much less importance is whether the Christian religion will wither away, or whether there are emancipatory 'moments' in religion. Rather, here we may see that Marx argued that the creations of religion will act like a mist, in fact as an ideology, disguising the very conditions by which they are determined.[8]

IV   TWO EPISTEMOLOGICAL THEMES IN MARXISM

In the previous section, I concentrated on the Marxian critique of religion as a common area for dialogue between Christian theology and Marxism. I have tried to show that, if construed in a certain way, it is a critique that theology can respond to and claim to satisfy. It can do this by the stratagem of terminological innovation, and by stressing that theology,

[8] To my knowledge there is no sustained engagement in liberation theology with a critical (negative) Marxist conception of ideology. Míguez Bonino (1983: 51–2) regards the distinction between the negative and positive senses as so unimportant that he decides not to distinguish between them: '... an ideology is "a system (possessing its own internal logic and rigor) of representations (images, myths, ideas, concepts) which have an existence and an historic role in a given society". In this rather formal definition, I do not distinguish between ideology in a negative sense (as hiding reality) and ideology in a positive sense (as a mobilizing force) nor do I distinguish between an unconscious and a conscious ideology.' Assmann (1975: 93) grasps the distinction between positive and negative: 'This leads us to a double concept of ideology: the negative side, which idealizes and legitimates the existing order; and the positive, which is an "ideology of struggle", an ideology expressing our ethical and political decision.' But he links the positive (after Lenin?) with the competing ideologies of conflicting classes, thereby downgrading the importance of the 'negative side' which he seems to regard as abstractly methodological. Segundo (1984: 16) uses the term ideology in a very general sense: 'I shall use the term "ideology" for all systems of means, be they natural or artificial, that are used to attain some end or goal.' Gutiérrez (1974: 12, 235) grasps the negative sense – 'ideology ... rationalizes and justifies a given social and ecclesial order' and again 'ideology does not offer adequate and scientific knowledge of reality; rather, it masks it' – but fails to develop this insight.

previously on the side of the big battalions, in fact can support the exploited and oppressed. The key condition it failed to satisfy is that of the method that Marx suggested for the study of religion: in sum, that the analysis of religion begins with material life. This suggests that a theological response to the critique of religion is not what is required in the attempt to secure the liberative 'social location' of Christian theology.

If we accept the Marxian *method* for the analysis of religion outlined in *Capital*, we are obliged to consider two epistemological themes in Marxism: ideology and determination. (Indeed, as I hinted above in my comments, these two themes are present in the excerpt cited.) Material life determines the theoretical form that religion takes; religion as an ideology obscures and mystifies the conditions which produced it. This suggests that responses to the critique of religion are not sufficient as a response to the weightier Marxist epistemological objections to religion which lie in the accounts of ideology and determination.[9]

In *The Peasant War in Germany*, Engels suggests just this: terminological innovation and commitment to the revolutionary struggle do not guarantee a liberative status to the theology of, in this instance, Thomas Münzer. Rather, Engels argues that these theological ideas need to be seen in their context, which he understands as the birth pangs of the bourgeois revolution. The revolutionary, communistic ideas of Münzer are simply inappropriate in that they anticipate by 300 years the proletarian revolution. They are ideas ahead of their time, which means inappropriate to their time, which means non-liberative. So Engels writes:

Münzer's political doctrine followed his revolutionary religious conceptions very closely, and just as his theology overstepped the current

---

[9] It may be important to note here that this is a *Marxist* enquiry. Marx's contribution to the criticism of religion occurred early in his theoretical development, and did not, apart from some important asides, persist in his later work. The richness of Marx's later work, as it might be applied to Christianity, in fact lies in the conception of ideology. But even here, Marx's thinking is not fully developed. It is therefore incumbent on the commentator to reconstruct an intelligibly Marxist conception of

conceptions of his time, so his political doctrine went beyond the directly prevailing social and political conditions. Just as Münzer's religious philosophy approached atheism, so his political programme approached communism ... (Engels, in Marx and Engels, 1975: 98)

What Münzer was struggling for as a political agitator was not so much 'a compilation of the demands of the plebeians of that day than a visionary anticipation of the conditions for the emancipation of the proletarian element that had scarcely begun to develop among the plebeians ...' (Engels, in Marx and Engels, 1975: 98).

In response to Engels we might want to quarrel with his understanding of theology and his strictly progressive historical schema, but the general point is well made. An appropriate terminology is not enough; what is also required is a correct 'connection' with the situation. To use the terms I have suggested, Münzer's theology can be seen as determined in such a way as to reinforce the status quo *despite* the revolutionary nature of its language. On account of this, such theological and political discourse can be seen as ideological in that it confuses rather than clarifies. By this I mean that it wrongly suggests that the gains from the proletarian revolution can be achieved in advance of the growth of the proletariat, and even before the bourgeois revolution. The two Marxist concepts of ideology and determination are therefore central to the establishment of a theory's ideological or liberative status. This gives some indication of their importance in Marxist epistemology – I shall say more about them shortly.

I began the previous section by arguing that this book is not an argument in the Marxian critique of religion. Perhaps now it is somewhat clearer what this book is about: an argument in Marxist epistemology toward a liberative theology. Specifically, it is an argument concerning the ideological and determined status of theology. In order to assess this status, what is meant within Marxism by 'ideological' and 'determined' needs to be established.

ideology to address to Christian theology. The criticism of ideology must govern and complete the critique of religion (see chapter 2).

V HIERARCHIES OF EXPLANATION: THEORETICAL PRACTICES AS IDEOLOGICAL

To secure its claim to be liberative, I have been arguing, it is important that theology has some sense of its social location. Theology is of course a discursive practice, which raises questions as to its importance. Althusser, for instance, has suggested that there are four areas of practice: production, the political, the ideological and the theoretical (Althusser, 1979: 166–7) – which suggests, at the very least, the relativising of theoretical discourse. And a number of Marxist commentators have been at pains to suggest that non-discursive practices, especially labour, are central to capitalism.[10] Further, in terms of its status as a theoretical practice, Christian theology is perhaps not central to the reproduction of capitalist society. Indeed, Althusser has noted that although it may have been true in the past that the Church was a crucial Ideological State Apparatus, now the main such Apparatus is education (Althusser, 1984: 24–6).

This may of course be so. And it may also be that there are other areas of theoretical discourse – social theory, philosophy

---

10 Terry Eagleton stresses the material bases of ideology in comments on ideology and discourse (1991: esp. 199); Alex Callinicos (1985: 38–9, 46f.) argues for the centrality of the 'redirective' and 'transformative' aspects of Marx's account of labour, although he later argues that in the full account of historical materialism the notion of labour is transformed into more scientific terms, avoiding the 'humanist' terminology of the *Economic and Philosophical Manuscripts*; Bhaskar insists on the irreducibility of social relations of production, indeed, he considers them a transcendental condition of knowledge and action (1989: 4, *et passim*); Jorge Larrain stresses in his reconstruction of historical materialism that 'practice is the basic social fact [although] it is not absolutely free or unconditioned' (1986: 93); Istvan Mészáros argues that if there is a transition in Marx's thinking it is between 1843 and 1844 (the date of the *Economic and Philosophical Manuscripts*): what is crucial for the development of Marx's thinking is the movement to centre stage of the concept of alienated *labour*. This concept marks the beginning of Marx's crucial contribution, not the end of a period of youthful philosophical extravagance (1970: 232); Terrell Carver argues that 'Marx's interest in the social production of life can now be traced back to his view that political economy (the science of production, distribution, consumption and exchange) was the key to civil society (our economic activities and relationships). From an understanding of those material conditions of life Marx expected to grasp legal relations and forms of state, that is, contemporary political life' (1982: 24).

of science – that are more central, at the theoretical level, to the reproduction of capitalism. But much Marxist commentary has been at pains to suggest that theoretical disciplines do make a contribution to the reproduction of capitalist society, and theology, at the very least, is part of the Ideological State Apparatus of education. Although, as Marx and Engels pointed out, the world cannot be changed simply through reinterpretation, yet there can be no revolutionary change without adequate theorising of the workings of capitalist society. Further, they considered that many of the ways in which capitalist society was interpreted were indeed ideological. The real workings of the capitalist economy and civil society differed from most descriptions of those workings, whether the description be one of common sense, or philosophy or social theory. Such false theoretical interpretations inhibited revolutionary possibility, and demanded criticism.

So theoretical practice does have its own importance within Marxism. More than this, theoretical practices have their particular determined place within the social relations of capitalist society. An example from the philosophy of science may help to make this clear.

Roy Bhaskar has argued that there are two 'traditions' within contemporary philosophy of science. The first he calls the orthodox tradition, and has roots going back to Hume and Kant. This strand of interpretation 'has depended upon an implicit ontology of *empirical realism*, on which the real objects of scientific investigation are the objects of actual or possible experience' (Bhaskar, 1989: 13). The second 'tradition', termed 'super-idealist' and based in the work of such theorists as Bachelard and Kuhn, 'has secreted an implicit ontology of *subjective conceptual realism*, on which the real objects of scientific investigation are the products of scientific theory (that is, of the spontaneous activity of mind, unconstrained by sense-experience)' (Bhaskar, 1989: 13). Bhaskar proceeds to argue that his own position is in fact the only one that accounts for the theory and practice of science with any degree of adequacy. That point need not concern us here. What is of interest, if Bhaskar's interpretation is correct, is the consequences of adhering to an account of science based on either empirical realism or subjective realism.

Bhaskar argues that the implicit ontology in the empirical model (the term is appropriate), and generally unanalysed within it, offers an account of the scientist as an atomistic individual engaging in the investigation of a closed system (which is not open to transformation by human beings). How is this? Bhaskar argues that the empirical model 'has uncritically accepted the doctrine, implicit in the empirical realist dissolution of ontology, of the actuality of causal laws; and it has interpreted these, following Hume, as empirical regularities' (Bhaskar, 1989: 21). What, crucially, is left out of this account, Bhaskar maintains, is some sense of scientific procedure as *work* (Bhaskar, 1989: 22). Science, on this empirical model, seems to be a passive intellectual exercise: 'people are regarded as passively sensing (or else, as conventionally deciding upon) given facts and recording their constant conjunctions, that is to say, as passive spectators of a given world, rather than as active agents in a complex one' (Bhaskar, 1989: 22). We may immediately note the displacing of the connected issues of agency and social transformation.

Of greatest concern to Bhaskar is that this model issues in the notion of a 'given world', especially when the principles of science, in 'its [inappropriate] role as the guarantor of justified belief', are transposed into the social sciences. Drawing out some of the consequences of this implicit ontology and the account of scientific work it generates, he argues:

... the Humean theory depends upon a view of conjunctions existing quite independently of the human activity necessary for them, and hence upon the *fetishism* of the systems within which the conjoined events occur. And it depends upon a view of what is apprehended in immediate sense experience as a fact constituting an atomistic event or state-of-affairs, and existing independently of the human activity necessary for it, and hence upon the *reification* of atomized facts, apprehended by autonomized minds. (Bhaskar, 1989: 22)

Marx noted that '*Thus everything appears reversed in competition*' (Marx, 1959: 209). So it is in Bhaskar's trenchant critique of the empirical realist account in the philosophy of science. The social character of knowledge becomes its givenness in experience; and the 'reality' of the world is transformed into its independence of the individual enquirer (the bourgeois centred subject). This is a good example of the epistemic fallacy: ontological matters are transformed into epistemological considerations.

I mentioned above that one of Bhaskar's central worries about this account is its consequences for social theory. He comments: ' . . . the Humean theory of causality, presupposing a view of the world as closed and completely described, encourages a conception of the social world as unstructured (hence as "obvious"), undifferentiated and unchanging, so underpinning certain substantive theories of social life' (Bhaskar, 1989: 23). The possible political implications of this need no further comment.

The other report in the philosophy of science, subjective conceptual realism, is also commented on briefly by Bhaskar: ' . . . the super-idealist ontology of subjective conceptual realism involves a *voluntarism*, on which theory is unconstrained by either nature or history, which readily lends itself to the rationalisation of so-called "revolutionary science"' (Bhaskar, 1989: 23).[11] Whether this is quite fair to this particular tradition is not germane to my argument here. It is rather the basic point that Bhaskar is making which is important: an inappropriate form of scientific realism would be one which tended to suppress the character of science as work.

What makes this argument interesting for my purposes is that it highlights the character of ideology. Bhaskar does want to say that as accounts of the theory and practice of science both subjective and empirical realism are flawed. They are both, in a straightforward sense, false. But they are also both ideological.

What is involved in making this further claim? Here I am

---

[11] This is not to deny the important 'hermeneutical' insights of, among others, Kuhn and Feyerabend: for instance, the stress on 'tradition' and the acknowledgement of the importing of criteria from outside the domain of science into scientific work (on this, see Peukert, 1986: 78f.). Perhaps here Bhaskar is misled by his suspicion of hermeneutics.

suggesting that these accounts in the philosophy of science have a particular relation to the pressures of the class divisions of capitalist society. As intellectual practices, they are determined by these pressures to such an extent that they misdescribe, here, the operations of science. They do this in such a way as to offer a theory which either reinforces a conception that individuals are prior to and distinct from society and that society itself is not open to change, or that 'reality' is not so much 'theory-dependent', but changed by developments in theory 'independent' of historical development. The real history of human beings, with its natural basis, is thereby overlooked (cf. Marx and Engels, 1970: 42, 46, 48). 'Reality' is misunderstood, but in an 'interested' way – that is to say, to the benefit of the dominant order.

Such intellectual practices are thereby inscribed by the pressures of a class society. They offer us ways of conceiving scientific activity which relativises practice and reinforces atomistic passivity in face of the apparently closed character of social systems. Thus, both accounts in the philosophy of science have particular *ideological* functions to perform (of which both theories are unaware). Of course, this is a particularly important victory for the dominant order to secure in the area of the philosophy of science, because science is regarded as a key expression of rationality, and so functions to underpin other forms of rationality (cf. the now classic critique by Adorno and Horkheimer (1979)).

The discussion above on the philosophy of science shows how Marxism understands intellectual practices as being determined. It also illustrates strategies of ideological containment (Fredric Jameson): here the misconstrual of agency and the character of society. Does theology demonstrate such tendencies to be ideological? Certainly, all theoretical practices are subject to the determining limits and pressures of capitalist society; theology is no exception to this rule. Furthermore, Marx was convinced, as we have seen, that ' ... in religion, man is governed by the products of his own brain' (Marx, 1954: 582). Of course, human beings fail to grasp that religion is the product of their minds. But more interestingly, human beings fail to grasp that in religion they are *governed*.

The crucial question here is: what sort of 'regime' is it? And, what is the source of this 'government', and in whose interest is it? Marx connected this account of religion to capitalism: in a similar way to the mistake enacted in religion, human beings fail to see that capitalist production is also the product of human hands and so within the control of human beings, and yet it governs human beings. The full sentence from *Capital* reads: 'As, in religion, man is governed by the products of his own brain, so in capitalistic production, he is governed by the products of his own hand' (Marx, 1954: 582). Again, the same questions might be raised concerning the sort of regime we have here, and whose interests it serves.

What is crucial is the connection which Marx forges between these findings on religion and capitalist production. As Kee notes, for Marx: ' ... religious commitments constitute an obstacle to the advancement of the [proletarian] cause ... as long as religion continues in its present form it will reinforce and legitimize all forms of the inversion of reality' (Kee, 1990: 86–7). In other words, religious alienation and commodity fetishism are related, and involve the same basic mistake. This is a mistake over the roots of religious and economic practices respectively. But more important than noting that these are human products, is to enquire after the 'order of government', the material governing of human bodies, which these human products (as embodied practices) secure, and the material basis from which they arise (and, simultaneously, obscure).

Christianity does, for Marxists, have its particular determined place. Indeed, Marx argued that some forms of Christianity were especially suitable for capitalist society: ' ... for such a society, Christianity with its *cultus* of abstract man, more especially in its bourgeois developments, Protestantism, Deism, etc., is the most fitting form of religion' (Marx, 1954: 83). It may well be that Christian theology is not as important here as the theoretical practices of science. But it still has its place in the reproduction of capitalist society. The question remains: what is that place? Is its place determined as ideological?

This need not lead us into the area of a crude economic reductionism. It is rather to ask after the social place of the theoretical practice called theology (that which is the practice in the domain of theory to the practice of Christianity in the social domain). And the manner of asking will be Marxist. If Marxism insists that Christian theology is thoroughly determined, then if the epistemological grounds for such a judgement might be ascertained, perhaps Christian theology might show how it is not, after all, identical with its social determinants.

But before getting to this matter, we must note that Marxism is itself a theoretical practice. And as such Marxism is also determined. But Marxism claims that its own determined status is precisely the ground of its 'scientificity'. And for most other theoretical practices, this determined status is the ground for their description as ideology. In exploring this difficulty we come now to the issues of determination and emancipation.

VI   CLOSENESS AND DISTANCE; OPPOSITIONAL, ALTERNATIVE, SPECIALISING

A social materialism is not concerned to reduce all actions and communication to their material determinants (even if this were possible). Indeed, the reverse is the case: from pillow talk to detective stories, from oil slicks to elections, the materialist position sketched here seeks to affirm the importance of such practices. What it does not do is affirm their equal importance. Writing from the perspective of his 'critical realist' position, Bhaskar has argued:

Critical realists do not deny the reality of events and discourses; on the contrary, they insist upon them. But they hold that we will only be able to understand – and so change – the social world if we identify the structures at work that generate those events or discourses ... Social phenomena (like most natural phenomena) are the product of a plurality of structures. But such structures may be hierarchically ranked in terms of their explanatory importance. (Bhaskar, 1989: 2–3)

Events and, important for my purposes, discourses are not all determining, and some account of their production by structures may be given. Theology is such a discourse, generated in its turn by a plurality of structures. Perhaps, if this were an enquiry in the sociology of religion we might now begin to investigate these structures. But this is an enquiry in theology. So what follows is an attempt to set out how theology, as a discourse and as a social phenomenon, might understand itself as situated in relation to 'the structures at work that generate ... discourses'. In order to do this, I use a spatial metaphor taken from the work of Raymond Williams: 'closeness and distance'.

I am using the phrase closeness and distance to refer to the 'location' of theology (and other theoretical practices) to the determining pressures and limits of capitalist society. I am suggesting that Marxism understands itself to be at the correct 'closeness' to and 'distance' from these determining pressures and limits. And a theology that takes seriously Marxist claims to 'know' this distance, and seeks to respond to Marxist strictures, may also 'know' the distance. That is, it may be neither too close to nor too distant from the determining pressures and limits of the class division of capitalist society.

A theoretical practice that is too close to such determining pressures we might call reactionary. A theoretical practice that is too distant from these pressures we might call utopian (in the bad sense[12]). Marx and Engels, while not using the terminology, offer in the *Communist Manifesto* excellent examples of theories that are too close or too distant. I am referring here to their discussion of various types of socialism. In section III of the *Manifesto*, Marx and Engels identify certain socialisms to which they oppose their own, communist, variant. Three types are identified: reactionary, conservative–bourgeois and critical–utopian. For my purposes, it is possible to see the first two types as examples of contributions too close to determining

---

[12] Jameson offers a rather different account of utopia: see Jameson, 1989: chapter 6; also Jameson, 1991: chapter 10. Jameson's account turns upon a conception of ideology which, as may become clearer, I do not fully share.

pressures; the last type might be understood as too distant from such determining pressures.

In the discussion of the first two types, the common complaint made by Marx and Engels is that such contributions wish a return to a previous form of economic organisation, e.g. manufacture based on guilds, or desire the present form of economic organisation, but 'minus its revolutionary and disintegrating elements. They [the bourgeois socialists] wish for a bourgeoisie without a proletariat' (Marx, 1977: 242). The complaint against the third type is that it mistakes the historical economic development and so proposes inappropriate remedies: the critical utopians offer only ' ... fantastic pictures of future society, painted at a time when the proletariat is still in a very undeveloped state and has but a fantastic conception of its own position, [and which] correspond with the first instinctive yearnings of that class for a general reconstruction of society' (Marx, 1977: 244). So Marx and Engels are less dismissive of utopian socialism, but they still regard it as unhelpful. It offers an inappropriate way forward, doubly inappropriate in that, by the time of writing, Marx was suggesting that the proletariat was of a sufficient size and (latent) power in some countries to carry out the revolutionary change required for the 'general reconstruction of society'.

It is instructive that Marx and Engels, in such an important programmatic[13] document, should have offered an assessment of various forms of socialism. The significance of such an assessment is plain: these socialist interventions all mistook in a fundamental way the material circumstances and the possibility for change (and there cannot be the assessment of the latter without an assessment of the former).

Here then, implicitly at least, is the issue of closeness and distance. What is crucial is that theoretical practices are thought through against Marxist epistemological strictures so that they may be situated. (We have seen that Marx and Engels themselves carry out such a critique in closeness and distance.) The argument of this book is that the theologian

---

[13] In the sense of 'translating ideas into action' (Daniel Bell, cited in Geuss, 1981: 11).

may be able to do this, and yet – even when this is attempted – too often, despite its best intentions, theological thinking is ideological.

To help further in setting out the difficult epistemological grounds of this argument, I employ another set of terms, also taken from the work of Raymond Williams: oppositional, alternative and specialising.[14] Against the use made of these terms by Raymond Williams, I characterise a theology as oppositional when it is neither too close nor too distant to determining pressures. The argument developed in part II and the theological construction of part III are concerned with precisely this: how might theology meet Marxist strictures and so secure its location as oppositional?

Too often, so my argument runs, theological interventions remain alternative – just as the socialism of the utopians remained alternative. Some theological contributions may claim a liberative status, but do so as alternative, a fresh way of doing theology. These are not oppositional theologies. There is an effective, practical difference between an alternative and oppositional theology – as will be evident in the argument of parts II and III.

VII AN EPISTEMOLOGICAL ACCOUNT OF IDEOLOGY

My argument so far turns upon a particular interpretation of ideology. Furthermore, the interpretation of ideology is a contested area within Marxism itself. I do not seek to defend an account of ideology nor pick my way through the controversies. But we may note that the Marxist account of ideology proposed in this book might, following Eagleton, be called 'epistemological'. Eagleton argues that some 'formulations [of ideology] involve epistemological questions' (Eagleton, 1991: 2). And the framing of these epistemological questions affects the way that ideology is interpreted. Commenting on the

---

[14] I am not employing the terminology in quite the way that Williams does. Indeed in Williams' work the meaning of the terms seems not to be fixed, especially the meaning of 'oppositional' as contrasted with 'independent': see 1977: 114, 1989a: 54 and 1989b: 308.

interpretation of the term, Eagleton identifies what he sees as two traditions:

Roughly speaking, one central lineage, from Hegel to Marx to Georg Lukács and some later Marxist thinkers, has been much preoccupied with ideas of true and false cognition, with ideology as illusion, distortion and mystification; whereas an alternative tradition of thought has been less epistemological than sociological, concerned more with the function of ideas within social life than with their reality or unreality. (Eagleton, 1991: 3).

The account of ideology I am working with here resides firmly in the first tradition raised by Eagleton. But I am unhappy with the sharp distinction between the two traditions (as is Eagleton, I think). Indeed, it is precisely on account of its strange epistemological status that ideology 'acquires' its social force. The notion of theory as a practice is perhaps helpful here as a way of understanding the social force of ideology. Theology is the intellectual discipline that may – for the persons and groups writing and reading theology and seeking to live a life thus 'disciplined' – allow the misperception of reality in ideological ways. Ideological theory is a form of practice that is ambiguous as to its social location. In other words, ideology has no sense of the plurality of structures out of which it is generated – it has no sense that it is determined. (We have already seen this in the empirical and idealist accounts of the philosophy of science, and in Marx and Engels' accounts of types of socialism – the common feature of these accounts is that they have no sense of their relationship to society. Their 'actual' relationship to society, as identified by the Marxist critique of ideology, is that of the legitimation of domination, or, at least, of being less than adequate in the criticism of domination.)

This seeming 'innocence' of ideology suggests another point: ideology is about power: 'Ideology has to do with *legitimating* the power of a dominant social group or class' (Eagleton, 1991: 5). And the complexity of the epistemology of ideology is such that ideology may be implicated in domination at the most subtle level. As Eagleton notes: ' ... some at least of what we call ideological discourse is true at one level but not at another:

true in its empirical content but deceptive in its force, or true in
its surface meaning but false in its underlying assumptions'
(Eagleton, 1991: 16–17).

This point has been the cause of much discussion among
Marxists. Here is the claim that there is a distinction to be
made between the surface appearance and the essential relations of capitalist economic practices or, to put it in cultural
terms, between manifest and latent text. We saw it above in
Bhaskar's criticism of philosophies of science. Such accounts
have a certain prima facie plausibility. But, in questioning
their assumptions, it is possible to understand their surface
appearance as ideological. In other words, such philosophical
accounts of science offered descriptions of scientific practice
and of society that reinforced the way that society presents
itself: closed, incapable of being grasped in its totality (by the
individual observer), and thereby obscuring society's 'essential' relations.

Ideology, then, for Marx, and for many Marxists, is about
power and domination: 'to study ideology is to study the way in
which meaning serves to establish and sustain relations of
domination' (Thompson, 1990: 56; italics removed). Although
it is only one in a range of meanings of ideology, the Marxist
account of ideology maintains 'an emphasis on false or deceptive beliefs but regards such beliefs as arising not from the
interests of a dominant class but from the material structure of
society as a whole. The term ideology remains pejorative, but a
class-genetic account of it is avoided' (Eagleton, 1991: 30).
And although ideologies arise from the material basis of
society, they serve only the interests of the dominant groupings
of society.

Quite how a theology might be ideological is perhaps not yet
clear. Different theologies may well be ideological in different
sorts of ways. In parts II and III, I begin by offering some hints
as to how theology might be approached from the perspective
of the critique of ideology, and suggest a number of ways in
which some theologies might be understood as ideological.

But I think that now we have some sense of the nature of

ideology. The location of ideological discourse is thus: either too close to or too distant from the determining pressures and limits of capitalist society. These have no sense that they are so determined and have a particular social location. Such discourses may well appear plausible. They may well claim to be oppositional. But patient analysis of their assumptions or connections will reveal that they offer unhelpful ways of thinking about human possibilities for the general reconstruction of society. Such ideological discourses may indeed speak the language of liberation, but, at the same time, mislead as to the actual human capacities for liberation.

What is the central effect of ideology? The effect of the production of ideology (as in other forms of production) is that human beings are denied 'the necessary human qualities of foresight, decision, consciousness and control' (Williams, 1983: 27). How theology contributes to the effect, and how it might avoid doing so, is the controlling concern of this book. Such an account of ideology I shall call 'negative', following Jorge Larrain (1983). It is to be contrasted with an account of ideology as general and positive. It is my argument that the negative account is thoroughly Marxian, and has been adopted by some theorists in the Marxist tradition.

Ideological discourse in this book, thereby, does not refer to the cognitive structure of ideology as 'descriptive' or as 'positive' (Geuss, 1981: 4f., 22f.). So, by the term ideology I do not mean to signify 'the beliefs of the agents in the society, i.e. only to the "discursive elements" of the ideology (in the purely descriptive sense)' (Geuss, 1981: 7). Nor do I mean by ideology what Geuss calls the positive sense, which is close to the notion of world-view, but including the sense that a world-view confers meaning: 'Starting ... from the wants, needs, interests, and the objective situation of a given human group, we can set ourselves the task of determining what kind of socio-cultural system or what world-view would be appropriate for that group, i.e. what "ideology" (in some descriptive sense of the term) is most likely to enable the members of the group to satisfy their wants and needs and further their interests' (Geuss, 1981: 22). Rather, in my argument, the cognitive structure of ideology promotes an account of ideology as 'negative' (Larrain), 'critical' (Thompson) or 'pejorative' (Geuss): here, the critique of ideology becomes 'a program of criticism of the beliefs, attitudes, and wants of the agents in a particular society. This research program is initiated by the observation that agents in the society are deluded about themselves, their position, their society, or their interests' (Geuss, 1981: 12).

Ideology is negative in a further sense: the transcendence of forms of delusion, false consciousness, etc., may be coincident with, or at the very least is a necessary pre-requisite for, emancipation and enlightenment. In this regard, in a comment on the critical theory of the Frankfurt School of Marxism, Raymond Geuss has argued: 'A critical theory . . . is a reflective theory which gives agents a kind of knowledge inherently productive of enlightenment and emancipation' (Geuss, 1981: 2). Ideology is to be contrasted with this: ideology is counter-productive to enlightenment and emancipation. Why is the critique of ideology important? Geuss' answer for 'critical theory' can stand for mine: 'The very heart of the critical theory of society is its criticism of ideology. Their ideology is what prevents the agents in the society from correctly perceiving their true situation and real interests; if they are to free themselves from social repression, the agents must rid themselves of ideological illusion' (Geuss, 1981: 2–3).[15]

If theology, as the theoretical practice 'governing' the practice of Christian praise and action, is ideological then commitment to the Christian 'way of life' becomes a contribution, in theory and in practice, to ideological strategies of containment (Jameson).[16] Rather than being the criticism of social domination and repression, theology is in collusion with these.

---

[15] This is a crucial hermeneutical element in the critique of ideology – see Thompson, 1990: 275–6, 292–3.

[16] This is not an abstract, or solely theoretical, matter if discourse is accepted as material. The following appropriate example offered by Dowling (1984: 130) may serve as a useful illustration: 'Our usual tendency, that is, is to think of seventeenth-century Anglicanism primarily as a state institution – the Church of England as a state religion, with Oxford and Cambridge as its seminaries, its cathedrals and bishoprics embodying a national administrative structure, its parish churches and their vicars an institutional presence reaching into every village and hamlet – and only incidentally as that body of abstract thought or theological discourse repre-

How theology might, *as theology*, avoid such collusion, and how it might make *theological* criticisms of the dominant order, is the concern of this book. And whether or not Marxism may help in the identification of this collusion cannot be decided in the abstract. If you are persuaded by the arguments of this book then the truthfulness of Marxism may be established. This lies in the very nature of critique.

sented in sermons, controversial pamphlets, works of systematic theology, university curricula, and the like. Yet the whole point of thinking of Anglicanism as a discourse is to see that a reverse perspective is also possible, that "Anglicanism" as an ideology or hegemonic theology may equally be said to have generated the Church of England as an institution, to have created its flesh-and-blood vicars and bishops and its actual cathedrals and village churches as the outward expression of an inner imperative.'

CHAPTER 2

Hegemony, ideology and determination

I CLOSENESS AND DISTANCE AGAIN

Marx contrasted true knowledge with what he called ideology. Hence the importance of the latter term throughout my argument. The nerve of the argument might be summed up in the question: is Christian theology ideological? And, following from this point, is it possible to conceive of a Christian theology that is not ideological? This is centrally a question about the production of knowledge. Here the spatial metaphor of closeness and distance is important as it offers a way of highlighting the problem concerning the social location of theology: what is the relation of theological discourse to the material basis from which it arises? And can the incorporation of theology as ideological discourse be avoided?

So far the critique of ideology has been restricted to examples from political theory and the philosophy of science. This has been quite deliberate. I wanted to show that the critique of ideology has no favourites; the task of critique is common across all disciplines. By taking this route I also wish to make another point. Marx and Engels do appear to have taken the view that Christianity was inherently reactionary. It is not perhaps fully clear why they adopted this argument, nor why (see Turner, 1983: 168–9; Lash, 1986a: 133–4) they found it so persuasive. But structuring the argument in this way has enabled me to suggest a way of proceeding: the interpretation of Marxist strictures and the reconstruction of a Christian theology which might meet these strictures. This, I think, is to take Marxist objections seriously, but also to seek to respond to

them *theologically*. If my argument is persuasive, then one implication we shall be able to draw is that theology is an intellectual
practice like others. As such, it has the same 'character' as other
disciplines: the capacity to be ideological but also the capacity
to be liberative (to be the criticism of forms of oppression and
mystification).

The difficult problem is: what sense can be made of the
notion that theology is ideological? This is our theme: how is
Christian theology true and so liberative knowledge under
capitalism, and not ideology?

II HEGEMONY

The aim of the previous chapter was to secure a rather different
criticism of theology than that associated with the Marxian
critique of religion. It was an attempt to suggest the important
epistemological issues at stake in the relation between theology
and Marxism. I suggested that theology needs to be seen as a
material practice and thereby in principle exposed to determining pressures. And I proposed a Marxist account of ideology (without seeking to pretend that it is the only account in
Marxism) in which ideas and arguments may be understood as
performing a 'negative' function: the mystification in theory of
wider material practice.

Yet this is persuasive only if some account of these determining pressures and limits may be given. There has been extensive
discussion of this within Marxism, much of it centring on the
metaphor of base and superstructure. I plan to offer an account
of determination but, closely following Raymond Williams, to
do so employing Gramsci's concept of hegemony. After this discussion, I return to the matter of theology as a material practice
and the issue of its social location. Finally, I rehearse again
what I think is the central Marxist objection to Christianity: its
(nearly constitutive) incapacity to engage with social forms.

But first we come to the matter of hegemony and the determination of ideas. Much discussion of determination within
Marxism has concentrated upon the metaphor of base and

superstructure (see Marx, 1977: 388–91 for its classic formulation). It has its weaknesses – among these, according to Raymond Williams, are a dualistic structure, and tendency toward reductionism in particular analyses (see Williams, 1977: 75ff.).[1] But the emphasis that Marx was seeking to secure remains important: ideas cannot be abstracted from the social and historical process. The problem with the base/superstructure model, Williams continues, is that it has been understood in such a way that its relational character has been lost. The heuristic device, intended to focus upon the difficulties in establishing the interconnections between the economic base and intellectual practices such as theology, becomes a principle: from tentative metaphor to abstract methodological procedure. During this process of false and inappropriate abstraction, what is lost is the connection between base and superstructure. The base and superstructure come to be identified as two separate areas: the metaphor becomes a 'picture' of society; what was tentative becomes fixed.

We might at this point note the fate of embodiment and language within this model. With so much interest invested in work, both in itself and as causal agent, embodiment becomes that which is structured by work. In effect, the actual practices of embodiment – particular bodies, particular geographical locations, particular histories, particular attitudes toward death – are overwhelmed. As a result of this, as the Frankfurt School noted, a certain variety of Marxism does not have the conceptuality for an engagement with fascism. The understanding of language in this model is also interesting: it either becomes distorted as ideology, or limpid as 'science'. Either way, the practice of language, as inscribed by particular pressures and as marked by sites of conflict, in which people are partly constituted, is lost. Indeed, paradoxically, in its emphasis upon materialism, the base/superstructure model often loses materiality; in stressing work as production (as it surely is), it

---

[1] Althusser's writing has done much to draw attention to the weaknesses of this approach: see Althusser in Althusser and Balibar, 1979: 182–93. Yet even Jameson, whose position owes so much to Althusser, makes some concessions to the 'expressivist' view: see Jameson, 1989: 23–58.

loses sight of the fact that language and embodiment are also productions.

The result of the abstraction of the metaphor, according to Williams, is deeply ironic: the separation of thought from activity, and consciousness from material production in a way that Marx was trying to *avoid* by his use of the metaphor.[2] What is required, Williams argues, is an 'adequate recognition of the indissoluble connections between material production, political and cultural institutions and activity, and consciousness' (Williams, 1977: 80). They are not, in this interpretation, separate areas, but 'whole, specific activities and products of real men' (Williams, 1977: 80). Further, although much attention has been paid to the superstructure – Williams refers to affirmations of its complexity (and, indeed, its autonomy) – the same compliment has not been paid to the base. Williams contends that any analysis must be aware of the possibility of 'deep contradictions in the relations of production and in the consequent social relationships' (Williams, 1977: 82).[3] He concludes that we need to pay attention, not to the base and superstructure, however defined and however related, but to the concept of determination.[4] From this position Williams offers a redefinition of determination that avoids understanding the base as some form of causal agent. Instead, Williams defines determination in two ways: as the 'setting of limits', and as the 'exertion of pressures' (Williams, 1977: 87). This, he maintains, is an account that can operate in a Marxist theory not predicated upon the base/superstructure model.

Williams understands the setting of limits as 'negative': there are specific historical conditions in which human beings work (cf. Jameson, 1989: 148). Williams' argument is a subtle one in that he maintains that a misunderstanding of these limits can lead to various forms of economism, but the central point is that certain conditions are objective and historical, and are

[2] Jorge Larrain specifically agrees with Williams on this point: see Larrain, 1986: 110.
[3] Williams' point, and sometimes his terminology of residual, dominant and emergent, has enjoyed a wide currency: see Jameson, 1989: 95–8; Best and Kellner, 1991: 279.
[4] This position is contested in Marxism: see Timpanaro, 1980: 114–17, who argues that the base and superstructure need to be kept separate (thereby in effect defending the metaphor itself).

thus the conditions into which we 'enter'. But this is an 'historical', not an 'abstract' objectivity: such conditions are open to change.[5]

Determination is not only negative. In its 'positive' sense, it is the exertion of pressures toward the constitution and 'construal' of social actions:

[Determinations] are at least as often pressures derived from the formation and momentum of a given social mode: in effect a compulsion to act in ways that maintain and renew it. They are also, and vitally, pressures exerted by new formations, with their as yet unrealized intentions and demands. 'Society' is then never only the 'dead husk' which limits social and individual fulfilment. It is always also a constitutive process with very powerful pressures which are both expressed in political, economic, and cultural formations and, to take the full weight of 'constitutive', are internalized and become 'individual wills'. (Williams, 1977: 87)

Through these pressures, we are constructed. We can grasp this if we consider that range of habits, that disposition of energies, which are the patterns of activity secured within the dominant hegemony. Small examples are easily identified: respect for authority, and an unwillingness to act unlawfully; a greater respect given to those who speak with particular accents; greater credence given to the testimony of men than women; a man may interrupt a woman, but not the reverse.[6]

---

[5] In discussing what he regards as unhelpful Marxist accounts of history, Fleischer argues that for Marxism 'the historical actuality of the "future"' is not 'something coming to us, but coming to us as the result of practical intentions' (1973: 87). Fleischer proceeds to reject various accounts of history: Marxism, he maintains, is not a religious communism, nor concerned with laws of historical development, nor is communism a moral requirement. Rather, 'It is not history that has an aim, but men who have historical aims' (1973: 90). Williams is similarly suspicious of laws (see 1977: 102). Such an understanding of Marxism as a philosophy of practice has implications for an understanding of human freedom in the context of determination: for an interesting discussion, from a different perspective, see Timpanaro, 'Engels, "Materialism" and Free Will', 1980: 73–133.

[6] Having said this, there may be significant variations in these habits across classes. A friend told me of his difficulties in not paying his poll tax during the campaign illegally to withhold payment of this tax in Britain; yet he reported to me that a colleague of his, from a different background, found no difficulty with the issue of illegality. Perhaps there are class modulations in determinative pressures. Indeed, a person with a decisive Yorkshire accent told me that, in unfamiliar surroundings, he was embarrassed by the way he spoke, saying that such a way of speaking was 'common'. This concern manifested itself in a certain reticence in speaking publicly.

These examples are, in one sense, trivial. But they all can, without too much difficulty, be connected up with rather larger motivational structures: patriarchy, the domination secured through class division, nationalism. In these interconnecting, multidimensional structures, we encounter the range of positive pressures: 'Determination of this whole kind – a complex and interrelated process of limits and pressures – is in the whole social process itself and nowhere else: not in an abstracted "mode of production" nor in an abstracted "psychology"' (Williams, 1977: 87).[7]

The objection often made at this point is to interpret determination in monocausal terms in order to reject it. But this tactic is only persuasive, as Helmut Fleischer has noted, if determination is taken to be uniform and total. Such an interpretation is not, he insists, properly part of a Marxist position: 'Politics, religion, art, etc., are not the results of the production of material goods; all that Marx claims here is that changes that take place in them correspond to changes in the sphere of production' (Fleischer, 1973: 109). 'Correspond' is an unhappy choice of terminology. Staying closer to the conception of hegemony allows us to say that politics, religion, art – as production – will be informed by, and will also inform, other social and economic practices. The construction of a social order means also the securing of that order, the construction of a 'regime'.

Indeed, if we are serious about characterising Marxism as a theory of practice, then it follows that economic determination 'must be described in terms of the motivated and conditioned behaviour of living men' (Fleischer, 1973: 110). Fleischer proceeds to argue that determination needs to be understood in

---

[7] It may be the issue of an 'abstracted psychology' which weakens the progressive/regressive method of determination in Sartre (1968). Sartre's existentialism leads him to consider determining pressures on individuals: somehow determining pressures affect the psyche of the individual. Sartre's difficulty is the mediating process between the individual and society. He is therefore right to argue that Marxism needs an account of determination, but I suspect that his solution is more individualist than Marxist. For a severe critique of Sartre's contribution to Marxism, see Aronson, 1977. (It would be interesting to consider whether Sartre's approach is more suggestive for literary theory than political theory: see Jameson, 1989: 42–3.)

two senses: in the first place, certain types of cultural, social or political activity cannot be achieved without the attainment of a certain level of economic productivity – although we must qualify Fleischer's account by noting that some economic forms of production may act as limits to other types of production. The second sense concerns 'the economic motivation of extra-economic activities, systems and organisations, that is, social stratifications, political institutions, formations and actions, and finally artistic, religious, philosophical and other productions and ideas' (Fleischer, 1973: 110). The reference here then is to a whole way of life or, better, as E. P. Thompson reminded Raymond Williams, a 'whole way of struggle' in which extra-economic activities are informed by economic production.

But this is not to suggest that naked economic interest can be traced in every aspect of cultural production. For instance, politics is concerned with the securing of the basis for the general reproduction of capitalist society, and does not straightforwardly reflect economic interests. Williams argues for this in his discussion of hegemony, given below. Fleischer argues this also: what the Marxist account of determination seeks to show is not 'that a special economic interest is the motivating factor in every case' but rather 'in quite generally demonstrating the class interests rooted in productive relations' (Fleischer, 1973: 111).[8]

[8] I do not enter here the debate as to the centrality of class. Certainly, I wish to affirm that there are other 'sites of struggle': race, gender, environment, and that these enjoy their own forms of autonomy and effectivity. I hope that the conceptuality being developed here works against the hypostatisation of class, and does rather insist on the importance of economic production as an indissoluble part of the wider process of social production. This sort of analysis insists on the specification, in particular instances, of levels of effectivity between different domains. Indeed, Marx himself argued in the *Grundrisse*, as Stuart Hall (1981: 32) has pointed out, that the unity of a social formation may sometimes only be grasped in terms of difference. (This point is thoroughly obscured by Susan Thistlethwaite (1989: 21–2) in her tendentious comments on historical materialism.) What is more important is the hegemonic strength of particular domains: to insist that capitalism is a novel form of the circulation of exchange value is not to reduce all forms of struggle to struggles over capital. It is rather to insist on the 'place' of such struggles within a structured whole. Of course, such claims to totality are contested today, but I think that such claims are hermeneutic claims in which the issue of interpretive horizons is raised (see Jameson, 1989: 89f.). Lastly, it is quite wrong to suggest that the concept of

Williams grasps the indissoluble nature of the material process through the concept of hegemony. He claims to follow Gramsci's distinction between rule 'expressed in directly political forms and in times of crisis by direct or effective coercion' (Williams, 1977: 108), and hegemony, either 'the complex interlocking of political, social and cultural forces' or 'the active social and cultural forces which are its necessary elements' (Williams, 1977: 108). The concept of hegemony tries to capture the dynamics of the development of a society. In so doing, it attempts to give some account of the uneven nature of this process: to explore how the self-understanding of agents is constituted by hegemonic theoretical and cultural practices which remain, nonetheless, open to challenge, amendment, revision and, possibly, radical change. Yet, these meanings, values and beliefs permeate our entire way of living, and the hegemonic is thereby deeply resistant to change. Thus Williams concludes:

Hegemony is then not only the articulate upper level of 'ideology', nor are its forms of control only those ordinarily seen as 'manipulation' and 'indoctrination'. It is a whole body of practices and expectations, over the whole of living: our senses and assignments of energy, our shaping perceptions of ourselves and of our world. It is a lived system of meanings and values – constitutive and constituting – which as they are experienced as practices therefore appear as reciprocally confirming. (Williams, 1977: 110)

Hegemony, in Williams' interpretation, goes beyond ideology understood as the reflective and theoretical upper stratum of consciousness.[9] Hegemony is the criticism of the notion that cultural practices may be understood without reference to the total social process. Put another way, the concept of hegemony

totality refers to something fixed (cf. Marx, 1973); hopefully, the discussion here of the concept of hegemony dispels such an impression.

[9] I am not sure that ideology is necessarily as 'formal and articulated' as Williams suggests. If it is right to insist that the primary locus of ideological strategies of containment (to borrow a phrase from Jameson) is 'ordinary language', then the power of ideology resides not so much in its formal structure but in its capacity to mobilise meaning in the interests of domination. The 'interpretation of doxa', as Thompson (1990: 279) puts it, is central to ideology critique. But such a reservation does not undermine Williams' central point: the notion of hegemony enables the conceptual engagement with a social *order*, and thereby resistance to that order.

introduces the notion of suspicion. What is at stake here is the maintenance of capitalism through its hegemonic pre-eminence. It is the task of cultural analysis to investigate and assess the contribution made by cultural and intellectual practices to the maintenance of that pre-eminence. (And this allows for 'the concepts of counter-hegemony and alternative hegemony' (Williams, 1977: 113).) Analyses in ideology and culture, if they are to be fully materialist, must always refer back to the question of hegemony, and the contribution of the practices under evaluation to that hegemony.

But this is no abstract matter. Hegemony refers to a way of living, and 'thus constitutes a sense of reality for most people in the society, a sense of absolute because experienced reality beyond which it is very difficult for most members of the society to move, in most areas of their lives. It is, that is to say, in the strongest sense a "culture", but a culture which has also to be seen as the lived dominance and subordination of particular classes' (Williams, 1977: 110). This captures the difficulty: it is not that within a dominant hegemony we are 'oppressed' by hegemonic discourses. This culture, in which we move 'freely', is already constructed upon, and is also the construction of, dominance and subordination. It is a culture which turns upon the production of work in certain social relations, and yet also the production of embodiment and language in such relations. We are not concerned here with those sorts of arguments that suggest: first, we must create the wealth, and then we will see if we can 'afford' our bodies. Rather, as a range of constitutive pressures, hegemony is to be understood as the securing of a series of practices: economic, cultural, discursive. (Of course, it is precisely from this position that the sort of argument just mentioned – wealth first, healthcare, etc., later – may be criticised.)

On this account, ideology is that lived relation in which dominance and subordination is experienced as a matter of freedom, personal choice or 'natural' limit. This last point is splendidly caught in a line from Ken Loach's film, *Riff Raff* (1990), in which one of the characters (a construction site worker), on learning that his girlfriend has been through a nervous breakdown, insists: 'Breakdowns are for the middle classes; the rest of us have got an early start in the morning.' This, then, is the internalised discursive expression of cultural dominance and subordination: the ascription of certain 'permitted' illnesses by class. And yet, of course, there is a serious point here: breakdowns are for the middle classes in that they can afford them – in the sense of enjoying white collar conditions of employment. Here then, in such a statement, is the acknowledgement of a material limit, together with the implicit assertion that it is a *social* (hence amendable) limit.

Williams draws the following deeply political conclusion when he specifies the advantages of working with the concept of hegemony: 'If the pressures and limits of a given form of domination are to this extent experienced *and in practice internalized*, then the whole question of class rule, and of opposition to it, is transformed' (Williams, 1977: 110). The concept of hegemony allows for connections to be made between various movements that might see themselves as concerned with the development of a new way of living and therefore in some sense as working for an alternative hegemony. In this perspective, a number of groups and movements may be seen as having things in common, and so therefore be understood, in a variety of ways and perhaps always in tension, as being part of a common struggle. This suggests of course that these groups and movements, of which the alternative hegemonic is comprised, do indeed have something genuine, and not ideological, to contribute to this common struggle. Indeed, the alternative hegemonic may acquire oppositional status.

Moreover, such an approach suggests 'a whole different way of seeing cultural activity, both as tradition and as practice' (Williams, 1977: 111). In other words, the concept of hegemony allows cultural and intellectual practices to be taken with full seriousness. No longer can they be seen as merely superstructural accretions, but as part of the social order – and as determined to a greater or lesser extent. In other words, this type of analysis, based in the concept of hegemony, allows for discrimination between various types of intellectual and practical activity. This is a consequence of the uneven character of hegemony, or perhaps the uneven nature of the process of the establishing of the hegemonic. What it cannot mean, despite the overstatement by Williams above, is that all experiences are 'coordinated' by the dominant hegemony. All practices may be encompassed by the dominant hegemony, but this does not rule out significant breaks within and against such dominance.

Perhaps some will wish to resist the direction of my argument in that it raises awkward questions about our complicity through our practices in the dominant hegemony; particularly so, if theology makes its own contribution to the dominant hegemony. In order then not to be too polemical, let me offer two non-theological examples of what I take to be theoretical practices effectively incorporated within the dominant hegemony.

The first I have in effect outlined in the previous chapter. Recall the lengthy discussion of Bhaskar's critique of some dominant arguments in the philosophy of science. A key objection made by Bhaskar was the account of the isolated individual and of a closed society 'secreted' by some interpretations. In perhaps the central site of rationality for the West – science – an understanding of practice is secured that not only seeks to offer an interpretation of scientific work, but at the same time secures a particular conception of the individual and society. (And this is achieved through the transfer of natural scientific 'rationality' into the social sciences – a classic hegemonic move, containing strategies of legitimation and domination.)

Second, I offer an example from social theory. In a trenchant critique, Norman Geras has argued that the work of Robert Nozick may be understood as profoundly ideological. Nozick, according to Geras, argues for a strong entitlement theory of ownership and possession. If you can show that you acquired your possessions rightfully, both morally and legally, then no agency has the right to take them from you. And yet, there is an interesting tension in Nozick's argument regarding rectification. What if you have not achieved your possessions in such a manner? Here Nozick's account runs into difficulties because what we are not always able to obtain – and this is exactly what Nozick's account *requires* – is '*precise* knowledge of the *precise* historical path to every current property holding' (Geras, 1990: 12). Rectification is only possible on this knowledge, and yet this knowledge is not always available. So Nozick, according to Geras, manages both to entrench property rights, affirm rectification in principle, and yet deny it in practice.[10]

In one way then, these attempts to secure a particular account of society or of property are perhaps theoretically not that strong. But they are part of a wide-ranging, although uneven, process to secure a particular range of meanings. (Nozick's is perhaps particularly interesting here as it connects immediately with a very important 'feeling': my property is *mine*. This is its crucial hegemonic 'performance'.)

III THE MATERIALITY OF IDEAS

But, it will be objected, is Christian theology truly implicated here? Might it not escape such determining pressures? It may well be that there are determining hegemonic pressures, but this is not the same as accepting that *theology* is 'exposed' to them, is it? It is important to get the answer to this question correct otherwise all sorts of confusions abound. The answer may well be that theology is not necessarily ideological and is not necessarily incorporated into dominant hegemonic forms. But this is not secured through any special quality inherent in theology. Rather, theology may secure such self-reflexive status through an affirmation of the material nature of theological practice, and through particular attention to the epistemological matter of closeness and distance. In this section I want to concentrate on what it means to suggest that an intellectual

---

[10] You may immediately see the difficulties of such an account of rectification: I live in Bristol, one of the key ports in the 'slave trade' in Britain. Indeed, such a trade was (and remains) one of the sources of the city's wealth. But rectification? Could this acquisition of wealth be traced? And to whom should it be distributed? To the black people in Bristol? To the black diaspora? To the four winds?

practice, such as theology, is material. (We shall be returning to the issue of closeness and distance shortly.)

To argue that intellectual practices are material is to argue that knowledge is 'public'. Theology needs to recognise that it shares the public nature of all intellectual production: it cannot appeal to 'special' sources of knowledge as its epistemological basis. The 'public' nature of theological intellectual production is noted by Clodovis Boff: 'I am of the opinion that the process of theological cognition obeys the same structural laws as any other theoretical practice . . .' (Boff, 1987: 73). Christian theology is therefore not concerned with some 'special' source of knowledge, nor with delineating a specific area as sacred. It is concerned with the 'scientific' ground suggested by Marxism: that language is practical consciousness, and is thereby inscribed by the practices of capitalist society.

This then is a further point: not only is all knowledge public knowledge, but consciousness remains part of material life and part of the social and historical process, whatever the apologists for consciousness might themselves proclaim. (It is interesting to note that Marx and Engels (1970: 51) cite the emergence of priests as ideologists as concurrent with the separation of mental and material labour.[11]) An emphasis on the 'materiality' of ideas, and on the production of ideas as part of a distinct process open to scrutiny, allows for an analysis of the determination of ideas: the hegemonic pressures which in general 'generate' theoretical discourses and 'limit' them to alternative or specialising modes. This does not suggest that there are no ideas that can be described as true, or that all ideas are determined equally, nor that the ideas of an epoch need to be seen as homogeneous. What can now be established, although it is a difficult theoretical task on account of the complexity of

[11] As Williams (1983: 23f., to which my general argument is indebted) points out, Marx and Engels argue thus on account of their conception of the division of labour, in which it is seen that some people, the apologists of capitalism, are concerned solely with the production of ideas. But while such apologists appear to be at one remove from material life, and indeed often consider themselves as such, the very fact of the division of labour that allows for the exclusive concentration on such production is, of course, an aspect of the organisation of a particular society, and so of material life.

the determinations, is the relationship between the ideas and the organisation of society, as both are seen as parts, often in tension, of the same socio-economic development.

Such an approach allows both ideas and the material life of which they are a part to be taken seriously. So, for instance, analysis of the dominant material force does not necessarily give you the dominant intellectual ideas, and vice-versa. As Williams puts it, this is an historical not a categorical proposition, and needs to be tested by the available evidence through intellectual analysis and practical application. Theology therefore needs to be seen as more than public knowledge, although it is at least this. It also needs to be seen as the product of human endeavour and inquiry: the institutions and groups which produce it are part of a process which includes both 'material' and 'mental' activity. This activity not only produces the ideas, but also tends towards the legitimation and naturalisation of a particular social order – this is the consequence of determining, hegemonic, pressures (see Williams, 1983: 41). Such an account suggests that theological ideas will generally incorporate, in some fashion, the pressures of the institutional and class structures of society, and that theology, as all other intellectual disciplines, will tend towards the legitimation of the existing social order.

IV CHRISTIANITY AS INTERMEDIARY?

Two emphases come together here. Theology is a theoretical practice, but this is not to deny its 'materiality'. As material, it is exposed to the determining pressures toward incorporation into the hegemonic. The ideological function of Christianity – if such it has – is not random or arbitrary, but serves a particular end. That is, it makes a contribution to the securing of the reproduction of society (a point discussed in more detail in chapter 5). What are the consequences of this for theology? In this section, I discuss what I take to be the crucial ideological function of Christian theology. How theology might resist its incorporation into the dominant order is a matter for the next section.

The stress upon the materiality of ideas, a contribution in epistemology as part of a wider inquiry in (a Marxist form of) social materialism, insists then on the 'embodied' nature of theological discourse. If, as feminist theologies often contend, Christian theology has too often denigrated, and been a means of control over, the bodily and the material (particularly women's bodies and nature), and thereby sought to deny its own materiality, then my argument insists, methodologically at least, on the reconstruction of theology as an embodied discourse, determined by material pressures and limits. The connection with the sustained attempt in feminist theologies to specify and, in some instances, to redeem the incorporation of Christianity into the hegemonic is, I hope, evident.

One way of delineating this methodological continuity is to note that, in both my argument and for feminist theologies, Christianity is 'put into question'. In my argument, this is secured through the Marxist critique of ideology; in a somewhat similar fashion Christianity, for some feminists, is 'problematized' by women's experience, and sometimes by the subsequent insistence that women's experience be enacted, both ecclesiastically and theologically (see Young, 1990: 14). The connection lies in a common commitment to what I term 'materiality': the criticism of 'theology's dualistic vision of reality, which depends on the separation of mind and matter, and the resulting method of bracketing historical and natural existence ...' (Chopp, 1987: 240). Chopp even refers to her (1987) position as a 'social naturalism', although I prefer the term 'social materialism', with its resonance of material *practice*.[12]

Yet there are also substantial differences. I am employing the Marxist critique of ideology not as a general resource for theology to draw upon (as in Ruether, 1983: 41–5), but as the crucial epistemological stricture to which theology must

---

[12] A further difficulty with the term 'naturalism' is that for some (e.g. Roy Bhaskar) it refers to the primacy of the methodology of the natural sciences. This is a position I do not share.

respond if it is to be liberative.[13] Indeed, the argument of part
II is spent not in an engagement with central Christian doc-
trines but rather with the issue of the location of theological
discourse. The aim of that part, and part III, is to offer a way
of reconstructing the outline of a Christian theology which
self-reflexively enjoys some sense of its social location, and is
thereby enabled (as counter-hegemonic) to engage with social
forms. This point is perhaps more general than the concerns of
some feminist theologies, which concentrate on 'the primary
alienation and distortion of human relationality ... the
relationship of men and women' (Ruether, 1983: 161; cf.
Young, 1990: 11–12).

In short, I am concerned with whether Christianity may
speak a liberative word at all, or as Rebecca Chopp puts it
(1989), a consideration of the theological warrants of Christianity toward the proclamation of a discourse of emancipatory
transformation. It is only after paying attention to such considerations – here construed in terms of the epistemological
strictures outlined by Marxism which in turn highlight the
ideological function of Christianity – that Christian theology
may turn to the issue of theological engagement with social
forms.

---

[13] At this point, the relation between ideology and experience (especially women's
experience) is raised. Although Althusser's conception of ideology is not mine, his
stress on the fact that experience is the outcome of a sedimented process of repression
is very fruitful. Hall (1981: 33), in a discussion of the culturalist and structuralist
paradigms in cultural studies, goes so far as to suggest (which may perhaps explain
the weakness of Williams' (1977) account of ideology) that precisely the notion of
'experience' in some areas of cultural study functions as a 'barrier' to adequate
understandings of ideology. It is here that the notion of experience, including
experience forged in struggle, becomes problematic in that in its welcome stress on
agency, it does not perhaps take with full seriousness the decentring pressures of
ideology. There are important, nuanced discussions of women's experience and its
rôle in theology in Young, 1990; Carr, 1988; Chopp, 1987, none of which are
perhaps explicit engagements with the decentring pressures of ideology. As I hope is
clear by now, I would want to explore the notion of experience through the
conceptuality of ideology, determination and hegemony. It is in the resonances
generated by the last concept that the relation between agency and decentring
might be explored, as a way of connecting, in a critical, emancipatory fashion, our
experience(s)/doxa, our theoretical work, and our imaginative (utopian?) desires.
Crucial to the methodology here, and already central to much pioneering work in
feminist theologies (and regrettably too often absent from 'theology proper'), would
be the relating of theological insights to insights from the social sciences.

What then is the central ideological function of Christianity? How might this be understood? We might begin by noting Marx's contention that one of the ways in which religion alienates is by acting as an intermediary between human beings when an intermediary is not in fact required; and the positing of this intermediary leads to misunderstandings about the social nature of humanity – what Marx in the *Economic and Philosophical Manuscripts* calls 'social, i.e. human, being' (Marx, 1975: 348). Consider the following:

An organisation of society that abolished the basis upon which haggling exists, i.e. the possibility of haggling, would have made the Jew impossible. His religious consciousness would vanish like an insipid haze in the vital air of society.

The question of the *relationship of political emancipation to religion* becomes for us the question of the *relationship of political emancipation to human emancipation* ... We humanize the contradiction between the state and a *particular religion*, for example Judaism, by resolving it into the contradiction between the state and *particular secular* elements, and we humanize the contradiction between the state and *religion in general* by resolving it into the contradiction between the state and its own general *presuppositions*.

Religion is precisely that: the devious acknowledgement of man, through an intermediary. The state is the intermediary between man and man's freedom. (Marx, 1975: 236–7; 217–18; 218–19)

In these three excerpts, all from *On the Jewish Question*, we see Marx assessing the problem of the significance of religion. The evaluation is always negative, but it moves between an account of religion as only false consciousness and entirely determined by the organisation of society, to one in which central questions relating to the position of the state, and its emancipatory basis, are mystified in relations between political and religious emancipation. In this more sophisticated criticism, Marx argues that even when the necessity of emancipation from religion is grasped, as in the arguments of the Left Hegelians, the resulting 'emancipation' is not liberating; the issue is obscured rather than clarified if the relations between religion and politics are not understood correctly. We have here, also, the argument, repeated in the *Economic and Philosophical Manu-*

scripts, that religion affirms our humanity through an intermediary. Communists, by contrast, have no need of such mediation (see Marx, 1975: 357–8).

This suggests, against the argument that I have been proposing, that religion is at all times and in all places completely
determined by the hegemony of capitalism. To be sure, criticism alone does not remove its power (Marx's objection to the
approach maintained by Feuerbach), but it still has no
counter-hegemonic worth in its own right. I want to consider a
little further this charge of the Christian religion functioning as
an intermediary. It occurs in a number of places (one, in the
Economic and Philosophical Manuscripts, we shall meet again in the
next chapter). What is interesting to note about these instances
is that religion is used by way of an analogy with the restriction
of human capacities, either quite generally or with reference to
money. A closer look may make this point a little clearer.

In drawing this analogy with the Christian religion, Marx is
not, I think, positing an antithesis between money and human
capacities. He is rather saying that in the process of exchange,
money is to be understood as a '*mediating function* or movement'
(Marx, 1975: 260). The result of this movement is that 'human,
social activity, by means of which the products of man
mutually complement each other, is *estranged* and becomes the
property of a *material thing* external to man, viz. money. If a
man himself alienates this mediating function he remains
active only as a lost dehumanized creature' (Marx, 1975: 260).
It is this sense that must, I contend, govern the analogy with
the Christian religion: 'Through this *alien mediator* man gazes at
his will, his activity, his relation to others as at a power
independent of them and of himself – instead of man himself
being the mediator for man. His slavery thus reaches a climax.
It is obvious that this *mediator* must become a *veritable God* since
the mediator is the *real* power over that with which he mediates
me' (Marx, 1975: 260).

This is plainly a mediation of domination, in which human
capacities in the economic sphere are construed in a way
analogous to the Christian religion. And what is misrepresen-
ted in this mediation? Precisely 'human, *social* activity' (Marx,

1975: 260; my emphasis). The same argument recurs in the *Grundrisse*, where Marx comments more carefully on the rôle of money as mediator between use and exchange values. The analogy with Christianity is again governed by this 'economic' logic: 'Thus, in the religious sphere, Christ, the mediator between God and humanity – a mere instrument of circulation between the two – becomes their unity . . .' (Marx, 1973: 332). We shall have reason to see later that the mediating work of Christ does not have the theological meaning that Marx here ascribes to it. But this is not central to the point Marx is making because the analogy is governed here by the economic critique in which a false mediation denies human powers and capacities through their misconstrual, misrepresentation, etc. Such mediation is profoundly ideological. *This* is the sense that governs the connection with Christianity.

And yet, a difficulty remains: quite what is Marx claiming is the effect of this mediation? I think that the answer here is the misconstrual of the social being of humanity. The ideological 'effect' of Christianity is autonomous individualism, or, at best, an intersubjectivity. As Rebecca Chopp notes (1989: 80), interpreting an argument by Moltmann: 'Christianity locates itself within . . . transcendental subjectivity, securing absoluteness away from the social and material factors of modernity.' This is, I think, the force of the criticism in Marx's remarks: Christianity's ideological 'performance', its 'place' in the social order, is here identified. A related criticism is implicit in his assertion in the *Economic and Philosophical Manuscripts* that atheism and theism are mirror-images of each other, and socialism has no need to follow either, but rather move directly beyond them in its affirmation of the social being of humanity (Marx, 1975: 357–8). Social relations are the 'site' of the enactment of human beings' capacities. It is these social relations that Marx thought Christianity could not engage with.

Consider in this regard the sixth thesis on Feuerbach: 'Feuerbach resolves the religious essence into the *human* essence. But the human essence is no abstraction inherent in each single individual. In its reality it is the ensemble of the social relations' (Marx, 1975: 423). The mistake of Feuerbach, to whom Marx at least paid the compliment of describing as a materialist thinker, is that he is unable to escape the clutches of religion. These clutches are to be understood as an inability to grasp that human beings may only be understood within, in Marx's unhappy phrase, 'the ensemble of the social relations'. Indeed, Feuerbach proceeds, according to Marx, to make the same mistake as Christianity: a failure to identify the human 'essence' as social allows, it is true, the demythologising of the Christian individual, yet still within the presupposition of 'an abstract – *isolated* – human individual' (Marx, 1975: 423).

To develop this point, we may note that Colin Gunton has quoted Coleridge on the centrality of the Trinity: 'that *Idea Idearum*, the one substrative truth which is the form, manner, and involvement of all truths' (cited in Gunton, 1991a: 28). This connects with Marx's difficulties with religion. Marx is concerned to know how this affects human beings' understanding of themselves in specific social relations. Gunton comments on the quotation from Coleridge as follows: 'The underlying claim is that the notion of the Trinity takes us to the heart of our being and of our being in the world' (Gunton, 1991a: 28).

It is a Marxist question to ask: what does such a conception of God tell us of our capacities, enmired as we are in sets of restrictive social relations? Is such transcendentalism offering us a 'transcendental category of the universal [which] is individualist and idealist' (Hardy, 1989: 26), and which thereby has no way of conceptualising the social character of humanity? This is, I think, Marx's concern with Christianity. As too often individualist and idealist, it is restricted to a 'dimension of the subject's relationship to himself' (Hardy, 1989: 23). And if it is not idealist, it still tends to remain individualistic (even if this is extended into notions of intersubjectivity – a trap into which some Marxists have fallen!). Christianity, then, is understood to be implicated in the obscuring of community and in the protection of 'the individual', and thus is precisely working against the interruption or subversion of the social-symbolic order. Indeed, if the account of hegemonic determination is correct, we should expect to find evidence of this in Christian theology.

This point may be explored in a slightly different fashion by employing Mészáros' distinction between anthropological and ontological matters. In an unkind but perhaps not untrue comment, Mészáros attributes the following to the Judaeo-Christian tradition: 'It is an essential function of the mythologies to transfer the fundamental socio-historical problems of human development to an atemporal plain' (Mészáros, 1979: 36). According to Mészáros' interpretation of the theme of alienation in Marx, the way that the younger Marx envisaged this transfer taking place is through the confusion of anthropological and ontological matters. By misconstruing the relation between the two, it is possible to offer facets of historical development as brute fact – as to do with human 'essence' or 'nature'. For instance anthropological concerns about the pervasiveness of oppressive structures may be transposed into a theological formulation and thereby reappear as an ontological category. There is in Christianity a tendency to project an hypostasised account of a theological category, e.g. sinfulness, into an equally static account of the nature of humanity.[14] (Perhaps the latter governed by a transcendentalism individualist in tendency and idealist in operation?)

In other words, the notion of sin serves as the denial of historicity: it tends to offer a 'short circuiting' of the demanding theoretical and practical task of ascertaining how sinful structures are constituted by our technical and economic practices. (Mészáros makes precisely this point in relation to the affirmation of the equality of humanity. 'If for some reason the fundamental equality of all men is not recognized, that is *eo ipso* tantamount to negating historicity, for in that case it becomes necessary to rely on the magic device of "nature" (or, in religious conceptions, "divine order" etc)' (Mészáros, 1979: 39).)

Crucial here is the ontological framework in which anthro-

---

[14] Of course, feminist theologians have been making this point in the area of theological anthropology, particularly with reference to the doctrine of sin. See the pioneering essay by Valerie Saiving, 'The Human Situation: A Feminine View' in Christ and Plaskow, 1979: 25–42 (orig. 1960) and, for a fuller treatment, Judith Plaskow, 1980.

pological matters are considered. Or, to be more accurate, what is crucial is the relation between the two.

For there is one way only of producing an all-embracing and in every respect consistent historical theory, namely by positively situating anthropology within an adequate general ontological framework. If, however, ontology is subsumed under anthropology ... in that case one-sidedly grasped anthropological principles which should be historically explained become self-sustaining axioms of the system in question and undermine its historicity. (Mészáros, 1979: 42)

Christian (theological) concerns intrude into the basic ontological enquiry in such fashion as to inhibit the development of the social ontology that might, in tandem with anthropological matters, seek to offer some account of historical development. This is the spirit in which we might revisit the following comment: '... for such a society, Christianity with its *cultus* of abstract man ... is the most fitting form of religion' (Marx, 1954: 83).

It may seem strange at the outset of this enquiry to specify the ideological nature and function of Christianity. But, as Marx noted, beginnings are difficult and yet vitally important (Marx, 1954: 18). I do not intend here an *a priori* claim, but I shall rather be 'demonstrating' the ideological function of Christian theology as the argument unfolds. I think that the central ideological function is as I have described it. And we shall find 'evidence' for this in the following pages. But the character of Christianity as ideology is a conclusion arrived at 'outside' this text. The reader, perforce, joins the conversation rather late and after crucial decisions as to the organisation of the argument have been made. Whether my argument as to the ideological function of Christianity is persuasive will only be 'displayed' as the argument proceeds.

V A WAY FORWARD?

The charge is a tough one: Christianity is generally idealist and individualist. Is the case closed? The argument of the rest of this book is that it is not. Yet we shall see, in a number of critical excurses, theology performing precisely the function that Marx and Marxists generally ascribe to it: the inability to conceptualise the social character of humanity within a particular society together with a capacity to mystify or obscure the 'real' social relations of contemporary capitalist society.

But in suggesting a way forward we must remind ourselves of a key point. The articulation of the *discourse* of liberation does not secure for any theory, including theology, the status of being liberative. So, putting this matter 'negatively', Clodovis Boff writes: 'It is clear from what has just been said that it is absolutely insufficient to claim not to be ideological, or to wish not to be, in order actually not to be' (Boff, 1987: 44). The claim to non-ideological status is not proof of such status. If a properly political theology is interested in being liberative, not simply in talking about liberation, then the question of the contribution of Christianity to the liberation process is secondary to the issue of theology's contribution *as theology* (in other words, a question about the epistemological status of theology in relation to material pressures).

Or, to put the matter differently but more accurately, the issue of theology's self-understanding as material *is* the issue of the contribution of Christianity to the liberation process. The weakness of political theology as the 'free-ranging speech of the disengaged' (Charles Davis) is precisely a theological weakness. The issue here is how we are to understand in theological terms the interaction between material circumstances and the theoretical discipline of theology as a contribution to liberation. It is only on these theological grounds that I can see a way of articulating the theological contribution that is able to answer the charge of Christianity as inherently an intermediary.

In what way or ways should theology establish its claim to be liberative? I have argued that, at the level of theoretical discourse, ideology works to misdescribe, misrepresent or exclude issues which refer to collective human interests in enlightenment and human capacities for emancipation. This is a point relentlessly made by Marx, especially in discussions of bourgeois political economy. The categories articulated by bourgeois economists were often correct, he argued, but there remained a persistent failure to make connections between the categories at a fundamental level (and so reinterpret them). This failure inhibited the contribution of these theories to the process of critique towards enlightenment and the programme of emancipation. Here resides the issue of ideological status. (We have already seen that the same sorts of objections were made to various accounts of socialism – see Marx and Engels' discussion in the *Communist Manifesto* of various forms of socialism.) Althusser gives a good account of this: 'Even if Smith and Ricardo did "produce", in the "fact" of rent and profit, the "fact" of surplus value, they remained in the dark, not realizing what they had "produced", since they could not think it in its concept, nor draw from it its theoretical consequences' (Althusser, in Althusser and Balibar, 1979: 181). In order to avoid the fate of Smith and Ricardo, theology does not need to develop 'theologico-political theories' (Davis), but it does need an understanding of its position within society. Theology is therefore not required to give an explanation of how the historical situation came about; that is the task of other disciplines. But it is required to take account of the findings of these other disciplines in order to understand its own position within a society and so to be able to make a contribution to liberation. Like Marxism therefore, theology will need to assess the contradictions of the present social order and give some account, from its own theological perspective, of the theological possibilities given by these contradictions.

Let us agree that theology seeks an answer to the question: given that we have some assurance (in the form of testimony) that God is, what are the grounds for this assurance, and what is the character of Christian discipleship in the light of this assurance? In this study, these two issues come together: the grounds for the assurance are given (partly at least) if we can know that we are not talking ideologically in our theological discourse; and the criticism of ideology, and the concomitant revealing of our genuine interests and of the forces that

genuinely restrict us, is an essential pre-condition for Christian
discipleship toward human emancipation.

Furthermore, part of what theology knows will be tested by
the practice of Christians – not only political practice, but the
practice of worship, liturgy, spirituality, etc. A liberative theology will *partly* be proved by the activity of Christians (and I
include 'worship' here) seeking to grasp the possibilities offered
by the present in order to secure a fairer and more just future,
and *partly* by a liberative theology's capacity to evaluate the
lack of 'proof' given by the activity of Christians. Part of the
'discipline' of a liberative theology will be that its understanding of God, and the relation between God and the world, entail
a commitment to working for liberation, and part of the
'discipline' resides in such a theology's capacity to note the
lapses in such a commitment. There can be no more fundamental assessment of a liberative theology than this.

The central question here is: how might a political theology be
liberative? On what grounds, internal and epistemological, is a
political theology liberating? What are the internal and epistemological grounds on which liberation theology seeks to ensure
its own liberative status? Put another way, how are we to
understand the self-reflexive character of theology such that
theology demonstrates some awareness of its social location?

Such an approach refers to the analysis of closeness and
distance I made in chapter 1. In order to situate itself as being
true and liberative, an oppositional theology needs to regard
itself as determined; and it needs to grasp its own determination. If this could be shown, human beings in revolutionary
struggle could consider themselves not as affirmed despite the
fact of thinking theologically, but in and through it. Theology
affirms human beings in the struggle for liberation by virtue of
its being a liberative *theology*. The faith, spirituality and
worship affirmed and 'ruled' by such a theology commits its
adherents to the process of liberation. As such, Christianity
may be understood as the basis of the liberation struggle.

The remainder of the book is devoted to showing, by demonstration so to speak, that Christian theology can meet the

Marxist critique of ideology. Christianity need not function as an intermediary in and through which human beings misunderstand themselves, and that Christianity can make an important contribution to understanding the conditions of the possibility of liberation. There need be no diminution in liberative potential, in the capacity to work for justice, to secure peace, as a consequence of seeking authorisation for such liberative potential in the human witness and testimony to the hidden presence of (the triune) God.

VI   THEOLOGY AND MARX/ISM: DIFFERENT VOICES

I have sought to suggest the shape of the argument of this book. It concerns the 'self-knowledge' of Christian theology, the self-reflexive part of the theological task that seeks to understand how theology is located in capitalist social relations. By this I mean to suggest that theology crucially needs some sense of its place within modern society if it is to be liberative.

This is a rather curious claim. It is not really concerned with 'doing theology better', but with the ideological or non-ideological status of theology. To try to offer some account of this, I rehearsed what I take to be the standard response to Marx's critique of religion (see chapter 1, section III). I then sought to suggest that this book is not particularly concerned with this critique of religion, but rather with the Marxist critique of ideology, and the consequences of this critique for theology.

In arguing this point I am developing insights already available in the theological debate between theology and Marxism. Central here are the contributions by Lash (1981), Turner (1983) and Kee (1990). What follows has continuities and discontinuities with all three. I agree with Lash that the employment of the Marxist critique may help to purge Christian theology of its idealism, thereby taking seriously Donald MacKinnon's complaint that 'idealism remains a besetting temptation of the theological understanding' (cited by Lash, 1986a: 95). Marxist materialism is therefore to be understood as a way for Christian theology to respond to the charge of idealism and to guard against it. This issues in an attempt to show how Christianity might be understood as materialist (see Lash, 1981: 135–52). Lash's work is a persistent presence in the rest of the argument. The sharpest discontinuity between his argument and mine lies in the fact that it is out of the engagement with Marxism that I seek to develop the theological proposals that follow. I have some sympathy with Denys Turner's complaint: 'Each of these challenges [from Marx's work] calls forth a response from Lash the theologian who, on the contrary, seems always to have a pre-written theological text to refer back to, its construction seeming to have taken place elsewhere than within the conduct of the debate itself' (Turner, 1984: 70). In what follows, I seek to develop theological proposals out of the debate itself.

Denys Turner (1983) explicitly argues that the challenge of Marxism to Christian theology is in relation to the nature and production of true knowledge. So Turner begins with an extensive analysis of ideology, that which under capitalism is not true knowledge. This is, I suspect, the right approach: Marxism raises the question of true knowledge under capitalism in acute form. Can Christian theology establish itself as true by meeting the conditions that Marxism itself exemplifies concerning true knowledge? Or, to put it in Turner's terms: can Marxism rescue the truth of Christianity? The weakness of Turner's argument is that his is insufficiently *theological*. Turner's is more an argument in moral philosophy than it is in theology; indeed, Turner notes there is scarcely any explicit theology in his book at all. David McLellan has suggested that Turner's book is 'more about ideology and morality than about Christianity' (McLellan, 1987: 195). What is lacking is the sustained attempt to develop a theology on the epistemological conditions exemplified and maintained by Marxism.

There are certainly a number of continuities between Kee's work and mine, and also some substantial differences. The most obvious convergence between my argument and Kee's concerns the nature of the criticism generated by the Marxist critique of religion: the 'effect' of theology is the 'inversion' of reality. The weakness of Kee's approach is that although Marx's thoughts on reversal/inversion are outlined, he does not set out how theology functions so as to invert an already inverted reality. To my mind, Kee is not sure how theology contributes to this process of reversal.[15] This uncertainty informs his analysis of liberation theology. He consistently asks the question: in the appropriation of Marxism why does liberation theology not respond to the criticism that theology is reversal or inversion (what Kee calls the ontological critique)? I agree with Kee that this is a very important issue, and is *the* question that needs to be put to theology. Yet the outcome of Kee's argument is to lock itself into a position from which it cannot escape. On the one hand, there is the insistence that theology must meet the ontological critique and must not function as reversal. But, on the other hand, as no detailed account is given of what this reversal comprises, it is hard to know how theology can respond to this Marxian criticism. Hence the brief and low-key nature of the final chapter of Kee's book, wistfully entitled: 'Religion [sic] in the Next Epoch'.

This book, by contrast, tries to specify the epistemology of what Kee calls the ontological critique, the critique of reversal. Here is the crucial difference between my argument and Kee's. My suggestion is that if the contours of the epistemology of reversal might be drawn, then it might be possible to show how theology functions to reverse (acts as a false intermediary), and to suggest a way forward such that theology might avoid the charge of reversing reality.

I have not spent as much time as Turner and Kee setting out the Marxist critique of ideology. The weight of my argument falls on the construction of a non-ideological theology which, for different reasons, Turner and Kee do not develop. I am rather noting Marxism's own claim to take the issue of determination with full seriousness and its argument that *it itself is determined*: 'It is the task of Marxist criticism ... to recognise its own historical determinants, but to demonstrate that its validity is not identical with them' (Eagleton, 1978: 16). This is the

---

[15] I have made this case in greater detail in a review of Kee's book: see *Journal of Theological Studies*, vol. 42, April 1991, pp. 436–41.

task for Christianity also: to grasp its own determined status, and yet to demonstrate that it is not to be fully explained by the identification of its social location. In other words, it is neither too close nor too distant.

Why is marking this theological 'distance' important? The reason is a basic one: failure to mark the distance is also a failure to know truthfully. And knowing the truth, as Christianity puts it, sets us free; in truth we know our circumstances and how to change them. This, concretely, is what sets us free. There cannot, as Helmut Peukert notes (1986: 229), be any going back on the attempt to conceptualise God in categories of freedom, nor of conceiving the task of humanity as the extension of social freedom. Such is the heart of a theological theodicy. Yet, it is precisely in the relation of these two points that the practical and theological difficulties arise. How do we know that our theological thinking, even our theological thinking about a God of freedom, sets us free?

Here Christian theology is required to show that it is not identical with its material determinants, that its social location is an oppositional place. The reason for this is fundamental: if we cannot know this, then we cannot be sure that our theological discourse is not ideological. If we cannot be confident of this, then we cannot be confident that theological production is, in the sense required here, in fact knowledge at all. If it is not knowledge, but ideology, then the theological contribution will, all claims to the contrary, be inimical to the enlightenment and emancipation of Christians. This is the issue that Marxism embodies for Christian theology. To put the matter at its strongest: the Christian claim to speak of a God of freedom is systematically undermined if the claim is productive not of the knowledge of social structures and relations, but rather ideological strategies whose effect is precisely to obscure such structures and relations. And how can struggles for emancipatory transformation be founded upon strategies which persistently deny their own material determinants?

We are back at the issue of trustworthiness with which I began this part. On what grounds are we to trust our theological interpretations, particularly our interpretations of social structures? How do we avoid a theological engagement with social forms that has the tendency toward mystification? How might we counter the charge that the key ideological function of Christianity is the privileging of the individual toward 'a purely individual, a merely psychological, project of salvation' (Jameson, 1989: 20)? If ideology is the restriction of human possibility, how may we be assured that Christianity is not ideological?

The following chapters suggest a particular way forward. I suggest in part II that through particular attention to theological language and by marking the distinction of God from the world, that the Christian God does not necessarily need to be understood in terms of an intermediary. In part III, I argue for a particular theological basis of the social character of humanity, and its relation to Word and Spirit. In short, I suggest that a trinitarian engagement, governed by the appropriate protocols concerning theological language and divine 'openness', may allow a specification of how God might be understood as present to the social character of humanity. In this way – by attention to particular protocols and through an insistence on the placing of social life in the economy of creation and redemption – Christian theology may begin the slow and painful task of acquiring self-knowledge against the unfreedom and idolatry of ideology.

PART II

Liberating theology

CHAPTER 3

Against idolatry: two protocols

The next two chapters are an exercise in theological self-criticism in order to secure some awareness of the determining context that impinges upon theological construction: liberating theology from the prison of ideology. The argument of these two chapters is, above all, an attempt to ensure that the use of the word 'God' is not idolatrous. If the theological protocols for such non-ideological and so non-idolatrous uses might be persuasive, the way will be open for the more 'positive' proposal of part III.

This chapter responds specifically to Marx's charge of Christianity as an intermediary: theology only offers an account of God through which, in ways that are ideological, human beings interpret themselves to themselves. I argue (in the next two sections) that an important 'protocol against idolatry' (Lash) is the decentring of the subject, human and divine. Theology does not fund accounts of centred stability (of individuality, race, nation, economy, gender). I also suggest (in sections III and IV) that this decentred movement needs to be interpreted carefully if it is to make a contribution toward a theology that is neither too close nor too distant; featured here are issues of agency and language. The second part of the chapter is concerned with the simplicity of God: a further protocol which attempts to secure an adequate way of distinguishing God from the world as a safeguard against the misconstrual of human capacities in relation to a God who is too 'immanent'.

In the previous chapter I rehearsed an important Marxist criticism: Christianity privileges accounts of the individual.

More strongly, that Christian theology has difficulties in engaging theologically with social structures and social relations. These two points are separable only analytically, and, taken together, tend to contribute to oppressive or restrictive notions of stability. 'The basic suspicion of the modern critique of religion is directed against the assertion of reality by religious consciousness as illusory projections that are merely supposed to secure and stabilize the factual performance of one's own existence and are thus finally directed at one's own realisation of existence' (Peukert, 1986: 234). In this chapter, I am concerned with this reference to the individual, and to the stabilising of the conditions of individual human existence.

The claim here is that Christianity secures the stability of the individual, the centred subject, and, by implication, 'his' immediate relationships. It is no accident that, for example, much Christianity has ideological capital invested in the family and perceptions of women as 'equal but different', and in individualistic accounts of 'society'. If the Christian religion functions in this way – construing human living in stabilising patterns of individual identity – the question for a liberative theology must be: is this a necessary function of Christianity? Are there theological ways forward? I think that there are. I propose, first, to discuss Denys Turner's argument for theology as a decentred practice. I then proceed to develop this case through a consideration of human agency and language toward an account of theology as practical. The subject matter is theological, but the approach is not; the latter is derived from the social materialism outlined in part I.

I   BEYOND THE CENTRED SUBJECT

To engage in 'ideology critique' is to raise questions about human experience. It is not, as we shall see, to bracket out that experience, but it is to decentre it. If a critical conception of ideology is to be understood as giving insight into the denial of the social determinants in experience, then to invest heavily in experience is to invest in an ideological strategy. Instead, here we are concerned with 'the process of the interpellation of individuals as subjects through which they become the agents of specific ideologies, sustaining particular material social relations' (Chris Weedon, 1987: 31). Ideology critique is thereby concerned to decentre the individual subject.

The issue raised at the end of the previous chapter concerned the privileging of the individual in Christianity, and the closely connected incapacity of Christianity to engage with social forms. Part of its ideological function, perhaps the crucial part, lies here. How then does Christian theology contribute to this process of centring (which is coincident with the denial of ideology)?

Denys Turner, in a number of contributions (1986, 1987), has analysed the theological commitment to the centred subject and the theological implications of decentring. Indeed, he has explored an insight from Marx in the *Economic and Philosophical Manuscripts* (see Marx, 1975: 357–8) as a way of criticising the Feuerbachian account of the competition between God and human beings. Turner argues that there are two aspects of theological centring: a tendency to place 'God' at the centre, and a commitment to the centred autonomous human being. This tendency must be exorcised by 'the wholesale decentring of theology, the abandonment of its commitment to a universe centred upon the competing autonomies of God or man ... ' (Turner, 1986: 138).

The structure of Turner's argument leads always to the Marxist deconstruction of a Feuerbachian theology. Thus Turner traces evidence of the autonomous human subject in the work of Don Cupitt, and seeks to show how it is 'placed' in the current order. If it is ideological to claim to have control over something which escapes your control, to be bound and yet to 'experience' this as acting freely, to parade one's imprisonment as freedom, then it is precisely this ideological strategy which Turner locates in the work of Cupitt. What is it about Cupitt's theology that reveals it as fit for late capitalism? Turner argues that it expresses the illusion that Marx considered endemic to religion: 'the thesis of the autonomy of religious language'. Turner argues, following his interpretation of Marx, that such a claim to autonomy 'is at once the result of

secular pressures upon that religious language and at the same
time it represents the need to deny or to misrecognise those
very pressures which produced that result' (Turner, 1986:
135). Put differently, Cupitt's form of religion, and especially
in its contention about religious language, is an articulation by
the 'abstract man' of bourgeois society, unaware of the determining pressures upon 'his' discourse.

Here we have, in Rebecca Chopp's formulation (1989: 27),
the Word being 'forced to re-present man's intent: the referent
of man, the securer of his infinite freedom, his universal autonomy'. Indeed, the celebration of 'autonomy' is itself determined, as we have already seen in Marx's description of Christianity in *Capital*: 'Christianity with its *cultus* of abstract man,
more especially in its bourgeois developments, Protestantism,
Deism, etc., is the most fitting form of religion' (Marx, 1954:
83). Such an 'abstract man', with 'his' autonomous religious
discourse, fits well with, indeed, is 'produced' by, the Eden that
Marx with some irony proposes in the first volume of *Capital* as
being the place where Freedom, Equality, Property and
Bentham rule. It is an Eden where each is concerned with his
or her own welfare, and where all believe that they enter into
wage contracts freely and that 'fair' remuneration is not
exploitation. Of course, this 'takes place on the surface' (Marx,
1954: 172) and Marx is convinced that the 'real' or essential
processes of capitalism occur at another level. I shall return to
this point below.

II DECENTRING THEOLOGY

Cupitt's argument is thus an example of theological support for
an account of stability of the individual subject that Marx
thought was endemic to Christianity. Turner interprets Marx
as identifying the basic dynamic of this Feuerbachian position:
the decentring of the Feuerbachian God simply leaves in place
the Feuerbachian 'abstract man'. We have here two parties,
either God or humanity, competing for the same centre. But
this is to suggest that there is some continuity between the
parties – a position which Turner characterises as idolatrous.

There can be no procedure for comparing the superiority of God over human beings because such a procedure presupposes that God and human beings belong to the same class, or, put differently, that they enjoy a certain continuity, and that, of course, is an idolatrous suggestion. Turner concludes:

> If God were something we could conceive of as superior to humans, then the game would have to be conceded to Feuerbach. A conceivable, infinite God displaces the world and denatures humanity, not by virtue of some utter transcendence but, on the contrary, by virtue of being nothing more than humans, displaced from their material, contingent history and projected upon the infinite degree *of the same scale* – in short, by being all too *immanent*. (Turner, 1987: 102)

This continuity, and the dynamic which encompasses it, is, so Turner argues, the focus of Marx's criticism. Hence the indispensability of Marx in trying to overcome Feuerbach's idolatrous God, and the ideological misrepresentation of a humanity competing for God's place.

Of course, we should not let the fact that Turner's example turns upon Feuerbachianism mislead us. The continuum does not need to be understood in terms of a competition for the dynamic to remain. We should note that, as immanent, 'God' denatures human beings. Nor should the fact that Feuerbach's intentions were atheistic blind us to the fact that we have here to do with a debate over who occupies this 'centre'. The implication of Turner's argument runs more widely than he himself suggests.

What is the significance of this? In a paradoxical (what Jameson would call a dialectical) way, Turner insists on an interpretation of Marx (against Feuerbach) as a crucial protocol against idolatry: Marx denies that there can be a centre for God (or humanity) to occupy. If theology has too often employed an account of a universe centred upon God to fund discourses which affirm particular patterns and forms of social organisation, particular gendered patterns of work and denigrations of embodiment, then here is a protocol against such idolatrous employment. Theological discourse is not secured through reference to a centred Subject. To borrow another of Rebecca Chopp's formulations, theology cannot be understood as reflection on 'the Word of God as *channelled through* human words, the event character of the Word receiving no content or influence by human words or experience' (Rebecca Chopp, 1989: 6). We have here the identification of a key ideological argument that many forms of Christianity (and some forms of atheism) manage to perpetuate: there is a centre (of meaning, value, etc.). Christians call this centre 'God', and such an argument keeps alive notions of a centred world, a centred universe. (We might again bear in mind here Jameson's comments (1989: 67) on the imperative of predisposition toward myth if mythological thinking is to be secured. Does Christianity function as a predisposition toward such myths of stable individualism as the 'free market', the 'end of history', the 'autonomous individual'?)

Theological discourse is not to be 'centred' in this way. Rather, theological discourse, as embodied in creation, as material, is subject to the pressures and limits of material determinants (and thereby, of course, open to deformation as ideology). The only true form of theological discourse will be one that recognises the determined nature of all discourse; one that explicitly welcomes, and seeks to secure, its own 'decentredness'. Only a theological discourse that accepts its status as decentred can be in a position (and no more than this) to speak of its own truthfulness, that is, of its closeness and distance to the determining pressures and limits of capitalist society. And the epistemological 'distance' marked by closeness and distance cannot be sidestepped through affirmations of a centring God: a Word which fixes, secures or stabilises words. Indeed, we have met this point already: as public discourse, theology is exposed to determining pressures and limits of the dominant hegemony. Reference to a 'God' at the centre would be to short cut the process of thinking through the implications of this for theology. It would also of course be ideological as, in a single act, it would deny the material determinants of theology. A Christianity which keeps alive the idea – an idea deriving its resonance from the pressures of material forces – that there is a 'place' that can be understood as the 'centre' of the universe, here secured by reference to a centred God, is to be rejected.

We should note immediately and underscore the non-liberative aspect of this sort of immanent, centring God. This aspect may be traced to the result that, as displaced from the centre, human beings are denied their own powers and capacities. But then that is the ideological consequence of having this sort of 'centre': the centre (founded in 'God') *can* hold, but its price is the denial of the subjecthood of real, historical people. That is, subjecthood is denied because the possibility of transcending current social arrangements is made more difficult through the misunderstanding of the true 'place' of human beings, and of the social determinants which 'in fact' decentre the 'abstract theologian' and 'his' discourse. Human beings are displaced by this centring 'God', and in this displacement is the denial of subjecthood, the denial of the energies, capacities and foresight that human beings will need if revolutionary change is to be effected. In short, we have ideology.

Now the Christian God has never occupied this spurious centre, and in sections IV–VI I shall explore one way of understanding this. But two central points emerge: first, if Turner is right, there is evidence for theology funding accounts of the stability of the individual. Second, theology as a decentred theological discourse puts into question 'immanent' conceptions of God. To construe the matter otherwise is to trade in conceptions of stability that the critical conception of ideology identifies as an ideological strategy in theology.

III   THEOLOGY AS A DECENTRED PRACTICE: AGENCY, LANGUAGE

If part of the task of Christian theology is the critique of idolatry, it will be unable to carry out this critique adequately if, as Turner puts it, 'it stabilises itself upon the myths either of God or of man at the centre of the universe and of its order, whether that "order" is that of the ego, or of the nation or of the socio-economic system' (Turner, 1986: 142).[1] The critique

---

[1]   The importance of the decentring strategy inaugurated by Freud is also discussed by Turner.

of idolatry will only be possible 'when it [theology] abandons the illusory security of its own autonomy as a discourse, with its naming either of an autonomous God or of an autonomous man' (Turner, 1986: 142). A non-ideological theology, a theology which seeks to be oppositional, will therefore enact as part of its methodology its own decentredness as a discourse, premised upon an account of a decentred (unknown) God and a decentred humanity. God cannot be at the centre because, as we shall see, God's relation to the world cannot be grasped in such terms. Human beings cannot be at the centre because that would be to claim an autonomy that a Marxist critique of ideology encourages us to see is illusory.

But we need to go beyond Turner, into the areas of agency and language, to develop fully this claim to theology as decentred discourse. We can best begin to do this by noting Turner's argument that 'a theological discourse which can qualify as truly cognitive is that which knows itself to be the decentred language of a decentred world, a discourse which is above all a moment of "unknowing" in a contingent, semantically unstable world' (Turner, 1986: 142). We have here a further claim: an interpretation of the world in terms of contingency and semantic instability.

What are we to make of this claim? I have argued that there are pressures that inhibit clear vision and understanding under capitalism, pressures which 'produce' forms of consciousness lived out by agents 'freely' in which these agents understand their world as fixed in meaning. This very 'fixity' is ideological, part of the dehumanising practice of capitalism and crucial to its continued existence. But the appropriate response is not necessarily to encourage a view that the world is contingent and semantically unstable. (Question: is Turner arguing that the world is, in its constitution, unstable, or that there are pressures which encourage us to interpret it in this fashion?) In short, I wish to argue that Turner is misled by the ideological strategy which he identifies. If theology often functions to found forms of stability, an attractive way forward appears to be a radical affirmation of instability. This much might be learned from the Marxian corrective to Feuerbach. Add to this an insight from Aquinas as to the unknowable nature of God (see Turner, 1986: 138), of God as absolute mystery, then we do seem to be afloat on a contingent sea of semantic flux (which is, at the very least, more fun than the game of 'push me–pull you' refereed by Feuerbach).

The attraction of this proposal from Turner does in fact locate a difficulty in my argument in the previous two sections. I seem to have affirmed the decentring of the individual and yet criticised the displacement of human beings by a centred God. These two arguments might seem, formally at least, to be similar. Both refer to a removal of human beings from the centre. Yet, I affirmed the first (the decentring of the subject), and yet criticised the second (the displacement of human beings by a centred, immanent 'God'). Turner's argument seems attractive in this context in that both these 'movements' are encompassed in the affirmation of instability. But Turner's argument, I suggest, obscures the fact that we have here to do with two very different movements as the rather different terminology – decentring, displacement – is intended to suggest. In the next two sections I rehearse my reservations as this will allow the further development of my argument in theological materialism.

My reservations are practical: how are we to act in such a world of contingency? As Jameson notes, we need 'a way for "decentering" the subject concretely . . . in the direction of the political and the collective' (Jameson, 1989: 60). The problem might perhaps best be identified as a tension between agency and the 'centring' ideologies (enacted in discourses) of capital. So it is to the issues of agency and language that I now turn to develop a richer, practical account of 'decentredness'. The issue of agency is rooted in a point made in part 1: the crucial hermeneutical insight that we are, in the critique of ideology, concerned with the self-understanding of (social) agents. Thus, we are concerned with human agents as embodied, language-bearing social actors in particular relations of production. This is important because grounding knowing, and the conditions on knowledge, in the practical sphere is crucial if we are not to be overwhelmed by the straightforward negation that has been

traced in some current theories by Thomas McCarthy
(1991: 3). Much so called post-metaphysical thinking, he
argues, in fact presupposes 'metaphysics of a negative sort'. It is
negative in the sense that in the movement of negation 'one set
of hypostatizations typically gets traded in for another: the one
for the many, the universal for the particular, identity for
difference, reason for the Other of reason, the structures of
thought for the infrastructures of thought, the logical essence of
language for the heterological essence of language, and so on'.
But, despite the range of different deconstructive moves,
McCarthy identifies a certain similarity which turns upon 'an
abstract negation of the conceptual apparatus of rationalist
individualism; the individual is represented as thoroughly sub-
merged in some whole and the historical movement of the
whole is viewed as governed by sub- or suprapersonal forces
beyond the reach of reason. The idea of rationally influencing
the shape of social life comes to appear as naive, dépassé, and in
short, hopelessly modern' (McCarthy, 1991: 3).[2] Modern or
not, the point I wish to make here is that 'rationally influencing
the shape of social life' turns upon a sense in which human
beings are decentred precisely as a factor in the process of
production. In short, this is also the grounds for their capacity
to grasp the situation and change it: to transcend a situation
that requires the trading of hypostatisations. Such trading is
thus an invitation to consider more carefully what is meant by
such notions as decentring.

Decentring does mean the decentring of the Cartesian
subject because the actions and discourses of subjects are constituted in and through hegemonic pressures and limits. There
are no 'pure' discourses and actions. But decentring does not
mean that the self-understanding of subjects is thereby
negated. Such self-understanding remains important, although
not determining. McCarthy has made just this point in a

---

[2] Jameson also speaks of Deleuze and Guattari's schizo-analysis as a form of a negative
(my term), here, hermeneutic – 'an *anti*interpretive method' – and insists that such a
claim is a challenge to offer a more adequate hermeneutics, rather than to dispense
altogether with hermeneutics. See Jameson, 1989: 21–3, especially 23.

comment on the status of the self-understanding of human agents in the work of the critical theorists and of Foucault:

> While both approaches refuse to take participants' views of their practices as the last word in understanding them, critical social theorists do take them as the first word and seek to engage them in the process of trying to gain critical distance from those views, whereas the genealogist [Foucault] resolutely displaces the participants' perspective with an externalist perspective in which the validity claims of participants are not engaged but bracketed. (McCarthy, 1991: 49)

Destabilising the 'centre' is crucial, but it is a very curious form of academicist criticism if this issues in a radically decentred world that is permanently in semantic flux 'in which the validity claims of participants are not engaged but bracketed'.

It may well be, as McCarthy reports Foucault as maintaining (McCarthy, 1991: 56), that the early 'humanist' Marx does see humanity as seeking the 'conscious reappropriation' of the 'alienated objectification of subjective powers' – an alienation which 'compromise[s] "man's" autonomy and thus block[s] his true self-realization'. But this is not, I think, true of the later Marx. There the *process* of labour is at the centre, with human beings decentred in the process of production. The task is to change the process in order to establish the freedom of human beings. Fetishism here does not signify powers to be reappropriated but that which inhibits change of the productive process by the revolutionary agent (for Marx, the proletariat, but today a category which requires significant extension). The decentred agent needs to secure the right amount of distance, practically and theoretically, from the determining pressures of capitalism in order to effect this change: a curious form of 'decentredness', indeed.

Crucial therefore is not the unstable and contingent nature of the world, but the basic activity, labour, of human beings. This might *appear* as unstable and contingent or it might *appear* as fixed. In fact, it is neither. To accept the first would be to accept a 'surface' account of the multifaceted character of metropolitan living as a definitive characterisation of 'essential' economic and social processes. And to whose benefit would such an account be? To accept the second is to accept that the basic activity of human beings is fixed. But of course it is nothing of the sort: social forms are at least in part the outcome of human intentionality (more on this in chapter 5). And to whose benefit would such perceptions of 'fixity' be?

As Raymond Williams has argued, the political consequences of being seduced by the unstable and contingent appearance of the world, or the demand for such flux as a protest against the fixity of social forms, can be disastrous. The 'painfully acquired techniques of significant *dis*connection' (extended in Turner's account of contingency and instability) which are so crucial for enlightenment and as precursor to emancipation are re-presented but to very different effect: 'The isolated, estranged images of alienation and loss, the narrative discontinuities, have become the easy iconography of the commercials, and the lonely, bitter, sardonic and sceptical hero takes his ready-made place as star of the thriller' (Williams, 1989a: 35).

What is the political force of such discontinuities? For Williams, 'the innovations of what is called Modernism have become the new but fixed forms of our present moment ... in an act of pure ideology, whose first, unconscious irony is that, absurdly, it stops history dead. Modernism being the terminus, everything afterwards is counted out of development. It is *after*; stuck in the post' (Williams, 1989a: 35; 34–5). Is not this 'stuck in the post' a danger in too swift a deconstructive move to 'decentredness' in that the contingency and instability of the world precisely denies us our subjecthood and becomes another form of ideology? The Marxist critical conception of ideology is the criticism of this sort of move which projects the (apparent) indeterminacy of our present situation into the heart of an epistemology. Indeed, we might say that this is to oversimplify the complexities of a practical 'decentredness' which is a condition of revolutionary agency. (We shall come across this issue again in chapter 5 where I offer a 'transcendental' account of society.)

I am doing no more than draw out the implications of the crucial epistemological metaphor of part 1: closeness and distance. This metaphor, as heuristic guide, contains within the dynamism of its paired terms an emphasis on 'decentredness'. Too often, as we saw, discourses which are too close or too distant are either reactionary or utopian. But 'decentredness' cannot take its guidance solely from deconstructive negation. It must rather take as its guide a persistent engagement with the practice of social agents. This then is the practical aspect of theological discourse. A theological critique of ideology engages with the thought forms of Christian social agents to criticise idolatrous theological reconstruction that obscures the closeness and distance of the self-understanding of social agents to material pressures. It thereby seeks to explore, together with such agents, and to have its own insights challenged and corrected, the forms of ideological complicity in which Christian theology is too often enmired.[3] (The horizon within which it does this, of which more in part III, is of course theological.) It is thereby crucially concerned with the discursive relations of power which govern human bodies.

I have mentioned the criticism of theology as ideology from the perspective of human agency. This brings me to the second point: the privileging of *discourse* featured in claims of the liberating importance of 'semantic flux'. There are dangers in this, as Terry Eagleton has noted: these might be understood as putting into question the very conception of ideology, and a failure to grasp the 'material' character of language.

The conception of ideology is put into question if discourse is linked strongly to the indeterminacy of power in which 'all viewpoints are relative' (Eagleton, 1991: 165). If all discourses are reduced to the inflections of (the same) power in which everything becomes a matter of interest, the unfortunate consequence, so Eagleton has argued, is to reduce all kinds of

---

[3] The account of who does theology suggested here is close to that of Nicholas Lash (1986a: 6): 'If, by "doing theology", we mean giving symbolic expression to that meaning of "humanity", that account of human identity, significance and destiny, which Christian faith declares, then *all* Christian existence is, in varying degrees of explicitness, "theological" in character. It follows that theological *responsibility* is ineluctably borne by every Christian individual and by all Christian groups and institutions.'

struggle to one level. In this levelling the force of the concept of ideology is obscured:

> [Ideology] is not just out to affirm that ideas are inscribed by interests; it draws attention to the ways in which *specific* ideas help to legitimate unjust and unnecessary forms of political domination ... The postmodernist move of expanding the concept of interests to encompass the whole of social life, while valid enough in itself, then serves to displace attention from ... concrete political struggles ... A 'scandalous' vision of the whole of society as one restless will to power, one irresolvable turmoil of embattled perspectives, thus serves to consecrate the political *status quo*. (Eagleton, 1991: 166–7)

What becomes of ideology on this account? Plainly, as a critical concept, it is undermined. No 'distance' remains to be 'marked' epistemologically as all 'distance' has been abolished in the flows of power in discourse. Ideology, it must be stressed, is concerned with particular meanings. Take this book: it seeks to highlight the mobilisation of ideological meaning in Christian theology: the securing of the stability of the individual, and a related failure to engage with social forms. It is not the (ultimately reductionist) attempt to reduce all of theology to the rush of power interests. To do so would be to deny, in the name of 'power' and 'interests', precisely the material determinants of language (including power and interests).

An emphasis on the contingency and indeterminacy of our discourse also runs the risk of obscuring how ideology may 'inscribe' particular discourses in that it seems to undercut the account of closure required by a conception of ideology, and, more generally, a conception of language as material. Following the Soviet philosopher V.N. Voloshinov, Eagleton argues that discourse may also be a battleground for ideological struggle, a point nicely caught in a paraphrase of a claim by John B. Thompson: 'Ideological power ... is not just a matter of meaning, but of making a meaning *stick*' (Eagleton, 1991: 195; for the reference, see Thompson, 1984: 132). The notion of a semantically unstable and contingent world seems to fit ill with such a conception.

The attraction for theology of this sort of argument – a stress on contingency and indeterminacy – is easy to grasp. The attempt to view discourse as anything other than unstable and contingent runs the risk of 'firming' into a centre of meaning, an 'imaginary unity', of generating ideological forms of closure. Such a position lends itself to the justification of a 'spurious theological universe' (Turner, 1986: 143) in which human beings compete with God for the centre – an account, for Turner, of one form of idolatry.

The question here is whether all forms of closure are in fact always reactionary. Does such a suspicion of closure betray a certain 'anarchistic suspicion of institutionality' which is in effect counter-revolutionary? Eagleton argues that 'a certain provisional stability of identity is essential not only for psychical well-being but for revolutionary political agency, ... since the subject would now seem no more than the decentred effect of the semiotic process ...' (Eagleton, 1991: 198). The 'suspicion of institutionality' is an important reservation, and in chapter 5 I suggest that it is important to understand social forms as the *condition* of human agency – in other words, social structures may be seen as enabling as well as coercive. The danger here is that the decentring of humanity and God leaves us in the theoretical position of being unable to say more than that we are in a contingent and semantically unstable world.

We encounter the need for a materialist account of language: a social structure with material determinants. Such an approach incorporates an account of determination, and thereby allows for a critical conception of ideology, and so of the possibility of oppositional discourses. A Marxist transformational model of society (considered more fully in chapter 5) that understands social activity to be governed by structures insists upon such an account of language. Such an account accepts the constitutive nature of language by understanding language as a social structure. As such, it is only reproduced through the social activity of human beings, and therefore must be understood in connection with the social relations of any given period. Hence the tendency toward ideology. The 'grammar' of language, the rules governing its use, are only intelligible – on a relational conception of society – upon a wider network of '*social* rules' based upon 'the relationships between people and between such relationships and nature (and the products and functions of such relationships)' (Bhaskar, 1979: 51). In other words, language is not 'innocent'. Language is a condition of the social world, and as such is governed by social rules in turn governed by social structures. What is not at all clear is whether social structures are benign, let alone emancipatory.

Discourses (the historical forms taken by language), if so determined by social structures presupposed by and given in social relations, may oppress; and, second, such discourses do not exhaust the real. Fundamental to society are social relations, without which intentional activity would not be possible, and social structures (other than language).

We need then to incorporate and yet go beyond arguments of a neo-Wittgensteinian type which suggest that what is fundamental is discourse, language, communication. For what is constitutive of social life is *work*, both mental and material. This emphasis upon language as constitutive may be seen as the expression of the division between mental and material labour, rather than its criticism. In stressing the importance of *language*, we must not lose sight of the fact that the rule-like character of language has a wider reference to the rule-like character of society. From this follows an ancillary point, that what characterises society is labour of various descriptions, governed by various structures and yet open to transformation. Language is a structural condition of social activity, but not language abstracted from social relations.

The neo-Wittgensteinian view is welcome in its hermeneutical stress on the discursive practices of social agents. Yet it remains insufficient in that it encounters difficulties in accounting for discursive deformation in ideology.[4] It does not articulate a materialist account of language, of the antagonistic discourses which compete within cultural, linguistic pro-

---

[4] 'Wittgenstein ... take[s] the "rationality" of an established form of life for granted, or at any rate as beyond question'; '... the later Wittgenstein's criterion of "everyday usage" ... has a strong tendency toward idealism and sceptical relativism and thus toward a toleration incompatible with criticism of any sort, however vestigial' (Edgley, 1983: 278, 280).

duction, and thereby does not specify ideological strategies of containment. The privileging of discourse must therefore be transformed by an emphasis upon the material determinants of language. The theological example given – Feuerbachian claims to a conception of a stabilising continuum between God and humanity – must not be allowed to shape the response: a leap into contingency and instability. (Of course, it is a competitive relationship, but it is one that takes place within what Jameson (1989: 84) refers to as 'the general unity of a shared code'.)

A more appropriate response, I am suggesting, is again to trust the metaphor of closeness and distance. What is required is an engagement with the practice of historical subjects and a commitment to specifying the ideological strategies toward stability which mobilise meaning in support of centring structures and practices. Such an approach takes embodiment and language with proper seriousness. In other words, it insists there are deep connections between language and other practices. From a materialist point of view, discursive amendments are material interventions, disclosing reality afresh and offering fresh paths to transformative practice. Emphases on agency and language come together here.

IV 'RECENTRING'?

I am arguing that the Christian God is not a projection through which human beings falsely mediate themselves to themselves. Christianity makes no such claim to the centre that this argument requires. Rather, in a way analogous to the rejection of 'placing' humanity, state, economy, race, nation, gender, at the centre, 'God' cannot be placed at the centre. Marxism invites Christianity to see this.

I have therefore accepted this stress on the 'decentring' of theological discourse. But I have not done so without restriction. The decentredness I propose here is an odd one: it refers to a 'decentredness' relating to social activity in order to grasp the possibilities of human action toward social change. It is not a 'simple' decentring but one which seeks to grasp the social character of this 'decentredness'. The 'decentredness' suggested here is not one that simply deconstructs conceptions of humanity into its 'negative' (into, perhaps, some impersonal force). It is rather a 'decentredness' that stresses such 'decentring' as a condition of human agency: a recognition of the majority's 'place' as a factor of production.

Jürgen Moltmann captures some of this in the following remarks: 'Human history always comes into being out of its interplay with the history of nature. In this warp and weft of humanity and nature, we cannot proceed from a centre, as do both modern anthropocentrism and the cosmocentricism which claims to be post-modern. If we wish to understand the history of the interplay between civilization and nature, we have to give up the notion of centricism altogether' (Moltmann, 1990: 245; cf. 272). Moltmann's argument has weaknesses: it is too static, the distinction between civilization and nature undermining precisely the point about the natural constitution of human life that he is trying to make; and the terminology is much too general. But I want to affirm the emphasis upon humanity actively shaping the conditions of its life. In current circumstances, any amendment to this active shaping will need to address the decentred 'place' of social agents (which of course includes Christians as social agents in the Church). Indeed, it is precisely from this place that such agents are enabled to see their true interest: not in some Lukácsian leap from a class-in-itself to a class-for-itself, but rather in the praxis of freedom (Jorge Larrain) that builds opposition to and extends the possibilities of action within and against the dominant hegemony of contemporary society. Indeed, in chapter 6 I shall be arguing that Christian practice will turn upon an account of being 'recentred'; and this account informs possibilities of social practice.

Second, I have questioned the privileging of discourse and its tendency to reduce 'decentredness' to a single quality: a reduction to discourse which, when understood 'correctly', cannot be understood as 'fixed'. If by this it is intended to stress the importance of grasping the emergent (that is, genuinely new practices), then this proposal bears a useful emphasis. But it tends to reduce all discourse to the emergent, and so obscure residual and dominant elements. Further, such a reductionist account fails to distinguish between the unstable and the emergent, and reduces all discourse to the same 'quality'. It does, thereby, as Eagleton suggests, display a tendency to cancel all the way through; in telling us everything, this position tells us nothing, apart from a shift into the 'negative metaphysics' of a cosmocentricism. What we require is assistance in identifying the counter-hegemonic, fresh possibilities in emergent practices, enacted in new 'structures of feeling' – not the 'freeing up' of all discourse.

Indeed, this 'emancipation' of discourse might be understood as caught in 'the separation of the social from the personal'. Williams writes: ' ... if the social is the fixed and explicit ... all that is present and moving, all that escapes or seems to escape from the fixed and the explicit and the known, is grasped and defined as the personal' (Williams, 1977: 128). Does the affirmation of flux move us beyond the disjunction between the personal and the social? The criticism of fixity can hardly result in the simple affirmation of flux, of all that is 'present and moving', because then precisely the social is excluded. Would not this be accounted an effect of the dominant hegemony: what seems lively and meaningful is characterised as personal, and what is 'fixed' – as 'beyond' the personal – is referred to as social? We cannot respond merely by saying that social forms are not 'fixed' as such a position remains within the contrast personal/social. A decentring critique must move us beyond the disjunction between the personal and the social, rather than stress one pole over the other. So, although this account is welcome, it cannot be allowed to stand unamended.

Finally, I wish to underscore the practical aspect of my argument here. I am maintaining that theology is practical: in this critical phase of its hermeneutical arc, it seeks to detect ideological strategies that fund myths of repressive or oppressive stability (primarily directed to individual identity, especially the psychological and the familial). It seeks therefore to pay attention to its social location, to the sorts of 'social experience' inscribed within its formulations, to the interests it serves, and the audiences it addresses.[5] The much favoured approach of giving priority to orthopraxis over orthodoxy, or of giving the practical primacy over the theoretical, does not really capture the complexity of this practical aspect. These are oppositions which are too static, dualisms which are too rigid, to engage with the subtlety and the persistence of strategies of ideological containment. I hope that part III will offer a more dynamic way of guarding against ideology: a way directed toward the abundance of God, and the richness and complexity of human living.

I am insisting therefore that Christianity – when attentive to a materialist conception of language – is the criticism of the idolatry of 'centredness'. But it is a 'practical decentredness'. The 'positive' side of this 'practical decentredness', in terms of the character of the theological contribution that might be made, I discuss in part III. In chapter 5 I suggest that, having argued that a 'God' at the centre is a form of idolatry, it seems inappropriate to reintroduce a kind of centredness by basing a relational account of persons or society 'on' the 'relational' being of (the triune) God. This, I suggest, savours too much of 'mediation'. The grounds for this opinion – God's 'openness' – are outlined in the next two sections, and developed in the next chapter. A fuller discussion of the being of God in relation to social forms is deferred until chapter 5.

V   GOD'S 'OPENNESS' TO THE WORLD

The previous sections stressed the decentred 'place' of our talk about God. This section seeks to maintain and develop this emphasis. To deny the 'availability' of God as 'centre' is of course a response to the charge of God-as-intermediary. It is a way of responding to the charge that the concept of God is ideological if human capacities are interpreted in relation to it. What follows from here is an exercise in disconnection: the

---

[5] See Metz, 1980: 58–9: 'Who should do theology and where, in whose interest and for whom?'

attempt to unthink ways of understanding God as the Subject who centres in order to make good the claim of previous sections that God occupies no 'centre'. But, I stress, to deny the 'availability' of God is not to deny God's presence to or God's involvement with the world. The God who does not occupy the spurious centre of which Turner speaks is not thereby to be understood as absent; the denial of immanentist, displacing accounts of God does not mean that God is 'lost'. To accept such a disjunction would be to deny or restrict God's freedom in relation to the world – a conclusion based, as we shall see, in the denial that the Christian God is the *creator* God.

In the remainder of this chapter I shall argue, through an exploration of the attribute of simplicity/simpleness and the creation perspective that it secures, for an account of God's 'openness' toward the world. Such an approach does, I think, rule out emphases on a 'suffering God', the notion of human beings in some form of univocal relation with God and the drive to pattern human relations on the 'model' of God's relationality. These matters will concern us in more detail in chapters 4 and 5.

What is meant by God's 'openness' toward the world? I am seeking here to get beyond the opposition between divine transcendence and immanence. In brief, immanence and transcendence are not to be understood as descriptions locked into competition with each other. Here meaning is produced through the fixing of this pair of terms in a strategy of contrast. I wish to move beyond such fixity by highlighting the ambiguity in the term 'openness', and the deferral of meaning through such ambiguity. 'Openness' may, as in the work of Rebecca Chopp (1989), operate so as to inhibit the ascription to God of notions of stability, hierarchy, and the denigration of embodiment. God's 'openness' toward the world resists such encodings. But 'openness' also has another sense, as when we speak of a person's openness to others, of a person's embrace or accepting stance toward the world, and – more generally – of solidarity. (Indeed, here 'openness' yields wonderful 'active' metaphors: involvement, engagement, embrace.) What follows will 'play' upon these two senses.

I am also proposing the term 'openness' because its decon-structive negation yields not one, but two terms. A God of closure in a first sense is one who fails to embrace creation (as in deism). But a God of closure in a second sense, is a God who is determined by God's relation to the world: a God who, to use an older category, we might describe as too immanent. In the first case we have a God whose freedom is so abstract that such freedom fails to engage with creation. In the second, we have a God whose freedom is curtailed. Freedom is here a crucial term: there persists an intimate relation between God's 'open-ness' and God's freedom. It is in part III that the connection between God's 'openness' in freedom and human social rela-tions of freedom will be explored.

Before moving on, I make two brief points. God's 'openness' remains a spatial metaphor. I see no way round the employ-ment of such metaphors.[6] Second, I stress here that this freedom is not arbitrary or formless. Indeed, we shall note in the trinitarian specification of God's economy of 'openness' and freedom in part III that this 'openness' is both structured and structuring.

To hint at the 'nature' of this 'openness', I begin, closely following the work of David Burrell and Brian Davies, with a brief discussion of divine simplicity. This might be described not so much as an attribute of God but as a 'formal feature' (Burrell). It does not have the same logical status as the attributes of omnipotence or omniscience, but rather assures us that, if we respect God's simplicity (Burrell prefers 'simpleness') in theological thinking, we can be assured that we are talking about God and not something creaturely. 'When we say God is simple, we are speaking not about God directly but about God's ontological constitution ... "Formal prop-erties" are not so much said of a subject, as they are reflected in a subject's very mode of existing, and govern the way in which anything whatsoever might be said of that subject' (Burrell, 1986: 46, 47). It is thus centrally a 'protocol against idolatry'.

---

[6] Gunton's proposal (1991a: 170f.) of otherness and relation to replace transcendence and immanence remains a spatial (although now personal) metaphor.

It makes an interesting contribution to the specification of 'openness' in that it suggests, as we shall see, both that the concept of God marks God's distinction from the world, and at the same time, invites attention to the mode of God's presence to the world. It is both these aspects – distinction and presence, freedom and embrace – that I intend in the use of the term 'openness'.

This 'formal feature' has been much maligned in recent theology and philosophy. Some theologians argue that it is a foreign import into Christianity and that its effect is to obscure God's relationship with the world (especially over the issue of God's capacity to suffer); and some philosophers regard it as untenable. I do not wish to enter into the details of the debate but simply to offer an account of divine simplicity. In offering this account I wish to suggest that it informs a conception of a decentred God. Second, it provides a basic control on theological epistemology, reminding us all the time that it is – just – possible to know God: to know that we do not know God. Why this is important as part of a response to the Marxist critique of ideology will, I hope, become clear as this chapter, and the next, unfold.

Such an epistemological control may be a way of ensuring that the 'concept' of God cannot function in a mediating fashion – a fashion of which Marx was so suspicious. The sort of relationship that God has with God's creatures is not one that can be construed in terms of false mediations – and it is precisely the 'concept' of God that tells us this. If theology claims more than this, it mistakes its own epistemological 'ground'.

To begin, I note an interesting comment by Burrell: 'Without a clear philosophical means of distinguishing God from the world, the tendency of all discourse about divinity is to deliver a God who is 'the "biggest thing around"'' (Burrell, 1987: 76). It is of course precisely this phenomenon that Feuerbach and Marx noted, and that Marx thought was endemic to Christianity. But the formal feature of simplicity/simpleness is part of an attempt to ensure that God is distinguished from all things creaturely and is a guard against thinking of God in such spatial terms. It is, centrally, an attempt to specify what God is not, and is thereby a defence against idolatry.

To argue this point, Davies quotes Aquinas: 'It is impossible to know of God what he is ... We cannot know what God is, but only what he is not', and suggests that the intention of such a comment is to invite us to see that God is not a puzzle to be solved, or some code to be cracked. Rather, in Davies' own words, 'God belongs to no class at all and that he defies the conceptual equipment by means of which we identify things and single them out as members of a world' (Davies, 1987: 51). This then may be considered an important resource for my argument. There resides within the tradition of 'classical theism', which is *not* the tradition of 'philosophical theism' in the philosophy of religion (see Surin, 1989: 110; Lash, 1988: 103), a stress on the distinction of God from the world as part of an inquiry that ensures that our talk of God is really talk of *God*.

Further, this formal 'feature' is closely connected with the idea of creation *ex nihilo*. It does not, as some might suggest, make God distant from the world; quite the opposite is true. But it does rule out notions of a suffering or changing God, and it does point away from notions of human beings in a relationship of, for instance, co-creation with God. These developments, in their infringement of the 'feature' of simplicity, raise questions as to whether such God-talk is talk of *God*. I am suggesting then that the implications of the notion of divine simplicity deny 'God' as an intermediary and stress God's involvement with the world. This may then inform our ways of thinking about God's relationship to the world. *How* the notion of divine simplicity denies God-as-intermediary is the argument of this chapter. *Why* this might be helpful in the development of a liberative theology is, I hope, obvious.

VI   THE SIMPLICITY OF GOD

What is divine simplicity? I quote Davies: 'God has no nature in any intelligible sense. He is divinity through and through without parts or aspects. On this account, everything that God is *is* God. Or ... God *has* no attributes but *is* his attributes'

(Davies, 1987: 51). Furthermore, as Burrell notes, it is important to grasp something of the importance of this 'feature' as a
way of disciplining our language of God: 'God's simpleness and
God's eternity are part of what assures us we are talking about
divinity' (Burrell, 1987: 77; cf. 1986: 46–7). We may now
appreciate why Burrell regards notions of simpleness and eternity as addressing the problem of the tendency to make God
into the 'biggest thing around'. Divine simplicity is a way of
disciplining our speech of God by ruling on the legitimacy of
certain conclusions regarding God's being. Although not a
description of God, and not to be placed with other divine
attributes, it enables the theologian not to confuse creator with
creature. It is centrally concerned with the 'character' of our
God-talk; it is a guard against idolatry through the distinction
made at the epistemological level between God and the world.
In making this distinction, the grounds of which we shall come
to in a moment, divine simplicity functions as a protocol
against idolatry in its insistence on the nature of the being of
God, a nature very different from that of objects in the world.

I want here to underscore the suggestion that the notion of
simplicity needs to be considered under the heading of 'what
God is not'. We must say, as the protocol invites us to, that
'God is not to be thought of (cannot be known) as something
with properties distinguishable from each other, or as something which we can conceive of as distinct from the nature we
ascribe to it' (Davies, 1987: 59). Further, if we fail to take into
account the centrality of simplicity (and eternity), we may not
be speaking of God at all. In other words, the doctrine of divine
simplicity invites us to 'think away from' how we conceive of
things in the world in terms of composition, in order to reflect
upon the simple 'nature' of God. Thus the notion of existence
employed here is a difficult one, for it is trying to show that
God's being is God's pure act of existing: *esse* is indistinguish-
able from essence.

A distinction is being made here, if you like, between the
'that' and the 'what' of God's existence: the nature of God
cannot be understood apart from its 'thatness', and vice-versa.
Thus God's 'existence' or *esse* is a special use of the word, and

insists that the only way to approach this simple God is by 'thinking away from' how we normally think of existent things. Hence, the emphasis that the simplicity of God governs an approach to the concept of God under the heading 'what God is not'. But how is it that failure to attend to the protocol of divine simplicity may lead to failure in our attempts to speak of God? What important point is the protocol intended to secure? Above all, according to Burrell, it is intended to mark the distinction between God and creatures, between creator and created. Aquinas – for Burrell, the most effective proponent of the attribute of simplicity – does this

by separating what is utterly without composition (or 'simple') from everything else, which is *composed* of essence and *esse* (or existence) ... [This] assures a clear creation perspective by insisting that the 'proper effect' of the simple One is the to-be (*esse*) of the cosmos. So the formal feature is intended to distinguish God from everything else – God's creation. That is, divine simpleness assures God's distinction from 'all things' as well as providing the ground for asserting the gratuity of creation. (Burrell, 1987: 77–8)

We may note two points here. The first is again to underline the 'negative' function of the doctrine: its formal effect is to enable the distinction between God and the world. The second point is to register that distinction – within such a 'clear creation perspective' – is not separation. (I shall return to this below.)

How might we understand this formal effect? How does simplicity enable the distinction to be drawn between that which is creaturely and that which is not creaturely? The answer to this question must lie in the fundamentally different character of the 'object' under discussion. And it is precisely this difference that the doctrine of simpleness or simplicity secures: 'What distinguishes divinity from all that is not divine, in such a way as to be able to characterize that One as the source of all the rest, must have to do with the *nature* of the subject in question and not simply its *attributes*' (Burrell, 1987: 78). Lack of attention to this formal feature, Burrell continues, invites, or tends towards, unhappy confusions between Creator and created, either because the 'nature' of the divine Subject is unclear, or because too anthropomorphic an account of the divine properties is suggested. Both these tend towards the mediation of human beings to themselves – a mediation of which Marx was so suspicious – via a conception of God understood as the 'biggest thing around'.

This will result, of course, in precisely a disjunction between God and human beings – which Marx rejected. It is this problem of disjunction that, it will be recalled, the strategy of 'decentredness' was introduced to address. Once a continuum is established, on which in effect the disjunction depends, then what marks God's difference from creatures is likely to be construed spatially or in crude accounts of agential power. We have the drift to the 'God' who is the 'biggest thing around'. (That this is a real danger can be seen from Nicholas Lash's characterisation of William James' conception of God: 'The God of William James turns out, then, to have been not only a creature, but a thing: a large, powerful, fundamentally friendly material object of which our more elevated elements form part' (Lash, 1988: 80). It is interesting to note that Lash reports James as specifically eschewing the notion of divine simplicity (Lash, 1988: 19).)

Burrell's arguments allow us to see why Marx, and the Marxist, might be suspicious: without attention to such a protocol against idolatry there is the tendency to be unclear about God's 'difference' from humanity, or about human powers in relation to divine properties. It is all very well to insist upon a liberating God, but this is plainly a problematic insistence if, in the very moment of insisting, what is human and what is divine, and their relation, are unclear. It is of course here that process theologians, those who wish to affirm that God suffers, and those who wish to place a heavy stress on co-creation, make their objections. For they are correct to note that there are consequences if we are to say that God's nature and existence coincide. Burrell spells these out:

This One whose essence is simply to-be cannot be limited by quantity (since it is not bodily) nor by genus or species, since its essence – to-be – 'overflows' both genus and species. So what is simple is also unlimited or, more traditionally, infinite. Nor can such a one be temporal, since it does not come to be, and so is not subject to motion or change, of which time is the measure. So what is simple must be beyond change – not unmoving, as the traditional term 'immutable' is often taken to mean, but beyond the categories of *kinesis* or of *stasis*. (Burrell, 1987: 79)

Difficulties arise at this point if 'immutability' and other terms are taken to be descriptions of God. Then, of course, the objections raised against these 'descriptions' by proponents of process theology and 'suffering God' theodicies (who may be one and the same) might be accepted. But we have seen already that the purpose and effect of divine simplicity is to distinguish God from the world, away from the problems of mediation. It is not an attempt to offer a 'description' of God, but rather to ensure that similarities between God and persons are not construed, on analogy with human properties, through a distinction between the divine nature and the divine properties; nor that there is presumed to be an easy continuity between human powers and divine properties – developments which have the unfortunate tendency to posit a 'God' who is the 'biggest thing around'.

VII   A CREATION PERSPECTIVE

We are now in a position to see how it is that the notion of divine simplicity secures the distinction of God from the world, and that it does so within a 'clear creation perspective' (Burrell). The implications secured by the distinction will be set out in the next chapter. Here I only want to explore how the notion of simplicity marks this distinction.

I have suggested that the notion of simplicity is directed to securing the distinction between God and the world. But this account also encompasses as constitutive of its position a doctrine of creation. Indeed, as Burrell notes, Aquinas develops the notion of simplicity along creationist, rather than emanationist, lines. This is suggested by the distinction given in the notion of simplicity: God is without composition (composition, of course, characterises things in the world). 'God is not one of the items in the world of which God is the origin' (Burrell,

1987: 77). But Aquinas' distinction between essence and *esse* to mark creaturely things, taken over from Avicenna, enables 'a clear creation perspective by insisting that the "proper effect" of the simple One is the to-be [*esse*] of the cosmos' (Burrell, 1987: 78).

Let us look at this a little more closely. We have seen that the notion of simplicity invites the identification of God's essence with God's *esse*. This is not to claim that we know what God 'is' – we cannot know what we mean when we say this, but we are forced to this conclusion. That *esse* is not a qualification of God's essence is the crucial move here. This move, in Burrell's interpretation, is systematised by Aquinas: it is the analogy of 'essence : *esse* :: potency : act' that allows Aquinas to insist that the activity proper to the simple One is creating or intentional activity. The One who is, by analogy, to be understood as pure act in relation to potency is the One whose proper effect is creation: 'a characterization of divinity as that One whose essence is simply to-be will allow him [Aquinas] to delineate creation as "producing to-be as such"' (Burrell, 1986: 28; internal quotation from Aquinas, *Summa Theologiae*, 1.45.5). Thus it is that the simple One is also the creator God. Things which enjoy material composition are to be understood in their existence as the effect of the One whose essence is to-be or *esse*.

In addition, we may note here that this position establishes a real relation between the One who creates and creatures: 'What *is* present in things, however, is the real relation to the creator ... which is displayed in the ontological unity possessed by each being by the fact of its existence ... [a] real relation to the One, really present in each existing thing in its ontological constitution by essence and existence ... ' (Burrell, 1986: 34). But this is not all there is to be said. 'Beyond' the composite nature of the world lies the simple One who is the creator. And this God is also beyond change, becoming, etc., as these are all characteristics of temporality. So, for Burrell, the second crucial 'formal feature' to be ascribed to 'God' is eternity; the Simple One is also the eternal One. God exists 'beyond' the world of temporality, and is thus eternal.

Yet this is not an account of eternity which suggests a God

who is disengaged. This stress on the simplicity or simpleness of God does not result in a God distant from the world. It does rather, through its stress on the distinction of God from the world, suggest God's presence to the world. The doctrine of divine simplicity places God beyond the 'composition' that marks the world. This 'beyond' is also 'beyond' temporality; such a God is eternal. But it is precisely God's eternal being that is the ground of God's presence. This is so, as Aquinas notes, because if time 'measures' temporal becoming, then eternity 'encompasses' all of existence. Existence is that which we 'enjoy' now – so eternity 'embraces' the current existence of things. So the eternal God is decisively *present* (see Burrell, 1987: 80). Thus it can be seen that the notion of simplicity informs a creation perspective: ' ... Aquinas' specific articulation of divine simpleness as the identity of God's essence with the divine act of existing seems tailored to a characterization of God as creator: the One who bestows existence' (Burrell, 1987: 79). The God, whose 'nature' is to be understood by analogy to the distinction between 'potency' and 'act', is the creator God.

Now, one interpretation of such a 'protocol against idolatry' has been to stress that the conception of God given in such grammatical considerations is not the God of the Bible, not the God of Jesus Christ – not a 'close' but a 'distant' God. I think that we are in a position at least to query this judgement. Indeed, this simple God is decisively present to creation. God is not eternal in the sense of timeless; rather God is eternal in the sense of being beyond temporality. But this is not to suggest that God is not involved with creation. Indeed, eternity carries with it precisely the stress on God's presence because God's eternity refers us not to some timeless first moment of creation after which God 'disengages', so to speak, a good job done. Rather, God is here understood to be 'the cause not just of becoming but also of being' (Davies, 1987: 59). The eternal character of God's creating suggests God's permanent engagement with 'all that is'.

How God might be understood as present – and as present to social structures and social relations – is a different point. I return to this in the next chapter, and again in part III. But for now we must note an implication of this notion of creation. In the perspective of the formal feature of divine simplicity, the character of God's presence suggests a particular account of God's relation to the world. If it is not an account that suggests that God sets a process going and then (occasionally?) intervenes, what account of God's presence is authorised by these 'formal features'? Plainly, we do not have here an account based in mechanical causality. God's activity is not to be understood in terms of alteration: God creates out of nothing. Such a position is not without its difficulties. It would depend upon, I suspect, a defence of a notion of 'activity' separable from the notion of causality – and I do not intend to offer such a defence here. But we may note the main conclusion to which the doctrine of simplicity drives us: that the distinction between creator and creature needs to be made (as a defence against idolatry); and the making of this case does not infringe upon God's involvement with the world.

We have a thoroughly intrinsic account of grace in which God's presence to the world is the 'action' that constitutes the being of the world. 'God's "capacity" to act is hardly in question; it is simply that divine action does not involve movement from potency to act, so is only metaphorically a capacity. And what is not subject to change is not itself in time, so God must be eternal' (Burrell, 1986: 49). So God's simple nature, and eternal presence, are 'rules' of theological discourse that insist on God's distinction from the world (protocol against Feuerbach) and yet insist that God is the 'cause' of all that exists. God, of course, is not present in the sense of changing things: that would be to understood God's activity under the rubric of temporality (and of mechanical causality). It would be to understand God as a 'thing' alongside other things. The God who creates *out of nothing* does not 'form' creation out of any pre-existing material, does not change anything. Rather, God's presence constitutes the existence of the world.

There are matters of some importance here which we might approach through a straightforward question: on what grounds is God worthy of praise? Let us say that one ground that is firmly to be ruled out is to consider God as one of the 'creatures' in the world. Such a 'god' would of course be an idol, and could hardly be 'the mover of history' (McCabe) and the maker of heaven and earth. It is to this matter that the doctrine of simplicity is directed. We are concerned here with the 'grammar of divinity' and 'the proper formulation of divinity as distinct from whatever else that is' (Burrell, 1986: 2). It follows that the distinction will not be a distinction in the world, in that it points us towards that which is different from 'all that is'.

Burrell argues that there is a strong tendency to place the distinction in the world, and points to the 'endemic tendency we have in attempting to distinguish God from the world. We cannot help, it seems, treating this distinction as though it were one *in* the universe – like every other distinction we make' (Burrell, 1986: 17). If the distinction is placed within the world, there is certainly no difficulty in locating the connection between God and the world. But what then becomes of the distinction? If the distinction is placed within the world the consequence is that we are left describing all that we know as 'God-plus-world'. Burrell again: 'For if the distinction of God from the world is treated as one in the world, then either God will be exalted at the expense of God's world, or God will be seen as part of a necessary whole – since in each case the attempt is to understand the entirety: God-plus-world' (Burrell, 1986: 17).

We cannot, of course, as Burrell points out, go to the other extreme and deny the connection entirely, because that puts in jeopardy the notion of creator and the 'accessibility' of God in our discourse that the notion of simplicity establishes. The problem remains: how to grasp the distinction between God and the world in such a way that marks no division in the world. We must have a distinction in order to respect the difference between God and creatures, but it must be 'a distinction which makes its appearance, as it were, within the world as we know it, yet does not express a division within that world' (Burrell, 1986: 17).

It is interesting to note that three religious traditions, Jewish,

Muslim and Christian, wrestle with this issue because at its heart lie the crucial issues of praise and idolatry – as we have seen.[7] We are searching then for a distinction that does, so to speak, make its appearance within the world without marking a division in that world. Moreover, this will be a distinction that marks God as the creator of 'all that is', as the beginning and end of all things.

We are of course now in a position to identify this distinction. The distinction may be found in existence, or rather our attitude toward existence (more on this in the next chapter). Existence itself marks no division in the world, it does not order the furniture of the world in any different way, it offers no explanation for the way things are – it is 'part of the grammar of the matter that the "fact of existence" [does] not name a kind within the world' (Burrell, 1986: 21–2). I shall be returning to this in the next chapter. Here it is important to note two points. First, such a conception is radically anti-dualist: the distinction marks no difference in the world. Second, the reference is immediately to existence: it refers us back to humanity and the attitude that we have towards our existence (and the particular difference that this may or may not make). Burrell argues thus: '[Aquinas'] proposal is rather like a call to a personal conversion, which one may ... ignore ... [a] call to conversion, as embodied and displayed in the distinction of essence from *esse* ... ' (Burrell, 1986: 36). If this is right, then the distinction is to be found in essence/*esse*: how this pair characterises God and invites conversion.

I have discussed the first at length above, and the second may be grasped by implication. It is also here, in fact, that the connection is to be found: in existence. It is in the bestowal of

---

[7] In a full materialist treatment, attention would doubtless need to be paid to the historical circumstances in which the doctrine of simplicity found such favour. Such an historicising enquiry I do not undertake here. Nor should the claim that 'the Thomist doctrine of divine simplicity is an exercise in "logical grammar"' (Davies, 1987: 59) be misunderstood. I am not thereby claiming that sorting out the grammatical rules is what is crucial to interpreting God's relation to the world, as if that were sufficient. I am rather suggesting that, as a kind of rule, the doctrine draws attention to the sorts of investments being made in the specification of the God/world connection.

existence that the distinction and connection between God and human beings is to be found. It is an absolute distinction; not one found 'in' the world. And it invites a reappraisal of one's attitude to 'all that is', because, as Burrell suggests, God's connection with human beings is precisely through the fact of existence, indeed, the existence of actual subjects.

The conversion that is being invited here is then a conversion towards 'existence' (to which God is present, in the connection and distinction of God's 'openness'). We might say that here the 'question of God' relates to the 'question of humanity' – in the practical sense of the attitudes that we shall strike, the 'position' that we shall take on the 'call to conversion'. But these considerations take us into the next chapter.

VIII CONCLUSION

This chapter has been concerned with the rehearsal of two protocols that might govern our discourse on God. The emphasis on the decentring of theological talk, it was suggested, might enable us to ensure that God is not to be regarded as available as the centre of a universe of meaning, nor as in competition with human beings. Both human beings and God need to be understood as radically decentred: so radically in fact that such decentring is the condition of human agency against the centring pressures of capitalism. Yet this is a materialist account of decentring, turning upon a materialist account of language. As such, it invites attention to the practical aspect of the movement of decentring. This might be understood as a commitment to an engagement by theology with the material location of theological discourse which is neither too close nor too distant. It is in this closeness and distance that oppressive forms of stability, institutional and psychological, might be disclosed; and, further, in which engagement with the social relations and structures disclosed by a materialist account of language might also be possible. Through attention to counter-ideological strategies, and not through a straightforward priority being given to orthopraxis over orthodoxy, a materialist theology is practical.

The second protocol, the doctrine of simplicity, is offered against the charge that the concept of God is to be understood as a false mediation of human powers. Or, in the terms used in this book, that the mediation is ideological in that it invites those living Christian lives to misperceive their own situation, and this misperception is to their own disadvantage (and to the advantage of the dominant hegemony). But a liberative theology, that seeks to be neither too close nor too distant, may employ the 'formal features' outlined above. These 'formal features' have their own 'proper effect': to deny the idolatry of confusing divine capacities with human capacities and of denying God's detachment from the world. God is not in some disjunctive relation with human beings; God is not the 'biggest thing around'. But this simple God is, as eternal, decisively present, in the 'form' of God's 'openness'.

Of crucial importance here, is the creation perspective which the second protocol yields. Here then we see the valuation of embodiment in this perspective, and its transvaluation in terms of our attitude toward 'the world' seen in the light of the dependence of 'all that is' on the God whose essence is to-be. The creation perspective articulated here is precisely a way of affirming God's commitment to the created order, and thus an affirmation of our embodied creatureliness. Indeed, the social form of this embodiment is, as we shall see in chapter 5, to be ascribed to the action of this creator God. The notion of God's 'openness' to the world is an attempt to capture something of this negation and affirmation: God-talk resists ideological encoding in its marking of the distinction of God from the world; God's 'openness' marks God's presence to and active involvement toward the world.[8] The discussion of the formal feature of simplicity has therefore been an extended attempt to give some content to the notion of God's 'openness' toward the world. How we might understand God's involvement, the 'difference' God makes and our attitude toward the world are the subject of the next step in the argument.

[8] An adequate creation perspective is implicitly present in Rebecca Chopp's notion of the Word as perfectly open sign. The Word, in her account, marks both connection and transcendence, naming and abyss, and so is both ordered and heterogeneous (see Chopp, 1989: 31–2).

CHAPTER 4

God/world: distinction and connections

The previous chapter stressed the decentred 'place' of our talk about God and, through an exploration of the attribute of simplicity/simpleness and the associated notion of creation, insisted on God's 'openness' to the world. Such an approach does, I think, rule out emphases on a 'suffering God', the notion of human beings in some form of univocal relation with God and the drive to pattern human relations on the 'model' of God's relationality. (The reasoning for this claim emerges in this chapter and the next.)

To deny the 'availability' of God as 'centre' is of course a response to the charge of God-as-intermediary. It is a way of responding to the charge that the concept of God is ideological if human capacities are interpreted in relation to it. But plainly to deny the 'availability' of God is not to deny God's presence to or God's involvement with the world. We saw in the discussion of divine simplicity that, within this conception, is a firm creation perspective.

In this chapter I seek to do two things. First, I explore the notion of God's 'openness' a little further, and suggest that it is connected with an emphasis upon human responsibility. Of course, I recognise that in some current theologies these two – 'openness' and responsibility – are regarded as, if not antithetical, then at minimum as a pair of terms to be reconciled. But I am suggesting here, in line with the mainstream realist tradition of Christianity in the West, that the distinction of God from the world is the form of God's presence to the world; and that this presence is the affirmation and not the denial of human responsibility. Second, I suggest that what is required for Christian practice is an appropriate way of 'marking' the difference of God from the world.

1   GOD'S 'OPENNESS' TO THE WORLD REVISITED

A central difficulty I am seeking to avoid is a concept of God that might be understood as falsely mediating human beings to themselves, in terms of the 'protection' of the individual and the obscuring of the social basis of human life. To this end, we have seen that there is no centre over which we compete with God; and some forms of philosophical theology remind us that God is unknowable mystery: Aquinas' certainty of God was, strange to tell, a curiously 'agnostic' form of certainty (see Copleston, 1955: 138–9; McCabe, 1987: 41).

We have seen also that the conviction that God creates, and creates *ex nihilo*, is crucial for giving an account of how God relates to the world. God's relationship to the world is not one that is informed by our understanding of relationship between objects.[1] Curiously God's very 'openness' to the world is the condition for God's presence; it is precisely God's otherness, God's eternal character 'beyond' temporality, that is the ground for God's nearness; eternity encompasses 'all that is'. I shall return to this point in a moment.

Mistaking the import of this creation *ex nihilo* may have disastrous consequences. David Burrell has noted (1987: 75) that attempts to replace the notion of creation with that of *creativity* are often connected with attempts to avoid the importance of the 'formal features' of God's simplicity and eternity. Simplicity is crucial if some account of God's 'unknowable' character and 'decentredness' is to be maintained. And eternity is crucial if an account of God's presence is to be secured. A departure from this, toward a 'notion of *creativity* borrowed

---

[1] I suspect that a common understanding of the relation between objects stems from Hume: inimical to accounts of God's presence in the world, and determination. For a critique of such an account of causality see Althusser, in Althusser and Balibar, 1979: 186–7. For a defence of the restricted, local employment of a 'Humean' notion of causality in Marxist studies, see Jameson, 1989: 25–6. I am persuaded that Jameson is right about this, as long as it is subsumed under a rather different account of causality.

from Whitehead' (Burrell, 1987: 75), has the unfortunate consequence of informing a theological development which issues in the construing of God in radically *immanentist* terms. Pannenberg (1991: 29–30) writes in a very similar vein to Burrell:

The problem with process theology, however, is that it does not allow for a concept of creation. The Whiteheadian God is but a partial factor in the constitution of actual existence, which is basically conceived as self-constitutive. Therefore, the God of Whitehead is not the biblical creator God. Furthermore, the Whiteheadian God is one actual entity among others, though distinguished from them by being everlasting. According to this philosophy all actual reality is finite, even God.

It may be clear what the difficulties are for a Christian theology that is seeking to meet the Marxist charge of ideology of a God who is 'one actual entity among others'. I do not see how the fact that God and human beings are constituted through a common process can be helpful here. Such a theology seems the very epitome of the possibility of false mediation, and of course open to the charge of exemplifying the movement of the Feuerbachian dialectic (see Turner, 1986).[2]

This argument may be developed with the help of the work of Herbert McCabe, who has written of his sympathy with the political edge of liberation theology, but not with some of its formulations of the doctrine of God. In his essay 'The Involvement of God' (McCabe, 1987: 39–51), he argues that 'it is not in the nature of God to be involved in the suffering of the world as spectator, sympathiser or victim, but that it is in God's nature nonetheless to be involved with his creatures more intimately than any creature could be involved with any other' (McCabe, 1987: 39). In other words, to argue for an 'immanentist' account of God is, paradoxically, to deny God's

---

[2] Some strands in feminist theology would resist the claim that de-humanising consequences flow from conceptions of God that are too 'available'. See Mary Grey (1989: 126f.) for a defence of process theology in order, it is true, to go beyond the process position; and Daphne Hampson ('Theological Integrity and Human Relationships', *Feminist Theology*, no. 2 (January 1993), 42–56), who speaks favourably of Schleiermacher's concept of God, given precisely in some general 'religious awareness'. (I am not thereby arguing that much else links the work of Grey and Hampson.)

involvement with the world, and restrict God's presence. McCabe is aware that notions of a suffering God are sometimes understood to be more 'biblical' than the simple God, so he seeks to secure his interpretation by arguing that the main-stream western tradition – he refers to Augustine and Aquinas – has refused to talk about the mystery of God separate from the mystery of creation. The discussion in the previous chapter on divine simplicity may be seen as one way of ensuring that God is spoken of immediately as the God who creates *ex nihilo*. This conception of a creator God, McCabe suggests, was inherited by the writers of the New Testament from the Jewish tradition in which Jesus was situated, a tradition animated by the 'creation question'.

We have already seen in the previous chapter that the answer to the creation question cannot be given in terms of creation. The answer to the question 'why creation?' may be 'God', but this is not to say that God and the world are to be conflated nor that they are to be understood in terms of each other: two poles of a *known* relation. Indeed, the previous chapter suggested that it is God's radical 'openness', as the One who creates *ex nihilo*, that clarifies why 'God' is a response to the question 'why creation?'. The answer is radical in that it cannot be given in terms of this world; this is the affirmation of God's *simple* character contrasted with the composite natures of worldly objects; it is also an affirmation of God's tran-scendence.

One 'effect' of God's transcendence is the securing of God's presence to the world: '. . . the God of Augustine and Aquinas, precisely by being wholly transcendent . . . is more intimately involved with each creature than any other creature could be' (McCabe, 1987: 45–6). McCabe's insistence that an account of the otherness of God is to found in the biblical 'tradition' finds support in an argument by Pannenberg, who writes of 'the biblical intuition of a radical otherness of God . . .' which is to be contrasted with 'Aristotelian and Platonic metaphysics' (Pannenberg, 1991: 30). What needs to be rejected therefore is some easy antithesis between the God of the Bible and the 'God' of the Greeks. Indeed, McCabe proceeds, as does

Pannenberg, to insist on holding to an interpretation of the God of the Bible as radically transcendent. Pannenberg writes: 'it is precisely because of such transcendence that he is not bound to any place "up there" or "out there", but can also be present within the world of finite realities' (Pannenberg, 1991: 30). This perspective, according to McCabe's argument, is decisively biblical, and failure to hold to this perspective can lead to idolatry: of adherence to gods rather than to God.

The denial that God can be identified with the gods is then the glory of the Jewish tradition, and is rooted in a firm creation perspective. (This development might also be called the critique of idolatry.) Drawing out the political consequences of failing to hold to this creation perspective, McCabe notes the dangers of slippage towards idolatry: '... by contrast with this biblical God, the God spoken of by those who insist on God's participation in the history of his people, sharing their experiences, their sufferings and their triumphs is perilously like one of the gods' (McCabe, 1987: 42). Holding to the creation perspective which is the nerve of this protocol against idolatry allows for a rather different argument:

God the creator, who is not one of the participants in history but the mover of Cyrus and of all history, is the liberator fundamentally *because* he is not a god, because there are no gods, or at least no gods to be worshipped. This leaves human history in human hands under the judgement of God. Human misery can no longer be attributed to the gods and be accepted with resignation or evaded with sacrifices. The long slow process can begin of identifying the human roots of oppression and exploitation, just as the way now lies open for the scientific understanding and control of the forces of nature. (McCabe, 1987: 43)

Understanding God as radically 'other' in this way, we can begin to grasp God's permanent and pervasive presence through all creaturely structures. But God cannot be identified with any of them (not even, in the sense intended here, with Jesus of Nazareth); God remains decentred. Nor is God the partner or object of mediation; God is not available to human beings in the way that Marx plainly took Christian theology to be suggesting. God cannot be in competition with human beings, because there is no 'centre' over which to compete.

Indeed, in this construal of God's 'openness', the 'concept' of God is precisely the critique of such attempts that seek to 'use' the concept of God to buttress or support political positions. God, radically decentred, not available for human manipulation, cannot be used as a reason for avoiding the task of establishing what are the *human* causes of misery and oppression. Human beings have their own freedom to address the issue of the roots of exploitation. God's very 'openness' enables this. It is not that God allows us to be on our own, as Míguez Bonino claims, to be active in history (Míguez Bonino, 1975: 98). It is precisely in 'otherness' that God is present as the mover of history, as the One who encompasses all that exists.

Strangely then, the sharp account of 'openness' to which the doctrine of simplicity invites us is not best understood in terms of distance, but rather in terms of God's eternal presence to creation. God's freedom in relation to creation is precisely the condition of God's presence to it. This presence is liberating in two senses. First, and negatively, God is not 'available' as some form of false mediation; as unknowable and decentred, God is not the guarantor of political, social or economic arrangements. Second, and positively, God's presence-as-'openness' constitutes an invitation to look to the human roots of social oppression and economic exploitation. The concept of God cannot be used as an excuse for evading this task; neither is the concept of 'God' a substitute for social and economic analysis in the sense of offering 'knowledge' for the resolution of practical problems. Uncovering and countering the human causes of oppression and exploitation is a human task, under the judgement of God. How we might understand this judgement is an issue for part III.

II   MARKING THE DISTINCTION

This is all very well. The question we might ask here is then: what difference does God make? Put another way, the direction of this argument suggests that God is not available so as to

interrupt the 'secularisation' of our circumstances. In other
words, God does not interrupt the criticism in theory and
practice of the idolatrous 'gods' of the market, the economy,
etc. But then the question returns: what difference does God
make? If God is no 'interruption', does this mean that God is of
no use? Robert Jenson (1989: 27) has argued that 'God's first
debility in the Enlightened West is that he has become *useless*'.
Have I constructed an argument that has this debility as its
core? Of course, without God's 'practical knowledge' (Burrell)
which encompasses love, creation would not be. But is that all
we can say? God is intimately present, but not in a way that
makes a difference?

This may sound rather odd. But it is an issue raised, I think,
by McCabe's argument. Certainly God is involved in creation,
and the character of that involvement leaves us free to examine
our own circumstances; God is not a thing that might make
particular differences. And yet, in the previous chapter I
argued that marking the distinction of God from the world is
important – with the implication that God does make a difference. What then is this difference that God makes? Responding
to this question, Nicholas Lash has written:

If he does make a difference, he ceases to be God (because particular
differences are made by particular things, and God is not a particular
thing). If, on the other hand, he does not, in fact, make a difference,
then there is nothing useful or intelligible, or true, that can be said
about him. (Lash, 1988: 223)

To be sure, there is no absence, properly conceived, of God.
Such is the conclusion to which we are drawn by the creation
perspective set out in the previous chapter. Yet, even if we do
acknowledge God, such acknowledgement fails to make a
difference; it 'does not, in itself, rearrange the furniture of the
world or make any particular difference' (Lash, 1988: 230). To
find a way out of this difficulty – does God's presence make a
difference or not? – we need to go back to the distinction that
the doctrine of simplicity invites us to make. Recall that the
effect of the formal feature was to ensure God's distinction from
the world. God is definitely not the 'biggest thing around'
because God is not an existing 'thing'. This 'formal feature' is

corrosive of Feuerbach's idolatrous 'god'. But, we may ask, what precisely is it that marks the distinction? Where lies the distinction between God and the world?

The short answer is: existence. Or, put more accurately, our attitude toward, our way of relating to, our existence. Indeed, we shall discover that this distinction marks no division in the world. But, in order to get to this answer we must retrace our steps a little, with the help of David Burrell.

In the previous chapter I reported Burrell as arguing that Aquinas was not promoting a philosophical revolution. He was rather inviting us to strike an attitude toward the world or, in rather different terms, to acknowledge 'a call to a personal conversion' (Burrell, 1986: 36). Fundamentally, Aquinas is concerned with a question about our existence: '. . . how can we sustain our conviction that life – especially human life with its attendant relationships – is what is most precious?' (Burrell, 1986: 21). This is, of course, only a particular instance of the larger question that McCabe argued, as we saw in the previous section, animates the Judaeo-Christian tradition: why anything? How are we to explain *our*, *this* existence? If we are unable to answer as to why there is anything at all, how shall we specify the importance of particular relationships?

These are troubling questions, in either their general or restricted forms, for, as Burrell notes: '. . . existence does not mark a division within our world so much as something that *happens* within it, as when a baby is born. What before was not is now present in our midst, yet population statistics are merely increased by one' (Burrell, 1986: 21). Thus it becomes important to strike some kind of attitude towards this rather odd aspect of existence – that it makes no difference. Or, if a different word has somewhat stronger, more active, force to it, it depends on how we *relate* to that which exists. Such relating does not of course rearrange the furniture in the world – it speaks of *our* relating, *our* conversion. We are now in a position to appreciate Aquinas' demand a little better: Aquinas, in this account, is issuing an invitation 'to reflect on our characteristic ways of approaching the world' (Burrell, 1986: 22), because the sum of these ways expresses both our attitude toward the world and the enactment of that attitude in relationships (with others and with non-human nature).

But why should we reflect on our basic stance toward the world? Burrell argues that our ways of grasping the world are constitutive of who we are. These are the habits and assignments of energy of which I spoke in a previous chapter, and which comprise our 'performance'. We are concerned here with 'our relationship to all the things in our life': our relation to the totality of our existence, the horizon of our engagement with the world as it is constructed through the uneven process of hegemonic constitution. We are not then concerned with our relation to the various compartments of our life, but with our relation to the world; we are concerned here with oppositions, not alternatives. The reconstitution of this relation, the transformation of this horizon, we might call conversion. As Burrell writes, if '. . . some power [were] able to alter *that*, then our relationship to each of the items would be altered *tout d'un coup*. Such is normally called *conversion*, and justly regarded to be beyond our own power to execute' (Burrell, 1986: 23). But this does not really answer the question. Why should we reflect on our attitude toward the world, the basic stance that we take towards it? It is here that the character of the invitation becomes clear. The distinction, we recall, between God and the world is precisely to be found in existence. To ask the 'question about God' is also to ask the 'question of our existence'. Of course, we do not know God – as McCabe has pointed out. But we do know something, although perhaps not much, about human beings (and our world). In the extension of our understanding of ourselves and our world, God makes a difference; in the asking of questions about our creatureliness, God makes a difference.

We can explore this a little further if we return for a final time to Burrell:

If this level of articulating 'the distinction' is to be in the service of knowing an unknowable God, we had best remind ourselves that the traditional analogue for divinity – the human creature – is also quite unknown to us. Were we to presume to begin with a self we understood, and wonder how divinity surpassed our understanding, we would be off on a false start. Yet here too, all is not mysterious, for the progressive consciousness we can gain of our characteristic attitudes to the world can offer us some insight into that self which is its microcosm, and whose 'sense of reality' expresses – in whatever we do or think – our grasp of that inexpressible dimension of the world which is its reality. (Burrell, 1986: 24)

Some of the terminology here is unfortunate. But we can note the main drift of the argument. We have seen in the previous chapter that the distinction of God from the world is inexpressible. Or, although we may put it in words – God is the One whose essence is to-be – we cannot say what this means. In this sense, it is inexpressible, and marks the distinction of God from the world – both epistemologically and ontologically. By analogy, our relation toward reality, our horizon of engagement, is equally mysterious. And yet it is in precisely this relation that we offer our own assessment of the 'reality' of existence – a reality we can never get outside, and is thereby always in part inexpressible. It is in such a relation, practical and theoretical, that we express and enact our relations 'toward' existence. This horizon is thus to be understood as an active commitment toward the world: a sense of a reality by which we are already 'cultured', and which we in turn refashion. This is the analogy to knowledge of and relation to God.

At the same time, it seems to me that there is a difficulty in the general nature of the language. My concern here is with conversion away from social forms of idolatry – a practical matter. But I think that Burrell's account can be moved in this direction. Burrell's terms are perhaps somewhat unhelpful: 'consciousness', 'insight', 'self', perhaps even 'attitude'. But the dynamic of his argument is not restricted to these terms. I have already suggested that the material dimension of ideas needs to be grasped, and in this context we may begin to grasp the insufficiency of the terms in which Burrell casts his argument, even if the general direction may be sound.

The 'materiality of ideas' insists that ideas need to be understood as practical consciousness, informed by and informing our material circumstances. Thus our attitude toward existence is not existential, in the technical sense. Indeed, 'existence', although in one sense appropriate – with its implicit reference to 'all that is' – may be somewhat misleading if it generates images of the individual confronting his/her own, *individual* existence. In short, I am seeking to stress here that conversion is not solely a matter of attitude. To seek to take and enact a stance toward the 'givenness' of the world cannot be summarised only in terms of attitude, although that may be part of it. As Lash puts it: 'Conversion, turning, is a practical matter, a social matter, with material conditions. It cannot occur through the mere exercise of will power, or through wistfully wishing that it were so' (Lash, 1988: 205).

The call to conversion is a practical matter that engages with the criticism, theoretical and practical, of forms of social idolatry. It is to enquire into the circumstances that inhibit our conversion, and it is to enquire into the circumstances that generate, and seem to require, such forms of idolatry. If God marks no division in the world, and is not available to restrict Christianity to private moments or personal matters, then what emerges is an enquiry into idolatrous human relations and into the forms of life of those relations. Or, to put it in the terms of Burrell's argument, it is in trying to grasp our attitude toward our existence that the distinction between God and world is enacted. Human relations, as Lash says, are the metaphor for God's relation to the world. Thus we may say that our manner of our relating to the world marks the distinction of God from the world. Furthermore, this 'mark' invites us to pay attention to the manner of our relating to others and to our environment toward the mitigation of idolatries of the social.

At the beginning of this section I posed the question: what difference does God make? We are now in a position to grasp a possible response to this question. Existence makes no difference; existence certainly marks no division in the world. And yet there is another sense in which it makes all the difference.[3] How is this?

---

[3] This section is deeply indebted to Lash, 1988: 221–31.

Existence, I have said, makes no difference. Yet existence does invite us to think differently about the world, to take up a different attitude towards it (Burrell). We have already seen McCabe's argument that the 'creation question' animated the Jewish sensibility – a contention he repeats elsewhere (see McCabe, 1987: 16). Once we grasp this we begin to understand that it is this creation that demands from us a response. Here resides the possibility of a change of attitude that, Burrell argues, Aquinas is inviting us to see in his distinction of God from the world as secured by the attribute of simplicity.

We might note also that this perspective guards against unhelpful construals of the relation of God to the world. For instance, it guards against an identification of God as 'monarchical'. Sallie McFague has incisively criticised such an account on the grounds that God is understood to be 'distant from and basically uninvolved with the world' (McFague, 1987: 65). Such a position is ruled out by the creation perspective proposed here. Neither does the distinction God/world mark a division in the world. The distinction between God and the world is not to be found in the world, nor beyond it; it is neither 'pantheist' (Burrell's 'God-plus-world'), nor Platonic. Here we could not do better than accept Ruether's rejection (1983: 70) of the 'dualism of nature and spirit' that such unhelpful distinctions between God and the world invite us to make. We can thereby reject 'both the image of mother-matter-matrix as "static immanence" and as the ontological foundation of existing, oppressive social systems and also the concept of spirit and transcendence as rootless, antinatural, originating in an "other world" beyond the cosmos, ever repudiating and fleeing from nature, body, and the visible world'. Rather, the distinction neither denigrates the material world, nor denies the distinction between God and the world. It is a distinction that makes no difference, and yet invites a response. An epistemological revolution is not in prospect. Instead, the invitation is that we should relate differently to 'all that is'.

We can specify this more carefully if we follow Lash's argument that we have here a distinction that makes no *particular* difference. Yet although it makes no particular difference, this distinction does refer us to the basic stance that we make towards the world, and does thereby make a certain difference. Lash constructs his argument by developing Burrell's notion of relating to 'all that is' as the site of conversion in terms of relations with others. Lash suggests that, strangely, 'being in relation' makes no particular difference: '... People who find themselves to be "in relation" to each other still need food ... still get toothache, still require work and shelter, and still live under the threat of nuclear war. In some sense, then, being in relation does not, in itself, rearrange the furniture of the world or make any particular difference' (Lash, 1988: 230). Here we have the transposing of Burrell's argument that existence does not make a difference into the form of relationships. In a suggestion analogous to Burrell's that existence does not make a particular difference, it marks no division within the world, so here Lash argues that 'being in relation' marks no division in the world. And the same is so of God's relationship with the world. 'And the suggestion is that the same is true of our relationship with God': it makes no particular difference.

Yet this, of course, is a play on words: to argue that being in relation makes no particular difference is not to suggest that it makes no difference at all. Just as the birth of a child marks no division in existence, but 'merely' increases the population statistics by one (Burrell), so being in relation marks no particular division in the totality of our relationships. Yet, in another sense, being in relation makes a (if not, initially at least, particular) difference: '... people in relation, in acknowledged mutual dependence, may find that they are newly enabled to *cope*, with fresh energy and clear sightedness, with all the particular problems that engage their attention and responsibility. And this may serve as metaphor for our relation to God (except that here, of course, the dependence is not mutual)' (Lash, 1988: 230). Here we have the transposing of Burrell's suggestion that it is in the manner of relating to 'all that is' that the distinction between God and the world may be enacted. Just as Burrell suggests that Aquinas is inviting us to make a conversion which of course makes all the difference, so Lash is suggesting that 'being in relation' makes all the difference – and may, indeed, go on to make particular differences.

Yet I must also note that although Lash's argument is in fact a transposing into different terminology, and the development, of Burrell's argument, Lash resists the employment of the attribute of simplicity. Lash offers two reasons for such resistance. First, he maintains that the recovery of the distinction of essence/*esse* in the notion of simplicity is too difficult an interpretative task. Further, the connections that simplicity tries to break are those of a neo-Platonic scheme of 'emanation', a scheme which does not picture the connection for modern people (Lash, 1988: 228). I have much sympathy with this, and with Lash's alternative: relationship (and its enactment in community) against a universe where 'connection' is understood mechanistically. Yet Burrell's interpretation of Aquinas' scheme does have two advantages. The stress on *creation* avoids the immediate narrowing to human relationships that Lash's scheme invites, and, by holding to a creation perspective, secures God's presence to the world.

The second point is: because, for Lash, human relationships are the metaphor for God's relationship with the world, and the latter is fundamentally unknowable, there is a tendency towards a lack of detail in Lash's account of human relationships in community. This has been noted by Gregory Jones: 'It is perhaps surprising that, given the prominence of the language of community in *Easter in Ordinary*, it remains such an unspecified notion' (Jones, 1990: 400). I intend to keep the wider term in order to include 'the natural' and as a warning that the notion of creation, as it relates to social relations, requires some specification. (This last matter is the subject of sections IV–VI of the next chapter.)

Indeed, as will become clearer in part III, only in a theological interpretation of society, I shall be arguing, can the dynamic of the argument set out in this part secure its full theological force. Indeed, such an argument is given, implicitly at least, in holding to the creation perspective of this chapter and the last. Failure to think through the implications of this perspective leads to the indeterminacy of Lash's argument as regards a theological interpretation of society: if the analogue for an *unknown* God is the human being, then on theological grounds the specification of the social organisation of the latter is obscured. Such a deficiency can only be made good by taking the constitutive force of holding to a creation perspective: we require the development of an aspect of a theology of creation in order to secure the 'being in relation' of which Lash speaks. If it were possible to secure such a placing of human beings in a doctrine of creation, then it might also be possible to understand how this 'being in relation' is reconstituted through the event of Jesus of Nazareth. As the Logos enfleshed, in Jesus is the reconstitution of that which is created.

Indeed, Lash's failure to think through this creation perspective in relation to the second Adam may be traced to Lash's lack of attention to Christology. Again, it is Gregory Jones who has caught this weakness of Lash's theology in an acute comment on the character of Lash's argument:

To be sure, Lash frequently refers to the importance of Jesus Christ and the centrality of discipleship of the crucified; but a particularistic christology does not decisively affect the structure of his argument. Indeed the people Lash discusses in developing his argument have frequently been criticised precisely for their inadequate christologies ... Lash discusses Schleiermacher, but not Barth; Rahner, but not von Balthasar; Buber, but not Sobrino.[4] (Jones, 1990: 400)

In part III, I shall seek to avoid such a criticism by placing an interpretation of society in a theology of creation, and by exploring in relation to this the concentration of God's activity in the life, death and resurrection of Jesus of Nazareth.

We may conclude this section by affirming that the account offered here still protects the decentred 'openness' of God. But God does make a difference: the question of God's presence to the world becomes a question of our humanity, and, particularly, the conversion of humanity. Of course, God is always present. Yet the sin of idolatry here becomes crucial in that sin is the expression and enactment of our ideological and idola-

---

[4] Although perhaps it is not really to the point to criticise Buber for an inadequate Christology!

trous tendency to mistake the distinction: either to 'get a fix' on God, '. . . to set up some object of our mind's construction, some idol of our imagination and desire, which, coming between us and Him whom we sought, would further darken our vision and render the "eclipse of God" more or less total' (Lash, 1988: 203); or as well as attempting to 'secure' God, also to seek to 'fix' humanity. In other words, to lead us away from the consideration of our own circumstances toward idolatrous forms of stability, and thereby to obscure the possibility and necessity of material conversion away from such idolatry. We see here the important practical point that 'the truth of theological formulation lies in its effects' (Carr, 1990: 109). But such considerations lead us to the matter of the eclipse of God.

III   AGAINST THE ECLIPSE OF GOD

We are now in a position to begin to see why it is that human beings are enabled by God to confront their human circumstances. God cannot be applied to as some metaphysical buttress for forms of economic or social organization. But then neither does God's 'openness' simply leave human beings free to secularise their circumstances. We have here a closer connection between the presence of God and human responsibility. And we can see why: the manner of God's presence to the world is in the denial of difference: existence does not make a difference to anything. But this denial is enabling in its invitation towards conversion, to a fresh relation to existence. This is no necessary connection (that would be a division in the world). But it is a real, if not a particular, difference.

To ask the question of God is to ask the question of humanity, in the sense that human beings are invited in the face of the incomprehensible mystery of God to be converted away from all forms of idolatry. The doctrine of simplicity invites us to pay attention to the manner of our predication of the divine. If we follow its strictures we learn that our knowledge is of an unknowable God. But it is precisely this that is the invitation to conversion; to reaffirm that, although we do not know God, yet we do know that the condition for our living, the existence of 'all that is', is of God. The question becomes: how do we enact the reality of the presence of God as mystery in the world? Not in order to make God present – God's absence would mean the end of existence – but rather to secure the actuality rather than the latency of God's involvement with and presence to the world (the terminology is Buber's – cited Lash, 1988: 205).

Here we encounter the issue of sin. It may well be, as the protocol of simplicity suggests, that God is unknown by us not on account of our sinfulness but because we are creatures. But sin does matter because, although God is never absent, we may turn away from God. This, crucially, is a turning away from ourselves, away from a manner of relating to 'all that is' in a way that recognises, acknowledges and enacts the fact that the 'answer' to the mystery of creation is the mystery of God. It is in this 'relational' or 'attitudinal' sense, as we have seen, that God makes a difference. We may explore this further through a discussion of Lash's use of Buber's metaphor, the eclipse of God.

This metaphor allows for the insistence on the latency of God's presence (as we have seen, in this chapter and the last, this is the very condition of the existence of 'all that is'). As Buber writes: 'But ... an eclipse of the sun is something that occurs between the sun and our eyes, not in the sun itself' (cited Lash, 1988: 201; original from Buber, 1957: 23). Yet, human beings may live lives and construct forms of social organisation, as if God were not present: the denial of the actual (that is, the enacted), not the latent, presence of God in the eclipse of God.

The crucial question here is: what is it that lies between ourselves and God? What 'form' does the eclipse take? Lash, in his articulation of the theme, seeks to develop Buber's insistence on relation, and so argues that it is forms of 'irrelation' that obscure God: 'the living God is eclipsed in the eclipse of human community' (Lash, 1988: 200). The route my argument takes in part III has some similarities with Lash's position. Indeed, this is not surprising bearing in mind the discussion of ideology in chapter 1, and the emphasis on the relation between ideas and society outlined in chapter 2. Thus, I want to suggest that it is against the 'background' of the 'fetishism of relation', of which ideology is the guardian, that theological criticism needs to be secured as liberative. It is on account of this perspective that in the next chapter I begin to sketch a relational account of society, and in chapter 7 I suggest a way in which the trinitarian God may be present to the contradictions and tensions of capitalist society.

These points might be made in more specifically theological terms. In the next chapter I suggest a way of understanding society as created in the Word, and in chapter 6 suggest some Christological principles regarding a Christian engagement with social forms. In chapter 7, I consider the presence of the triune God in the Spirit to capitalist society. Thus it is that in the next part I consider the address of the Word and the presence of the Spirit (the terms are Lash's: see 1988: 199f.) in creation and redemption to society. This, however, is to anticipate the final section of this chapter.

The argument of this chapter so far has been to suggest that the very 'openness' of God is the condition for human liberation; the very 'openness' of God constitutes creation. But this does not mean that human beings are simply left to their own devices in front of a God whose ceaseless activity sustains creation. It is rather that, under the pressure of the suggestion that God makes no particular difference to the world, whose presence marks no particular division in the world, we may say the human task is to refer to our own circumstances within a call to conversion, toward the mitigation of the idolatry of the social. Human beings are invited, in front of the mysterious presence of the unknowable God, to reflect on their own attitude to existence. 'Attitude' is perhaps a rather anaemic word. Lash suggests 'conversion'. How are we to understand this conversion? Not 'religiously' (religion makes a particular difference and marks a division in the world). Rather conversion calls for transformation of those circumstances that eclipse the presence and silence the address of God. And this transformation is not one of the will or of knowledge – it is one of social relations and structures, because it is these relations and structures from which ideological forms arise. And it is in these ideological forms, in that 'very Eden of the innate rights of man

... [where] alone rule Freedom, Equality, Property and Bentham' (Marx, 1954: 172), that God is eclipsed.

IV ENACTING THE DISTINCTION

How then are we to conceive of the enacting of the distinction of God from the world? Sections II and III suggested that 'material' conversion is the acknowledgement of the distinction of God from the world. Does my account offer any guidance as to Christian praxis in the world?

I offer a fuller response to this question in part III. But a preliminary report is in order here. Out of the argument of this and the previous chapter we may recall that the 'openness' proper to God, and the decentred account of God offered here, free human beings to be for themselves. (It does not follow that human beings are freed to be *by* themselves.) The act of conversion is the affirmation of humanity in its denial of idolatry. How might this be understood?

A place to start might be to consider a point that will become clearer in part III. A Marxist account of society stresses that the location of human agents is to be understood in terms of social relations. These social relations are all relations of production (Bhaskar). The making of products is thereby governed by a range of social relations. This suggests that human beings are engaged in a number of practices, across a range of 'sites' of production, which constitute their lives. It is likely, therefore, that there will be a range of praxes required if these relations, and the social structures governing these relations, are to be transformed. There may well be a range of praxes that might be appropriate in relation to a specific practical issue.

An account of conversion against the eclipse of God needs to have some purchase here. In other words, we need an account of those irrationalities and contradictions that may not be available within theological discourse. We must confront the weakness of Lash's account, and insist that the enacting of the distinction of God from the world needs articulation with reference to relations of production, with reference to an interpretation of *society*.

Second, the position outlined here is the critique of the idolatry that human beings have no capacities for the achievement of such change. Or, rather, such an account of God's relationship to the world cannot be employed to deny human capacities for the extension of the rational basis of their social life. God-talk marks no intrinsic limit to the extension of the creative self-constitution of human being. This is not to say, in some moment of hubris, that there are no limits to human achievement; nor is this an exercise in Pelagianism. It is rather to suggest that 'social' limits cannot be set abstractly. Rather, we need, in order to assess human limits, to uncover, as Marx points out (1975), what are genuinely human needs. Ascertaining such needs can only be achieved through the practical establishment of 'full humanity' – an eschatological, and therefore sacramental, task. Only in this way does properly social, properly natural, human being emerge. The *locus* of such emergence is those places where the contradictions and irrationalities of contemporary living throw up a range of false needs (which, in turn, raises the difficult issue as to how we might distinguish between true and false needs). It is here that the enacting of the distinction needs to be understood as neither denying our capacities for change, nor as providing information 'from above' about social 'limits', etc. (I shall in the next chapter be offering an account of the crucial constitutive basis of human being – its social character. But an exploration of the nature of humanity is not restricted to social 'limits', in the sense intended here.)

That the distinction of God from the world fails to provide information about social 'limits', may also be explored in theological terms through a reappropriation of the contrast between the sacred and the secular. I say 'reappropriation' as the antithesis between sacred and secular is sometimes used to stress that Christianity is not (or should not be) concerned with, say, political liberation because its 'true' task is with sacred matters such as, say, individual salvation. I would prefer to argue for a different conception of the contrast: that the boundary between the sacred and the secular marks *for the time being* what human beings perceive can be changed and that which cannot. And of course this boundary cannot be fixed. If it were fixed, then there would be no possibility of social and economic change.

I am not using the pair of terms, sacred and secular, in quite the way it has been employed in some areas of sociology. Jürgen Habermas suggests that, for instance, the contrast between sacred and secular institutions is one of a number of contrasts or polar concepts that seek 'to grasp the structural change of the institutional framework of a traditional society on the way to becoming a modern one' (Habermas, 1987: 91). This movement into modernity is not my concern here. I am rather trying to argue that the contrast sacred/secular marks the irrationality and contradictions of contemporary capitalist society. We do not have to look very far to see these contradictions. As Claus Offe has put it:

The disparity between areas of life grows above all in view of the differential state of development obtaining between the actually institutionalized and the possible level of technical and social progress. The disproportion between the most modern apparatuses for industrial and military purposes and the stagnating organization of the transport, health, and educational systems is just as well known an example of this disparity between areas of life as is the contradiction between rational planning and regulation in taxation and finance policy and the unplanned, haphazard development of cities and regions. (Offe, cited in Habermas, 1987: 108)

If it is with these sorts of issues that a liberative theology must be able to engage, and be informed by, then the contrast sacred/secular is intended to direct the theologian precisely to areas of irrationality and contradiction. Theology does not assume, in advance so to speak, what the contradictions are.

Third, theology offers a critique of the idolatry that the doctrine of God might confuse or obscure the practical, human, social task. This conception of 'God' does not 'centre' us through the empowerment of relationship (in a world that works against relationship), but rather as 'other', infinite, creator, and so intimately present, is the very basis of our activity. As such, the conception of God is the constant reminder that any retreat into the sacred marks the area where human beings claim that their social capacities do not extend. For this reason it is important that this God is 'decentred', is unknowable: such an account of God tries to ensure that it is difficult to mark the boundary between sacred and secular, and when the boundary is drawn it can be done so only tentatively and provisionally.

My suggestions here, although set out rather too briefly, are designed to deny that the more we affirm ourselves or are politically active the less God is present; there is no form of competition between God and human beings, no disjunction between an immanentist God and humanity. Rather, we have an unknowable God, whose unknowable presence makes no particular difference, and yet demands conversion. That Christian theology might be the theoretical expression of false forms of mediation remains, as we have seen, an ever present possibility – but not a necessary one. The account of the relationship suggested here between God and the world points human beings to the contradictions and irrationalities of our lives, and suggests that in the praxes dedicated towards the transformation of these 'sites', God is present. This is an affirmation of the God–human relationship, and an affirmation of human responsibility. How this might be understood more particularly, and in a way that includes a radical conception of the resistances of sin, I am deferring to the more constructive discussion of incarnation and the triune God in the next part.

V   CONCLUSION: TOWARD A TRINITARIAN THEOLOGY

I began part II with a discussion of the Marxist concern regarding Christianity: it alienates. And it alienates in a particular way: through the misconstruing of human capacities. Human capacities 'produced' in social relations do not require such a mediation. So the argument goes.

I have argued that the Christian God need not be so construed if attention is paid to the social 'location' of Christian discourse. In chapter 3 I suggested that attention might profitably be paid to the decentring of our talk of God (and of humanity), and that the doctrine of divine simplicity insists that God's presence to the world marks no division in the world. Proper attention to two theological protocols governing theological discourse suggests that such discourse cannot be employed to mediate human capacities falsely. What form does this 'proper attention' take?

The doctrine of divine simplicity acts as a protocol against idolatry by distinguishing God from the world and thereby ensuring that our God-talk is talk of *God*. With this formal feature come other emphases. I have highlighted 'openness': God is both present, and yet this very 'openness' invites attention to the types of ideological investment in theological discourse. I have tried to show how these two 'effects' of the notion of simplicity, and its related 'feature', eternity, might be useful in the development of a liberative theology. I stressed that God's 'openness' need not be construed as in opposition to God's intimate presence. I also noted that the 'openness' of God refers to God's involvement with the world, but without interrupting or obscuring the human task of countering oppression and securing justice. Indeed, this 'simple' God is the invitation to human responsibility. I also offered a way of understanding God's relationship to the world that insisted upon God's sustaining relation to it, but also that this relation includes God's judgement.

These arguments follow on from the first strategy outlined in chapter 3: the counter-idolatry strategy suggested by an insistence of the decentred 'status' of God and humanity. This was offered as an attempt to deny that the concept of 'God' can be used to 'shore up' particular social or economic arrangements. With this emphasis on decentredness came another: a stress upon practice, and of theological discourse as directed toward practice.

These two strategies emerged as a response to, and as way of 'incarnating', the epistemological issues raised in part I. There I argued that theology must grasp the material nature of ideas or, put another way, ideas are products, and therefore open to the pressures and limits operative within the wider relations of production. Indeed, the meaning of ideas can only be grasped fully by reference to these relations.

The arguments in this part are offered as a way of meeting a crucial Marxist objection to Christianity: the charge that Christianity always functions as an intermediary, as mediating human capacities falsely 'back to' human beings. The account of Christian theological discourse offered here seeks to meet that charge and, furthermore, guards against it. The denial of God-as-intermediary was pursued through this chapter. The denial of the 'fixity' of God, and that God marks no division in the world, developed into the suggestion, made by Nicholas Lash, that God's presence to the world makes no particular difference, and yet makes all the difference in the world. The matter here is one of conversion, conceived practically and materially: God's presence to the world makes no particular difference, but may be understood metaphorically in terms of our relations within the world. This argument was extended through the appraisal of Lash's appropriation of Buber's 'eclipse of God'. Here, the matter of conversion was given more concrete content.

One important matter does, however, remain unaddressed. Perhaps we may approach it thus: granted that God's relation to the world makes no particular difference, and is thereby not a form of false mediation, what is the theological context of material conversion, and how is God's invitation toward conversion to be understood? Implicitly responding to this question, Lash argues that trust in God is the prerequisite for other forms of relationship. Indeed, this can be seen as a central protocol against idolatry: God alone is to be worshipped, God alone is to be trusted. Our commitment to, our trust in human relationships is secondary to our commitment to and trust in God. Indeed, this may be construed in terms of God's simplicity: 'The simpleness or oneness of God (which is, in part, a matter of his reliability or trustworthiness) is not *graspable* by us. It lies the other side of all the complications in the world . . .' (Lash, 1988: 235). This of course puts in correct perspective our attempts to secure trustworthy social forms.

In the next chapter I shall be arguing, in sections III and IV, a different, although closely related, case: it is part of our created status that we are social beings. This position will take the form of an argument suggesting that society needs to be understood as a transcendental, and that human being is social, embodied and self-reflexive being. Further, that it is appropriate for human beings to understand their social being is part of God's blessing to humanity; it is a form of God's grace. From this point I shall, in a subsequent chapter, insist that the sociality of human being should not be understood uncritically. The affirmation of the sociality of human being is not an affirmation of *all* social forms; indeed, it is the demand, in some circumstances, for their surpassment. This suggestion will, in chapter 6, be located in an account of incarnation. In chapter 7 it will be considered in relation to an interpretation of God's Spirit.

The next phase is thereby concerned with the trinitarian development of the argument. To leave the discussion solely in terms of an appropriate use of theological discourse seems insufficient. It is insufficient in that it leaves crucial ontological matters undecided. A failure to articulate an adequate ontology only means that an implicit ontology will fill the space: theology abhors a vacuum in ontology. More than this, the theological context of the call to conversion articulated in this part requires some further specification. The final stage of the argument is thereby to offer a little more detail on some of the ontological considerations that must inform a liberative theology. (And yet, although these are substantial ontological matters, the 'form' of their appropriation is epistemological. The discussions of incarnation and Trinity, although having profound ontological implications, are interpreted epistemologically, insisting that Christianity is not restricted to the function of false intermediary.)

Above all, the next part is an attempt to secure an account of the Christian God that, governed by the protocols of this part, will show that God is not a false intermediary. Indeed, it is part of my argument in the next part that Christianity may indeed be more revolutionary than Marxism: that the practices of the Christian may be more revolutionary than those of the Marxist. Before, however, we get to such a contentious issue an important area of current theological debate requires discussion. This discussion occupies the first few sections of the next chapter.

PART III

Christian liberation?

CHAPTER 5

Theology and society

In chapter 2 I suggested that Marx considered the Christian religion to be a false intermediary; it informed human beings of their capacities but in a way that misconstrued those capacities. By contrast, communists did not require such mediation. Through chapters 3 and 4 I argued that Christian theology as second-order discourse may be interpreted in such a way as to avoid being understood as an intermediary. I stressed that theological discourse about God needs to be understood as decentred by the determining pressures of capitalist society. I sought to show that God's 'openness' is the mode of God's involvement in the world. This led to the argument that God's presence to the world invites material conversion.

The following chapters take the argument a little further. If part II was 'negative', recommending protocols that might govern a liberative theology, this part is marginally more 'positive'. It suggests that resurrection is both the nerve of the practice of Christian liberation and is constitutive of such an account of liberation. It also suggests that an account of incarnation must be articulated against the primacy of society for an understanding of a theological theoretical practice that is neither too close nor too distant. In the next chapter, my claim, 'narrated' rather than argued for, so to speak, is that an account of resurrection engages with the issue of political liberation in a fashion fundamental enough to avoid charges of false mediation, and yet makes a contribution to the understanding (and the practice) of liberation.

The two final chapters are both more circumspect and more speculative. The Christian trinitarian interpretation of God hinted at in this account of incarnation and resurrection is discussed, and some suggestions made as to how the trinitarian nature of God might be understood in relation to political liberation and the primacy of society. The study concludes with some thoughts on the unfinished character of this argument (for instance, there is a brief discussion on the relation between immanent and economic trinities).

But, before we approach the issue of incarnation and resurrection (chapter 6) and trinity (chapter 7), there are two particular issues that require comment. The first concerns the relation between trinitarian thinking and society; the second the issue of how society might be grasped conceptually, and interpreted theologically. In this chapter I shall discuss, and criticise as inadequate, what might appear to be an obvious way forward at this point: to stress the relational being of God and to suggest that such being has strong implications for interpreting the 'actuality' of the world. I discuss this option in the first two sections and return to it in section v. The second issue is concerned with the interpretation of capitalist society. In section III I offer a way of understanding the theological 'place' of society, and in section IV I offer an interpretation of society against which a liberative theology needs to show its value. This part of the argument (see section v) also indicates why a trinitarian critique of society is not necessarily a helpful approach. To this critique I now turn.

I   TRINITY, PERSONS AND SOCIETY

In this section, I wish to identify a form of argument not specifically raised in the previous chapter. We may grasp something of its attraction from the following paraphrase by Anne Carr of Segundo's identification of the Trinity ' ... as a community or society of persons in a way that leads to the socialized and interdependent understanding of human persons' (Carr, 1988: 156). She continues: 'The mystery of God as Trinity, as final and perfect sociality, embodies those qualities of mutuality, reciprocity, cooperation, unity, peace in genuine diversity that are feminist ideals and goals derived

from the inclusivity of the gospel message' (Carr, 1988: 156–7).
We may note two implications of this form of argumentation.
First, it is decisively trinitarian, and would reject, for instance,
James Mackey's claim (1983: 243) that it is a form of *superbia* to
presume to describe God in this detailed way. Second, a link is
forged between the trinitarian God and human living: what
Catherine Mowry LaCugna has called an intrinsic connection
between an interpretation of God and, among other things,
ethics and politics (LaCugna, 1991: 399).

These two implications raise the issue of the status of such
trinitarian thinking. A range of positions which I shall call
'realist', in the sense of 'the long realist tradition in theology
from Augustine to Hegel' (Dalferth, 1989: 22), stresses the
'reality' of God's being as trinitarian – Gunton, Moltmann,
Boff, Meeks all do, I think, belong to this tradition.[1] At first
glance, this realist position or range of positions might seem to
be an appropriate way forward: it enjoys a stress on sociality,
divine and human and has obvious social (not always political:
Gunton's is an apolitical position) implications.

But there is a tendency in this approach to offer a 'strong'
programme based upon the position that 'it is only through an
understanding of the kind of being that God is that we can
come to learn what kind of beings we are and what kind of
world we inhabit' (Gunton, 1991a: vii). The problem with
such a move is its tendency – no more than this – to 'read off'
interpretations of society or of personhood from the communitarian nature of the triune God. This 'from' is understood in a
variety of ways. But the result is to offer a social programme
derived from the nature of God. Such a tendency is perhaps
most marked in Leonardo Boff (1988).[2] Boff suggests that a

---

[1] It is important to note here that there is within this range of realist positions no
agreement on the question of God's suffering. Gunton, for instance, specifically
rejects such a development (Gunton, 1988: 96). So it is not possible to reject this
'realist' position on the grounds that it infringes the protocol of God's simplicity.
Some 'realist' trinitarian formulations do so infringe it, but it is not a necessary part
of this position.

[2] I have learned much about the weaknesses of this approach from Brian Marshall's
illuminating paper (1992). However, I fear that Marshall's position remains close to
that which he criticises: 'trinitarian social criticism' remains an (the?) appropriate
way forward.

Christian interpretation of liberation 'aims to bring about participation and communion, the realities that most closely mirror the very mystery of trinitarian communion in human history' (Boff, 1988: 152). Although there is a studied reticence in the text, Boff seems to suggest that a form of democratic socialism most closely mirrors this mystery. Interestingly, the criticism of capitalism turns not upon its individualism, but instead on the marginalisation of the majority, and the suppression of differences in the reduction of human living to mass consumerism in the domination of the market. Socialism, he argues, is at least founded upon a right principle: communion. Yet socialism is to be 'corrected' by 'basic democracy' which 'seeks communion with transcendent values, those that define the highest meaning of life and history' (Boff, 1988: 152).

The real difficulty with this approach concerns the status of various forms of 'social experience' that are 'written up' in the doctrinal thinking. As Marshall (1992) points out, it often appears as if a particular understanding of social life is read out of a determinate situation and into an account of the immanent Trinity; it is then no surprise that these considerations impinge upon the recommendations for social action which are then 'derived' from the doctrine. A hermeneutic circle, indeed! Marshall's substantial point is that it behoves Christian theologians to be more self-critical of the interaction between social experience and doctrine, and more open as to how this process informs theology and practice. Perhaps this point is made more persuasive if we note the range of the recommendations for social action that emerge from the style of argumentation, from Boff's preference for a form of socialism to Gunton's decidedly apolitical privileging of persons (in relation).

In part II I sought to avoid a 'reading together' of the being of God and the being of the world. Instead, I have argued for the 'inconceivability' and 'decentredness' of (the triune) God. This is not quite the same as maintaining that we learn nothing about human relationships from such a conception of God. Rather, such a conception of God serves as a permanent reminder that what denies and undermines relationship are dehumanising practices in the form of our social organisation.

God's relationship to the world is to be enacted in the form of turning away from idols. If the idols are those of economic management and social organization, then this conversion will be a practical matter with material conditions. Theologians need to be careful in offering 'resolutions' or 'programmes' that move too quickly from the triune being of God to human sociality. The Christian relational God may be an interesting and provocative criticism of the lack of relationship in the world. But this needs to be handled very carefully. It may be true that the Christian demand is for human social relations to be brought into 'correspondence' with the triune God. But we must be wary lest this form of argument obscures the actuality of current social relations – the matter of false mediation again.

We must begin with a tougher question: how is God present when the free commerce of social relations is denied under capitalism? To argue that we can ascertain the nature of 'true' relationships among persons in society by attending to the social nature of God is to suggest in theological theory some account of genuine relationship without consistent attention to the actual form of distorted relations under capitalism. Yet in the previous chapter I offered two reasons which suggest that we ought to be wary of attempts to demarcate between the sacred and the secular, of accepting a dualism that posits an 'abstract' account of relationality over actual forms of relation and irrelation. The first reason is that the demarcation cannot easily be fixed: praxis alters its position. Second, such a demarcation tends to mislead us as to the possibilities of change towards more open and freer social relations. Christianity is not the 'heart of a heartless world, and the soul of soulless conditions' (Marx, 1975: 244) in that it moves quickly to offer us the form of 'genuine' relationship amidst actual distorted relationships. Instead, Christianity should be the critique of such a parody of the possibility of relationship.

I shall argue that (the triune) God refers us to the contradictions of the present. In the contradictions of the present we may gain intimations of the possibility of genuine relationship, and of the possibility of radical change. I am proposing that the presence of the triune God is the demand for the relationship that is not given; not a substitute for it. The suggestion that the trinitarian nature of God as relational is the basis for speaking of human relationships and the empowerment of human beings has the tendency – no more – to obscure this. I specify the nature of this tendency more fully at the end of this chapter, *after* – and this is significant – a discussion of the nature of society.

What then, it may be asked, is the 'function' of the Trinity? Why can we not simply have done with it if its 'function' is so negative, so ephemeral? I shall argue below that we do not have here a sophisticated attempt to humanise circumstances that are radically dehumanising. Rather trinitarian thinking is the reminder of the possibility of relationship. This reminder, so my argument runs in the next chapter, is to be traced to the resurrection in the embodiment of Jesus of Nazareth. The abundance of God is here displayed in its most concentrated form, and it is from this concentration that Christian theology must take its cue as to the theological significance of society. In this event of redeeming reconstitution, the 'openness' of God is concentrated in cruciform materiality. Yet, I shall also be arguing that only in a trinitarian appropriation of resurrection can its full significance be grasped.

Indeed, the event of resurrection is at the heart of my objections to the sort of trinitarian realist position outlined here. The neatness, the orderliness of this realist approach, as it seeks to think through the social implications of the trinitarian God, are insufficient. It seems that we have to do here with the type of theological element identified by Deleuze and Guattari which, they claim, shores up the Oedipal person, who indeed must be cleansed from this element to release the reconnecting overflow, the flows of desiring-production. What must be avoided is: 'the extraction of a transcendent complete object from the signifying chain', the effect of which is to produce a 'despotic signifier on which the entire chain thereafter seemed to depend, assigning an element of lack to each position of desire, fusing desire to a law, and engendering the illusion that this loosened up and freed the elements of the chain' (Deleuze and Guattari, 1984: 110). Christianity, if my arguments concerning 'decentredness' are persuasive, has nothing to do with a God who is a complete object, who centres accounts of person or society. Christianity, in this interpretation, is witness to the actuality of the freeing of the chain of idolatry.

Indeed, we may now see the *theological* reasoning for this: the trinitarian programme criticised here does not seem to be constructed – risked – around this event that *is* the economic abundance of God. 'Economic' is an interesting word here: Frances Young and David Ford (1987: 166f.) have written of the importance of this metaphor for Paul, claiming that it has immediate, practical resonance in II Corinthians. We may reclaim this resonance here: the 'openness' of this decentred God toward the world is to be identified (as far as it can be) with this extraordinary abundance: a revolution in embodiment, which reshapes our conception of the world, of society, of community and of our hope. Resurrection is, so I shall narrate, the crucial way that God is toward the world. It is this dynamic of overflow, this creative 'energy' which reconstitutes the matter of the world, rather than strong trinitarian realist programmes, that might be understood as trustworthy.

Christian patterns of disconnection from the sensibilities of the dominant order are funded by this event. From respect for 'authority' to the impulse to consume in non-sustainable ways, an ecclesial culture, funded by resurrection, is the affirmation of the emergence of sensibilities and practices of disconnection which threaten and drain the interpellating power of such features of the dominant hegemony. The nerve of the Christian account of revolution is to be found here also (as we shall see in the next chapter). The abundance of God, enacted in concentrated form in resurrection, is thus central to my argument. Its strength may be grasped if we note that it allows a response to a question posed by Juan Luis Segundo. Addressing the relation between the temporal and eschatological orders in the theologies of Metz and Moltmann, Segundo reflects on the terms employed to grasp this connection: anticipation, image, outline. His question is a sharp one: 'But who dedicates their life to an "analogy"? Who dies for an "outline"? Who motivates a . . . people in the name of an "anticipation"?' (Segundo,

1980: 247). Such a question, which might also be put to Leonardo Boff, goes to the heart of the trinitarian position criticised in this chapter. My argument takes another route. Distinguishing between two issues raised by Segundo's questions, I shall be suggesting that resurrection is the nerve of the Christian motivation to revolutionary activity, and that Christianity is intrinsically concerned with the reconstitution of social life on account of the activity of the Logos in creation and redemption.

II   THE DENIAL OF PERSONHOOD

One way of 'testing' my argument is to see whether trinitarian thinking operates in the way that I suggest it does: by obscuring, as well as revealing, social relations. We may approach this issue by noting that theology and the social sciences are not on a par in dialogue. The objects of enquiry of the social sciences are social, and yet so are the social sciences themselves. The social sciences should incorporate into their method some account of how they too are to be 'explained' as a social product (see Bhaskar, 1979: 59–60): the social sciences are implicated in their own method. This is a permanent 'meta-critical' task of the social sciences. Any theology seeking to be liberative must also have some sense of its 'location' as a social product. This suggests that the social 'location' of theology can and must be explained by the social sciences. But theology can offer no 'explanation' of the social sciences.

Further, some sense needs to be given of determining pressures, of theology's inscription by the pressures of capitalist society, whatever position the theologian takes on the hermeneutic importance of an implicit or explicit account of society, and however acknowledged (or not). But it is perhaps not a lesson that theology likes to learn. The crucial point – perhaps not yet learned, never mind forgotten by theology – is that whatever weight the theologian deliberately and explicitly places upon an understanding (or pre-understanding) of society, and in whatever form, theological construction is informed by the wider hegemony – and must assess its liberative status in relation to that hegemony.

To make my case, I offer an argument from the work of Colin Gunton. In a critical comment on Marx, Gunton argues that an account of humanity/personhood cannot be fixed upon something impersonal such as 'species-being': 'It is as a species-being that humankind is free ... And however much Marx's later thoughts changed, the point remains: that a species-being, a universal, is impersonal, and it is not possible to base the freedom and society of persons on what is impersonal' (Gunton, 1991a: 89). I suggest that the weakness is Gunton's and not Marx's. For Marx, species-being does not give a normative account of human nature, but rather stresses the conditions for human self-creativity. And, more fundamentally, Marx discusses it in the context of his theory of alienation where it is not possible to speak of *alienated* labour without talking about its *transcendence*. For Marxists, there can be no personhood, except in a severely abstract and ideological sense, under present circumstances. The problem is precisely that people are in a sense 'things' (whatever their self-understanding and however much we might wish the situation to be different).

So in his interpretation of Marx, Mészáros writes: 'This real human being ... exists both as *actuality* (alienated "commodity man") and *potentiality* (what Marx calls: "the rich human being")' (Mészáros, 1970: 163). Mészáros continues: 'And thus we can see that the rejection of transcendentalism and ethical dualism does not carry with it the dismissal of *ideality* without which no moral system worthy of this name is conceivable' (Mészáros, 1970: 163). In other words, no transcendental notion of, say, the selfless individual opposed to the self-seeking individual is an adequate basis for a moral theory. By implication, the same must apply to the 'transcendental' of a theological category, if such a transcendental fails to be constituted by the tension secured by the notion of ideality.

Gunton may say that an account of personhood cannot be fixed upon the actuality of reified relations; and Marx might agree. The point is to attend to the circumstances giving rise to the reification and their transcendence, and not to propose that personhood cannot be so founded because God, in the divine

perichoretic community of persons and relations, is not so
founded. Gunton may wish to say that persons are not objects;
so might Marx, but Marx was aware that there is a sense in
which persons *are* objects. Here lies the root of the curious
Marxian ambivalence (and it has caused great difficulties for
subsequent Marxisms) between the proletariat as revolutionary agent and the proletariat as dehumanised object (see
Harvey, 1984: 113).

The central issue in this debate with Gunton may be
approached through Kolakowski's interpretation of the dis-
agreement between Marx and the utopian socialists (Kolakowski, 1978: 182ff.). Despite many points of agreement, Kolakowski identifies a number of areas of divergence. An
important one is the characterisation of the situation. Much
socialism argues, according to Kolakowski, that the problem is
poverty and the misery thus created (a moral issue); for Marx,
the character of capitalism is its dehumanising tendencies and
its related drive toward reification (a practical issue).

Gunton's argument has similarities with those of the socialists: the problem is to locate the proper humanity of people,
unique human personhood, enmired as it is in contemporary
misunderstandings of personhood: a theoretical problem open
to a theoretical solution and (I am not denying) plans of action
consequent to this. But the Marxist case is different: the issue is
not the basic personhood of human beings, everywhere misunderstood. The difficulty is to get the only agent that can change
this situation to realise that its humanity ('species-being') is
denied to it, and to acquire the consciousness that its circumstances need to be changed – ideality again – in order to
reappropriate its humanity (in the sense of the transformation
of its general conditions of production, and not in the sense of
the reappropriation of some 'human essence'). Such reappropriation might be described as emancipation.

We may now appreciate the weakness of Gunton's argument. It is not what theologians might normally call a theological weakness – although the argument of this book is to
insist that it must be described as such. The difficulty with
Gunton's argument is not its poor 'theology' (in a narrow

sense), but its lack of reference to, and its awareness of, its determined position. Marxism is insisting that we begin with the transcending of alienation, with the problem of 'non-personhood'.[3] Gunton is suggesting that we begin from 'personhood', whether or not it is 'instantiated' in the world. The practical and theoretical programmes specifically required to secure actual, living personhood are not fore-grounded in Gunton's position.[4] What is central is not the quality of the theologising alone, but the quality of the theologising in relation to the hegemonic pressures that aim to secure the ideological misperception and misapplication of human capacities towards social change.

The point here is not that an account of society is incorporated into theology, but the *nature* of that incorporation. It is not, as Gunton and the utopian socialists demand, that we need a pattern to which to conform – a moral issue and demand. Rather, we need to begin with the transcendence of alienation, and with the practical and theoretical forms that inhibit such transcendence – a practical issue. The theological task becomes one of self-criticism: is theology one of the theoretical forms that inhibit such 'transcendence'?

I have suggested that there are difficulties with this trinitarian critique of society. My basic question is whether the immediate interrogation of and emphasis upon the social being of God is the best way forward when considering the relevance of Christianity to liberation. Can an account of liberation be secured here? Not easily, is my reply. I am suggesting that an account of society is too easily 'read into' God's nature in a way that may distract from alienated, dehumanising relationship. Indeed, in a brief discussion of Gunton's criticisms of Marx, I suggested that the tendency of theology to misconstrue problems in social relations is given in Gunton's argument. This, of course, as we have seen, is precisely the function Marx ascribed to Christianity.

---

[3] For a theological critique of non-personhood, see Gutiérrez, 1983: 193.
[4] There is of course another point as to whether individuality in Marx is subsumed under the generic species-being – Gunton's charge. I think that, following Kolakowski (1978) and Mészáros (1970), it is possible to argue that it is not.

Now, I do not wish to deny that this trinitarian approach is an important theological resource for thinking about politics and social matters, and for making a contribution to Christian liberation. Rather, I am suggesting that the way that such an approach is usually handled is unhelpful. The root of my disquiet is set out below in section v. But, to make the point, some account of the circumstances in which theology is to make its contribution must first be given. In sum, we come to the issues of sociality, social relations and structures, and capitalist society.

III   SOCIAL BEING AS CREATED BEING

The argument so far notes the difficulties in trying to move from a doctrine of the Trinity to political and social matters (section i) and to conceptions of, for example, 'personhood' (section ii), without a proper regard for the (determining) context in which theological work is done. (Gunton's argument reported in section ii is intended as an example of the style of theologising criticised in section i.) My aim here is to argue that it must be against some conception of society, and so of human agency, that a liberative theology must develop. The primacy of society – the prior, crucial and determining condition, as well as the outcome, of (all) work – must be acknowledged. My claim is that an account of the primacy of society will help in the identification of the location, and the liberative potential, of theology.

I have raised questions about (and shall return to) the trinitarian critique of society. But theology is not silenced at this point, thanks to the 'clear creation perspective' (Burrell) set out in the discussion of the doctrine of divine simplicity in chapter 3 and reinforced in chapter 4. There I sought to show that the basic attempt to identify God as distinct from objects in the world led to the specification of the character of theological discourse in terms of the notion of simplicity. In the thought of Thomas Aquinas – if Burrell's interpretation is persuasive – this issued in a clear distinction between the God who creates *ex nihilo* and 'all that is'. (This, of course, is a permanent theme in the classical doctrine of creation.) But there is a connection as well as a distinction: God's presence is constitutive of 'all that is'; this is the 'manner' of God's 'openness' toward the world.

This creation perspective enables us to grasp human sociality as part of 'existence'. If, as I argue below, humanity is to be understood in terms of sociality then this is properly part of a theology of creation. Here, if you like, we begin to extend Burrell's emphasis on 'existence': existence is to be understood at least in terms of human social being (and thereby sharply contradicting the sub-existentialist character of some of his remarks). Here, we also begin to extend Lash's notion of relationship: the relational character of human living is not only a metaphor for our relationship to God but is to be understood as 'given' in a theology of creation.

Interpreting social being as created being is important in response to the Marxist charge that Christian theology has difficulties moving beyond notions of subjectivity. Indeed, I am proposing, learning from and developing an argument by Daniel Hardy, that an essential condition for a liberative theology will be a theological interpretation of sociality and a transcendental account of society.

Human society may be understood as part of creation, although not as a 'natural' necessity but as part of human freedom: 'This is not to suggest that human beings are subject to some kind of mechanical or organic necessity; the necessity is a social freedom which arises from the presence of the social transcendental' (Hardy, 1989: 37). This argument is important in that, although open to a Marxist reservation, it will enable us to grasp certain important theological possibilities. If the radical 'openness' of God invites conversion – an acknowledgement of the relation between the question of God and the question of humanity – this need not be interpreted individualistically. If society is a transcendental condition of human practical possibility, then conversion is precisely a social matter: directed to, and enacted by, persons as social beings. Here epistemological and ontological matters come together: the insistence on protocols against the idolatrous misuse of theological discourse generates a creation perspective. This perspective needs to be carried through to a consideration of sociality within a doctrine of creation.

In the next section, I shall set out in more detail an account of the transcendentality of society. Here we may note the main point: in the creation perspective of the previous part, sociality is to be located within a theology of creation. The social being of humanity needs to be placed in a theology of creation (and not, as we shall see, in a theology of the redemption wrought by Christ in the Spirit). In other words, creation and redemption need to be held together; and creation must not be narrowed through a 'reading' of creation only in terms of the redemption given in and by Christ.

The transcendental character of society – as putative enactment of the social freedom of humans to be for one another – is brought within, so to speak, the remit of a theology of creation. But this needs to be understood precisely: what Hardy calls the sociality of human beings, due to the presence of the social transcendental, is to be understood as attributable to the activity of God. Put another way, sociality as transcendental is to be ascribed to the triune action of God in creation. Daniel Hardy puts it this way:

[Transcendental sociality] should be traced to the Logos of God operative in creation. This divine ordering is what ultimately implants in the human condition the 'being-with' which is natural to it. And rather than trace the social dynamic (of bringing the use of the social transcendent [sic] to its true form) to the apostolicity of the Church, it should be traced to the truth of God present in creation. (Hardy, 1989: 42)

It is, in other words, to the trinitarian activity of God in creation, and particularly to the ordering and shaping power of the Logos, that the emphasis on sociality directs the Christian.[5]

---

[5] Nor is such an interpretation an import into Christianity: it is to be found in one reading of the biblical witness. In noting the distinctiveness of Jesus' teaching from apocalyptic thinking, Helmut Peukert suggests 'that Jesus incorporates not only eschatological traditions but also Wisdom traditions concerning God's action in creation: Divine creation only now is established; the damaged, exploited, distorted creation is now to be restored' (Peukert, 1986: 222).

The effect is to secure through the doctrine of creation, a Christian interest in, and desire to understand and change, what Hardy calls the created sociality of human beings. (The justification of this claim is the subject of the next chapter.) In this way Christianity secures the possibility of its relevance in 'the presence of sharply increased contingencies in modern life, not only those which have to do with the disappearance of external natural resources but also those related to crises in institutions and personal freedom and meaning' (Hardy, 1989: 41). This insistence on created sociality invites Christian theologians to think through the implications of God's presence in creation and redemption to these contingencies.

For Hardy, failure to place such transcendentality in a theology of creation has unfortunate consequences. If 'created sociality' is misinterpreted, and is mistakenly ascribed to God's work in redemption two errors manifest themselves: the restriction of God's activity in creation, and too sharp a separation of the Church from the world. In a discussion of Bonhoeffer and Forsyth, Hardy suggests that to move too quickly to the redeeming work of Christ in relation to the 'social problem' is thereby to obscure the position of society in creation. Further, the tendency is to separate off Christian communities from the rest of society in a way that suggests the Church confronts society.

What is the theological result? Hardy draws out the implications of his argument by suggesting that one effect is to deny the common sociality in which all are placed. In Hardy's words: 'First, in moving immediately to the specific gift of God in Christ proclaimed by the Church, they [Bonhoeffer and Forsyth] lose their commonality as created social beings with the society to which they speak. They put themselves outside the society to which they speak, and put Christian faith in the position of pronouncing God's work to society' (Hardy, 1989: 40). A second effect is the restriction of God's activity: 'in proclaiming the specific gift of God in Christ as one of the graces which comes through God's victory, without relating this to God's work in creation, they narrow God's work unduly' (Hardy, 1989: 40). Thus Hardy's argument suggests that to

obscure the place of sociality in creation is thereby to separate
the churches from the rest of society ontologically, so to speak,
and not in terms of, say, political expediency in the construction of a counterculture. Second, the scope of God's work in
redemption is artificially confined, because God's work in
creation has been conceptually restricted.

There are difficulties here, however, that cannot be glossed
over. We must take a look at these before returning to the
theological implications of this position. Hardy's account of the
social transcendental is rather general and abstract. This leads
him to specify a range of 'themata' that might act as the
intermediate link between practical or empirical sociality and
the social transcendental itself. These themata are, in themselves, unexceptionable: institutionality, economic practices,
personal relationships, and language and culture (see Hardy,
1989: 44). Now, although Hardy argues that these need to be
interrelated there is no indication given of the explanatory
'weight' that might be ascribed to each themata within a
hierarchy of explanation. It is perhaps this generality that
leads Hardy to concentrate on the notion of sociality or the
social transcendental. This generality can be explained, at
least in part, by Hardy's insistence on employing the term
sociality to refer to both 'ontological' and 'anthropological'
matters. We have already seen in Mészáros' use of these terms
how important it is to make this distinction in that it allows for
the question: how is sociality to be understood as 'given', and
yet not available except through particular practices (restrictive or otherwise)? I shall, in the next section, insist not on a
transcendental sociality and an empirical sociality linked by
themata, but on society as transcendental, and the 'performance' of sociality in particular social relations. So although I
have no difficulty with the term itself, sociality must, as we
shall see in the next section, be understood as being enacted by
real, living human persons in social relations, with the explicit
acknowledgement that social relations are determined by
specific social structures.

My interpretation is thus slightly different from Hardy's.
Rather than drawing the connection between the social

transcendental and empirical sociality in a range of themata, I prefer to see the issue in the terms of transcendental sociality as enacted in social relations. Such a conceptuality enables a properly embodied account of sociality. It is too abstract to describe sociality as freedom or 'being-with', and refer the 'actuality' of sociality to empirical sociality. Instead, I propose to refer sociality as transcendental to three particular 'marks' (following Eagleton, 1970: 57–8): work, embodiment and language. (The first is of course important to liberation theology, the second and third to feminist theology.) These are the 'marks' of 'being-with', the ontological determinants of social freedom, the material 'marks' of our distinctive humanity. When referring to the social being of humanity, these three material themes give the range of practices of social life; social practices are the instantiation of these 'marks'. Indeed, in the sketching of a social materialism in part I, in which I concentrated upon ideology and material culture, these three 'marks' were already present. As such, these 'marks' refer us to economic practices, the practices in which the bodies of human beings are governed and construed (indeed, perhaps denied), and the discursive embodiment in which human beings enact such practices.

These three material themes are, I propose, the ontological determinants of sociality. Yet these determinants are not to be understood either in abstract or essentialist terms; they are 'present' only in the form of particular social relations: for example, the economy, the family, sexuality, culture, discourses and so forth. Such is the active construal of the three 'marks'. Yet this active construal occurs in relations of production into which people enter. (I set this out in more detail in the next section.) Persons in society always take their place in particular relations which always pre-exist them. And these are relations of production in that work, embodiment and language require the labour of the past in order to be produced afresh: there is no discourse without an existing language, and so forth. This is not, as we shall see, to ground particular social relations in ontological determinants. Rather it is to maintain that sociality is only enacted in particular social relations, which may or may not be coercive.

Following the account of determination in part 1, the greatest explanatory weight in the capitalist mode of production is to be assigned to those structures which embody and enact the material determinant, work, and particularly the structures concerned with production and distribution. More particularly still, this production and distribution is marked by a division of labour that we may call class – and this has direct or indirect implications for all aspects of society. Thus, as we saw, although work is crucially important, yet embodiment and language are also material, and so part of the single process of cultural (in Williams' strong sense) development. Indeed, as material, cultural practices in which embodiment is both 'achieved' and practised, and discourses, in which particular interests in determinate contexts secure a certain range of meanings are, as we have seen, implicated in the relations of production. Indeed, cultural work, including intellectual work, is always *production*, and is thus open to deformation as ideology.

An example may help to make this clearer. Consider advertisements: these are, I suggest, the construal of the three determinants of sociality in particular social relations. Consider adverts themselves: often particular accounts of embodiment are evident, particularly sexual embodiment. Persistent connections are made between consumption and embodiment; and these connections are often the reconfiguration of important practices, such as the 'grossness' shared by sex and eating. An example here is the connection forged between sexuality and ice cream in the adverts of Häagen-Dazs. (Indeed, the precarious nature of the new connection has allowed it to be parodied in an advert for Foster's lager. This parody, though, turns upon principles as reactionary as those in the original advert.) But there is not only the advert itself, there is also its production and reception. Both these different processes take place in a discursive context: both production and reception require interpretation. Yet production takes place in a particular context: in a particular economy, producing and distributing goods and services in a particular way. The making of an advertisement requires advertising companies structured by the demands of the companies who require such adverts. In reception, the adverts are interpreted by social agents in particular relations to the goods promoted in the adverts. To take an obvious example, some will be in a position to buy premium brand ice cream; others will not. Some will be persuaded by the advertising; others will not. (The process of interpretation is complex, and may, as I have just hinted, have material determinants.) This means that those interpreting the adverts are in particular relations to the products under promotion which are precisely material relations (of wealth, etc.). Advertisements thereby turn upon a particular form of social organisation: 'producers', 'consumers' and the construction of a 'market' through advertising.

We can see the issue of social relations another way if we reflect for a moment on who has access to advertising. By definition, such access turns upon money, and also upon the acceptability of the goods to be promoted. This means that, in the main, those who receive the message are not in a position to promote a message of their own. You can grasp a different aspect of the issue of relations if you consider the division of labour implicit in the making of advertisements. It is highly unlikely that the company which produces the goods also produces the adverts. Thus a further company is involved, whose task it is to produce such adverts. In other words, in the process of production and reception which occurs in a particular set of social relations, the advertising message is constructed by people in the advertising company (or their agents) who produce the advert but have no control over it. Of course, executives in the advertising company have influence over the final form of the advertisement. But there remain several groups of people – secretarial, administrative, technical – without whom there could be no advert, and yet who have no, or virtually no, say in its production.

I offer this example to make three points. To insist, first, that the making of advertisements does not occur in a neutral context. It occurs in a situation where the few have (purchased) access to the many, and, further, in which it is the many who provide the material know-how that allows for the making of the advert to the (intended) benefit of the few. We thus have in the reconstruction of the production of advertisements a glimpse of the social relations in which society is organised. Second, we have here an example of hegemonic determination discussed in chapter 2: advertisements promote a range of signifying practices that seek to secure and render obvious or invisible a series of assumptions, practices and connections (about sexuality, for example – particularly women's sexuality). We have then in advertisements the construal of a strong sense of culture: of perspectives, sensibilities and assignments of energy, as Williams notes, that members of that society have difficulty moving beyond. In addition, we have the configuration of the three 'marks' of sociality: the organisation by particular economic structures of a social medium in order to maximise consumption which is both the enactment of embodiment (it is carried through by social agents in production and reception, who require the practical consciousness of language to carry out their rôles), and a particular construal of embodiment. We see also how it is that particular practices related to work organise aspects of embodiment and language. We see here then these three 'marks', but only as embodied in particular social relations.

In specifying the matter in this way, I have sought to overcome a certain generality in Hardy's account: a lack of specification of the distorting effects of capitalism.[6] To be sure, there is room for this in Hardy's account. In principle, as Hardy suggests, the conceptual possibilities enabled by a consideration of the social transcendental is one of the ways in which distortions may be grasped. But as to the particular distortions that restrict human capacities in the present – of these there is almost no discussion. In other words, no (or few)

---

[6] Perhaps on account of this weakness there also seems to be a very strong emphasis on rationality, which is belied precisely by the contradictions of modern life. At one point, Hardy suggests that there may well be 'manifest failure, through irrationality and wickedness, of human thought and life to appropriate a social transcendental' (Hardy, 1989: 35). But there may of course be other reasons for manifest failure: present conflict, the inheritance of the past, deeply sedimented practices, the 'limits' of finitude, ideology indeed. Irrationality and wickedness seem to be rather too narrow an account.

decisions have been taken as to the nature of our social relations. This point is particularly important in that there seems to be no acknowledgement of society as conflictual. Indeed, the centrality of conflict is smoothed over in the very writing. Here, I wish to insist on the antagonistic nature of society: its constitution in terms of dominant, residual and emergent elements, with the first seeking to incorporate the second and third toward a construction of the hegemonic.

But if there are these weaknesses in Hardy's position, there are important strengths. First, Hardy insists on an affirmative and critical dynamic, that governs the social transcendental as a protocol against the misuses, past and present, which have plagued (mis)interpretations of society or a social transcendental in creation and redemption. Indeed, Hardy's account may be seen to work with an implicit account of a telos of emancipation.

As affirmative, [the social dynamic] will be a projective realisation of society, and thus a raising of the most basic conditions for this by affirming them in thought and life. Furthermore, it will be capable of generating 'richer and more open-structured forms of order' in a social universe of constantly expanding complexity. As critical, it will identify and negate inadequate conditions based on unsatisfactory categories or particular societies, whether subhuman (e.g. mechanical, organic or animal) or human (e.g. particular human groups, practices, cultures, beliefs). In different terms, the dynamic is a dialectic of hope and 'reality'. (Hardy, 1989: 35)

Both parts are important here. The first stresses the telos of emancipation that must govern all our thinking about society, and makes the valuable point about an ever-increasing complexity. But there also needs to be constant attention to attempts to inhibit the dynamic by, for example, appealing at inappropriate points to 'natural' categories – as for instance in Nazi Germany and apartheid South Africa (both these are examples on which Hardy comments, although not in discussion of the dynamic).

In this section, I have avoided using the term 'social transcendental'. I prefer the term 'transcendental sociality', with its three 'marks': work, embodiment and language. Indeed, a glance back to the discussion of hegemony in chapter 2 will show that to see society in terms of an indissoluble material process is to note that hegemony is an account of the determining pressures and limits in which the practices governing work, embodiment and language exercise constitutive force across a 'culture'. These three marks are indeed the transcendental conditions of human life. In this sense we may say that they are 'the forms through which being displays itself' (Hardy, 1989: 25): these are the practical conditions of human living and sites of conflict, and thus disclose the actuality (and possibility) of human being. Relations of production into which persons enter are the enactment of these 'marks', as we shall see in the next section. These relations may be altered by purposive human action.

IV   SOCIETY AS TRANSCENDENTAL: A THEOLOGICAL APPROPRIATION

Locating the social character of humanity within the doctrine of creation is an important yet incomplete claim. Here I wish to specify more carefully this character, in such a way as to incorporate the welcome stress in Hardy's paper on affirmation and the social dynamic, and yet also to correct the tendency toward generality. In short, I here propose, following Roy Bhaskar (1979, 1989), an interpretation of society as transcendental in which both the tendency toward conflict and the potential for transformation are secured. I argue that society is the transcendental condition of all human action (including human personhood), that society is stratified and that strata 'beyond' the surface are real, and that an inquiry adequate to its object must encounter and disclose the relational character of society.

I suggested in the previous section that an important issue is the specification of ontological and anthropological matters in relation to sociality: ontological status must not be given to anthropological matters. We need therefore a way of grasping the ontological status of sociality, and yet its anthropological enactment (and its openness to transformation). The transformational account of society proposed here allows us to say that society is real, and yet is open to reconstruction by social agents; that we are always already determined as social beings, but not as *particular* beings. To secure this requires an insistence on society as condition and outcome: as produced and reproduced in intentional human activity. It is important to stress here that neither condition nor outcome can be understood too simply. To insist that society as condition cannot be surpassed is *not* to affirm particular social forms. It must also be insisted with equal force, that social relations are open to reformation. Both relations and the structures governing such relations are real, and may thereby be transformed.

On what grounds does Bhaskar argue for an account of society as transcendental? Perhaps we might start by noting his claim that social activities 'are essentially *productions . . . relations of production* of various kinds' (Bhaskar, 1979: 56). By this he means to insist that human beings do not create society, nor are they its products/effects. Social relations pre-exist human beings, and yet social relations do not 'fix' the activities of human beings. Human beings thus enter into social relations (of work, embodiment and language) that are all relations of production: the 'inheriting' and working over of existing materials. Human beings in their social relations produce (an outcome), which reproduces social structures.

That is, human beings engage in social activities which have the unintended outcome of reproducing society. When I buy life assurance my intention is to secure some financial security; an outcome (unintended by me) is that money is now available to be invested in the money markets. Hence, although society is not reproduced behind my back – I pay life assurance premiums quite 'freely' – yet *necessarily*, given current social structures, this money is invested in capitalist money markets. (And any request by me that investment might be otherwise – that I would like it invested in non-capitalist enterprises, or invested deliberately at a loss – would be senseless. The first request is reactionary, the second utopian – in the terminology suggested by Marx and Engels in the *Communist Manifesto*.) This we might call a transformational account of society: there is no society without human agency, and yet social outcomes are not identical with the intentions of social agents. To speak of society is thereby to speak of the reproduction of society, and the utilisation of already established social products: to speak is to use a language, to make is to 'work over' already existing materials, to act is to participate in a situation governed by social rules (see Bhaskar, 1979: 43). Although only available in the intentional activity of human beings, society is the condition of such activity. These are (some of) the properties of society, and ground the claim of the *transcendental* character of society.

Recall the example of the advert for ice cream in the previous section. The advert turns upon the recreation of existing sensibilities (relating to sexuality) in a fresh context (the promotion of ice cream). In a very obvious way, advertisements are productions: the conscious reappropriation of existing materials (here, sensibilities). And yet we have here to do with *relations* of production: the advertisement is made within a specific set of social relations which requires advertising, and by various groups of people in very different relations to the production of the advertisement. Finally, we may see in this example how relations of production are governed by structural, substantive activities. To purchase such ice cream is to fulfil a want for ice cream; the unintended outcome is support for the capitalist system of distribution and exchange. To make the advert is simply to perform a task for a fee (and thereby hope to secure more fees); yet one outcome is to make a contribution to the speed of monetary exchange. As commissioner of the advert, your only wish is to sell ice cream, but as the producer of ice cream one outcome is that you enter into particular social relations with your employees in which (if Marx is right, and over and above the matter of the wage contract) you benefit, and your employees do not. In making these points, I am suggesting that in these social relations we encounter the structures of the capitalist economy, only available in, and yet not reducible to, such relations.

Yet no one has ever seen society: the totality of society eludes empirical description and, perhaps, identification. But then we must ask: is society real? Or is it a 'convenient fiction', the best hypothesis we have? If the latter were the case, some social properties might be understood as comprising a (socialised) transcendental idealism: an aspect of social life (communication perhaps) is necessary as a universal operation of the human mind, and there is no knowledge without such a condition (a kind of universal pragmatics?). Bhaskar's position is a transcendental *realism*. He argues on causal grounds that social structures can be understood as real; but they are not 'available' except through their effects. That people exchange goods of different values suggests an economic system; but that economic system is not 'available' apart from this exchange. This means that an *empirical* description of the economic process will not necessarily yield the *structural* activities of the economic system. The task of an adequate social science will therefore be to *conceptualise* the relations of the economic system, to ask what structures and relations must pertain for such exchanges of goods (the outcome of production) to be possible – we are back to the transcendental nature of the enquiry. This, of course, is a very important practical point: if such structures are not real, how might we transform them?

Social structures are real and *material*. Society is (re)produced, not thought; we are concerned here with relations of production, not relations between subject and object (see chapter 1, section v). Even experimental scientific activity is work, not 'pure thought'. These social structures are organised in and through social relations: 'The *social* conditions for the structures that govern the substantive activities of transformation [and reproduction] in which human beings engage (and which constitute the immediate explanation of these activities) can thus only be relations of various kinds' (Bhaskar, 1989: 81). This much is given in the fact that society would not exist without human agency: social structures both govern and are the result of human agency. That is, they are the result of, as well as the condition of, relations between human beings, between human beings and their products, and between human beings and nature.

This allows us to make a further move: to say that some

structures are oppressive, some emancipatory, others perhaps neutral (see Bhaskar, 1989: 6). For instance, part of Bhaskar's argument points to language as a social structure: there could be no society without language, and yet without 'speakers' there could be no language. Of course, it is not given in this analysis whether language is oppressive. It may be in that, in particular instances determined by other material structures, it allows for the misdescription of social relations and social structures. It may, as we have seen, deny the reality of relations and structures. Such language we might call ideological.

But there are other structures that may also oppress: economic, social, political, familial. Although these may be known only in concepts (Bhaskar argues that the social sciences are inherently 'concept-dependent'), such structures are not exhausted by concepts. As Bhaskar puts it, the actual does not exhaust the real. Thus it is that although ' ... social structures are dependent upon the consciousness which the agents who reproduce or transform them have, they are not reducible to this consciousness. Social practices are concept-dependent; but ... they are not exhausted by their conceptual aspect. They always have a material dimension' (Bhaskar, 1989: 4). Yet the transformational model, with its emphasis on social relations, does of course leave open the possibility that people may, through purposive activity, alter the condition of production, social structures, as well as its outcome. That is, they may not only note the ideological function of language, they may also seek to alter those structures that 'require' such ideological discourses in order to secure more emancipatory construals of sociality.

This point needs to be underscored: there lies in this account of society the possibility of revolutionary transformation. The claim that human beings reproduce society means that human beings may also transform society; if human agents reproduce society, then they may also transform it. We meet here the Aristotelian distinction between material and efficient causes, which grounds the distinction between society and persons. This distinction avoids the errors of reification and voluntarism which suggest either that society is produced behind the backs of human beings, or that society is the direct product of human intentions. In other words, society is to be understood in terms of production: the transformation through human agency of existing material. The distinction also grounds the transcendental character of the enquiry: human activity is the efficient cause that can be explained only in relation to the material cause; but the potential of the material cause is only realised in the action of an efficient cause (the intentional activity of persons).

This gives us an account of society which suggests that society has a natural basis, and that it is open to be transformed. It also insists that society is concerned with relations of production, and that persons, working within these relations, will reproduce social structures – structures that may dominate or oppress them. Here the issue of class is raised, although it is not an issue foregrounded in Bhaskar's account. But it is clear where it fits: classes may be understood as particular relations of production which are governed by particular structures: in this case, the material production of wealth. It is of course Marx's central perspective that this access to material production needs to be transformed, in the sense of the radical change in social relations, which will result in radical changes in the productive capacity (or capacities) of some of the structures of society. Here lies a crucial dynamic of the conflictual nature of society.

The theological significance of the argument in this section and the last has been to secure an account of society as transcendental within the doctrine of creation. The account of the transcendentality that I am proposing here is not Hardy's. I do not object to the terminology of sociality or social transcendental, but I have sought to specify in some detail a stratified, transformative account of society as transcendental, in which sociality might be understood as organised. I have also stressed that an adequate conceptuality of the social must be able to incorporate notions of conflict and transformation.[7]

[7] I note in passing that there is something quite narrow about Bhaskar's account in the lack of consideration paid to cultural production. We do not need to grant everything to hermeneutics – indeed, the 'overcoming' of hermeneutics may be crucial – to

Such an account insists on the dynamic character of society, and turns upon the notion of transformation. Also secured in this account are some distinctions between the ontological and anthropological aspects of social life. The three 'marks' of sociality refer to real, active embodied persons. Such persons, we may now see, are always in relations of production: economic, cultural and intellectual work is always the refashioning of existing materials – in short, production. Yet, in this account, in these relations the substantive activities of society are reproduced in the intentions of human persons. (Here ontological and anthropological matters are distinguished.) Although we enter into particular social relations, the outcome of such a relation may be different from the agent's intention: I may not intend the reproduction of this society, and yet this is the likely outcome. Work, embodiment and language, enacted in social relations, persist as efficient cause in which the material conditions of society are reproduced. Indeed, social forms of work, embodiment and language which are inimical to my (and 'our') true interests may thereby be reproduced.

All social activity occurs in relations of production. Society is the condition and generally unintended outcome of such production. Social relations can be altered: the relation between a populace and the state might be altered; in this process the state structure might also be altered. But society cannot be overcome. Alterations to the state require a social context, a (social) language, rules for emancipatory action and so forth: the transcendentality of society. Yet such a claim must not be read wrongly. I am not arguing that society needs to be understood theologically as 'created'. Society does not enjoy the same 'status' as sociality. Particular societies cannot be traced to the presence of the triune God in creation. The point is rather that although particular societies may change – indeed, they may be changed by purposive, transformative social activity – there will always be the 'marks' of sociality –

note that human meaning as inscribed in the production of cultural objects is an important area of *work* within a range of relations of (cultural) production. Perhaps Bhaskar's militantly naturalist stance leads him astray here.

work, embodiment, language; this is a condition of human
living. As persons, we enter into these as a condition of being
persons. Indeed, we enter these as relations of production: all
aspects of society, from coal mining to theology, are productions, the 'working over' of previously existing material.

An important point must be recalled here also: the possibility of more emancipatory forms of social freedom, or less
restrictive configurations of social relations is given in creation.
It is secured in the very transcendentality of society (the
account of society proposed here is termed transformational),
in which the 'marks' of sociality are enacted in relations of
production. Such a dynamic is not to be ascribed to the gift of
Christ in redemption. This suggests that the next step is not
toward the Church in the Spirit, as the gift of Christ. Rather, it
is to an understanding of the place of society in the 'order of
redemption'.

Theologically speaking, these points come together in the
conception of resurrection – as we shall see. The desire that
might be animated by resurrection is a cultural production,
expressed in theology and in other (often ecclesial) practices.
Such desiring, focused upon and nerved by resurrection, may
provide the capacities for the transformation of contemporary
society, for the revolutionising in practice of social contradictions. Such desiring may be directed to the affirmation of
social transformation: the practical, as well as theoretical,
attempt to enact the sociality of human beings. Whether such
desiring might be truly practical turns upon an adequate
account of resurrection. This is the subject of the next chapter.

V   TRINITY, PERSONS AND SOCIETY AGAIN

I suggest that it is against such an interpretation of capitalist
society that some account of the liberative potential of theology
is to be given. It is in the specifics of an account of society, that
a theological contribution must illuminate.

At the end of section I, I maintained that the full case for my
suspicions regarding the trinitarian critique of society would
not be clear until after the discussion of society. We may now

see why it is inappropriate to begin with an account of the relational, personal being of God and its enactment in social life – this is only part of the required argument. We are now in a position to grasp the fact that society is already thoroughly 'relational'. From this perspective, we learn that a trinitarian critique of society is partly persuasive, and partly unpersuasive.

A trinitarian critique of society is right to argue that, in theory and in practice, the concept of relationality is denied: people understand themselves in asocial, non-relational ways. But we must note a further point: the existing relations of production are such as to deny the full creative capacities of human beings. From this, we may grasp that non-relational ways of thinking and acting are a 'product' of restricted social relations, not of a lack of clear thinking. Any conceptual reinterpretation of personhood and relationality needs to address both the non-relational perceptions of agents and the social practices that 'generate' and 'inform' such perceptions. Ideology has a dual aspect. The surface perception is one aspect – and many theologies rightly address this. But it is also an instance of ideology to fail to make a second move: to connect such surface perceptions with the 'deeper', essential levels of economic practice.

What is crucial here is to make the distinction between praxis as production and praxis as the reproduction of society. The function of ideology is, of course, to obscure this distinction, and is where a trinitarian critique of society misses its mark. The character of human society is relational; but its quality is not. These points – production and reproduction – are run together in a trinitarian critique of society – with the emphasis being placed on the former. Hence the demand for fresh understandings of personal being as relational – when in fact social activities are 'already' relational; they are relations of production. The issue is rather the difference between the productive practice of capitalism and the reproductive 'result' of that same practice, and how the criticism of the former connects with the material transformation of the latter.

A trinitarian critique of society, and perhaps other liberation approaches, grasp that contemporary accounts of person-hood and society are deeply compromised in their individual-ism. This is to engage with the matter at the level of the conscious production of social agents. But they fail to incorporate an anti-ideological strategy into their method by relating the productive actions of agents to the 'real', reproductive outcome of the acts of agents. To insist, with the trinitarian critique of society, that surface ideas are ideological is necessary but insufficient. The 'cause' of this ideology must be 'traced', and this can only be done with reference to the wider practices of society: those substantive practices that govern such alienated intellectual practices. In other words, the enquiry must encompass the perceptions and acts of agents, and their interrelation with the 'real' relations of social life by a conceptual reconstruction of those relations. Failure to do this suggests that such theological approaches are not sufficiently critical or self-critical. Such approaches lack an adequate engagement with an interpretation of society, and an awareness of their own collusion in the production of ideology. They assume that the theoretical task is complete in the criticism of inadequate formulations of personhood (and the actions and demands that follow from this). An anti-ideology strategy goes further, and seeks to connect such formulations to other relations of production so as to hold together the duality of praxis (Bhaskar).

The reconstruction of social relations will also require a reconstruction of social structures. Such structures are of course given in and maintained by social relations – there is no society without human activity. But these structures – the economy, the state, discourses, family – are a necessary pre-condition for human society. (Some of these may of course also function as relations.) To demand a fresh account of person-hood, or a fresh account of relationality, is right, but radically insufficient. It is to miss the fact that society is governed by social relations. If this is accepted, the issue becomes the nature of these relations, and the practical means by which these relations of production might be changed. This then raises the issue of those structures which govern and organise social relations. To demand a fresh account of personhood is to fail to take into account such social structures, given in social relations. The transformation of relations of production is always the transformation of structures of production also.

The fact that the trinitarian critique of society misses this brings us back to the issue of ideology. Indeed, precisely what Marxists expect from Christianity is here: subtlety and sophistication in large measure, but with this a fundamental reluctance to engage with the 'realities' of society. (We are back at the issue of Christianity as intermediary.) Yet when theology does address these issues, it does so only partially. In this, it is profoundly ideological, because the theological arguments are so deceptive. At one level these arguments are addressing important practical problems. But the categories of interpretation in which these issues are construed are seriously deficient. Thus theology is, generally, only engaging with the 'surface' of social issues.

This is no abstract or 'technical' point that demonstrates the cleverness of Marxists. It has immediate theological significance. If the Christian God is a God of abundance who is present to social forms, then God's presence must be grasped in relation to the *transformative* aspect of society. The possibility of social transformation in theological understanding lies in the making of the connection between condition and outcome: between society as produced in the intentional activity of agents and reproduced as the unintended result of such activity. The connection is, as noted previously, already 'given' in the work of the Logos in creation. It is ironic indeed if theology mistakes the liberatory potential of that which is already 'given'. Failure to make this connection theologically denies the presence of the abundant God and denies the 'openness' of God to the social being of humanity, a presence whose telos is the freedom of the Kingdom.

VI TRIUNE ABUNDANCE AND SOCIAL CONTRADICTIONS

I hope that it is now plain why I eschewed the insightful approach of the trinitarian critique of society. I am not denying the attraction of this approach; it remains an important theological development. But I am suggesting that it is insufficient. Its construal of the issue is too narrow and the effect of this is to 'dissolve' the social issues being addressed. Thus, I have spent some time closing off a route that might, at first glance, seem promising.[8]

I am suggesting a different way toward a liberative theology which explicitly leaves conceptual space for the abundance of God enacted in resurrection. The protocols introduced in part II suggested that an appropriate response to the presence of God is conversion. God, we may say, is present to society as the creator of 'all that is'. This demands from us a response – it is a call to conversion. We are concerned here with a turning away from false idols of the social so conversion will necessarily have a material dimension. There can be no only 'mental' turning away from idolatrous forms of economic management (and certainly no only 'spiritual' turning). This is a response to Marx's charge that Christianity is always implicated in forms of false mediation. Christianity – that is, a Christianity governed by the protocols of simplicity and decentredness, and which seeks to enact the distinction of God from the world – is intimately concerned with material conversion. In such manner, the eclipse of God might be countered: in the practical movement of conversion away from idols of the social, a movement in which the latency of God's presence to the world might become actual.

This position turned upon a stratified account of (social) reality. The account of the transcendentality of society given here allows for a greater specification of such a claim. I have suggested, following Daniel Hardy, sociality is, theologically speaking, to be understood as created being, traceable to the actions of the Logos in creation. *Practically*, the affirmation of the dynamic character of this social being toward richer forms of human life is not to be traced to the social being of God (as in

---

8   These criticisms apply also, I think, to rather different conceptions of God, such as those outlined by Anne Carr, 1988: 148–57: for instance, accounts of God as relational, suffering, may also be open to question here in that these accounts do not properly draw Christian attention to the relations of production (including those governing theology) of contemporary society.

the trinitarian critique of society). Instead, it is to be traced to the transformation of the structural activities that are the governing condition of social life. The ontic enactment of God's ontological presence to social forms thus depends upon a consideration of oppressive social structures: how these are perpetuated in social activity, and how they might be transformed. In this way the eclipse of God in social forms may be countered.

Here, the argument advances a little further. Marx was concerned that Christianity could not free itself from an individualism whose most collective form was 'intersubjectivity'; it was unable to free itself, and Feuerbach was also so unable, from understanding what was genuinely 'other' except in terms of the self. Now we may begin to see that this is not entirely so. There is a proper account of sociality within Christianity, seen as part of a theology of creation. This sociality is to be understood in terms of its three marks in relations of production in which occurs the reproduction of society. There can be no movement toward a liberative theology that sidesteps these two claims. The first indicates the theological significance of the issue; the second shows where practical possibilities for transformation might lie.

Yet this remains only a beginning in that an important theological question remains: if the practical affirmation of society (the gift of God in creation) is 'through' its transformational character, how is the *theological* reaffirmation of its dynamic character to be understood? The response to this question lies in an account of how sociality is to be understood as *re*created in the work of Jesus of Nazareth. For a liberative theology, this is a practical matter. It is not sufficient to incorporate an account of sociality within a doctrine of creation. If the emphasis on the dynamic of society, society as open to transformation, is to be taken seriously, then we require some theological specification of this dynamic in the 'order of redemption'. It may be that Christian theology is not restricted to the discussion of subjectivity. But how does it speak of 'redeemed sociality', of the recreation of social relations and structures?

This raises the final point for this chapter: abundance. Theologically, to speak of social transformation is to speak of God's abundance. We might note from Hardy's argument that a stress on the need for Christian theology to respond to the complexity and range of modern society comes with a denial that sociality may be restricted to spurious accounts of 'natural order' or the practice of resigned accommodation. Christian theology is concerned to engage, in theory and in practice, with society, rather than seek an accommodation with it. This is an important emphasis rooted in a particular understanding of the abundance of God in creation. We have seen, in Hardy's argument regarding the common sociality of humanity, an example of the structured 'abundance' which may be traced to the creative, ordering operation of the Logos in creation. This common sociality is, of course, open to abuse. Yet, as governed by the dynamic of the transformation of society, it resists abuse, and this structured resistance may be traced to the operations of the Logos. (This suggests that the suspicion of institutionality *as such* is no part of the Christian position being sketched here. Work, embodiment and language, as the constitutive, material determinants of social life, resist incursions into social freedom.)

But what about the abundance of God in redemption? In my argument the focus for understanding God's abundance in redemption is the eschatological event of the resurrection of Jesus of Nazareth, understood in its trinitarian dimensions. Theologically speaking, the transformation of society is to be referred not only to the work of the Logos in creation, but to the reconstitution of sociality in Jesus of Nazareth. Again the abundance here is not formless; it refers to 'attention' to a particular body. I shall consider the implications of this revolution in materiality in the next chapter, but if the connection can be made between sociality and resurrection, we might expect to draw out from this some account of God as present to the recreation of society in the perspective of this abundance or overflowing. This does, I suspect, give a theological context for the complexity of modern living. It does not follow that any and all such complexity is necessarily the abundance of God.

But it does mean that modern society, if God is present to it, is governed by the dynamic of the abundance embodied in resurrection.

The theological way is now open for the consideration of social transformation. Recall that God is present to society: as the 'shaper' of its basic status of its practical 'being-with', its common sociality. Christian theology does not always understand such a transcendental approach aright, nor does it always adequately inform a theological discussion of social relations. But misuse is not the same as lack. Perhaps, then, Christian theology does have some resources for a theological engagement with society, and not only an insistence on conversion. Put another way, there are Christian resources for beginning to specify how God might be understood as present to society: as the shaper of social life, and as the recreator of social life in Jesus of Nazareth. Here, then, there may be scope for some theological development as to God's relation to the contingencies of modern life – or, in a term I prefer, the contradictions of modern society. Here then we reach the full theological specification of social transformation.

Lastly, we may note that the contrast between social contingencies and social contradictions marks an important issue. My account of society as transcendental turns upon a number of decisions as to the character of social contingencies. The first of these, already raised implicitly above, is to insist that the relations that govern or embody society are relations of production; that is to say, that human society is to be understood as the 'working over' of existing materials, of a variety of types and at a range of levels. (This is the issue of determination.) The second is to note that – indeed! – modern society could be otherwise. And the way to this new 'form' is through particular *contradictions*.

The question then becomes: how is God present to these? How are social contradictions encompassed in Word and Spirit? How is a theological theodicy of freedom to be framed to meet this issue? It is important to note here that I am not suggesting that social relations are to be 'read off' the divine sociality. Rather, the action of the trinitarian God is the 'cause' of the social being of humanity; sociality has its place in the 'pattern' of creation and redemption. If so, then it sociality also governed by the dynamic of structured abundance, of proportioned and proportioning overflow which marks resurrection. The full theological articulation of the presence of God to social forms thus requires, in my terms, the relating together of sociality and resurrection. Only in this way will it be possible to establish the full abundance of the triune God, and show how such abundance nerves Christian practice and invites a way of interpreting society 'in the Spirit'.

Grasping this abundance becomes an important theological task. It will, in part, depend upon some specification of the variegated character of contemporary society, and some delineation of the nature of social contradictions. Although the forms of the dominant hegemony may be determining, these are not necessarily *all* determining, and neither do they exhaust all areas of practice. Society, comprising dominant, residual and emergent forms, is not to be understood as 'flat', as tends to be the account that comes out of the work of the Frankfurt School. There are sites of resistance around social contradictions, and activities directed against the dominant hegemony across many institutions and practices. The difficulty lies in ascertaining their character and their force. Here lies the possibility of the affirmation of social transformation as befits the abundance of God 'through' social contradictions toward different forms of social and economic organization. The issues of social transformation and God's abundance (in creation and redemption) meet here.

The issue raised by these remarks follows from my specification of some contingencies as contradictions: how is God's presence to these contradictions to be understood? This is the subject of the next two chapters.

CHAPTER 6

Incarnation, resurrection and liberation

I INCARNATION

It is, of course, a central claim of Christianity that the Logos is present in the flesh, in the person of Jesus of Nazareth. It will be recalled that in chapter 4 I began to speak of a God who is respectful in God's dealings with human beings, a God who is always reticent in the revelation of Godself. Here is the nerve of such suggestions. The personal God engages with human beings in the most personal way possible: such a God addresses us in and through a person. This is of course profoundly mysterious, and can be attributed to the graceful action of God; *that* it is, is fundamental to Christianity. Further, what needs to be understood aright is the *constitutive* significance of this claim – more on this in section II.

God's presence in the historical particularity of Jesus of Nazareth, accessible to us through the particular narrative witness of Christian scripture and the tradition – institutional, communitarian, individual, theological – of the Church, suggests that God has been present in social relations – not as the orderer of sociality, but living in the flesh as a person in such relations. Here perhaps much recent 'sociological' investigation of the context of Christian scripture is important (and perhaps the Christological essays that have come out of liberation theology – Boff (1980) and Sobrino (1978) – fit here also) in that such investigation enquires into the very texture of these social relations: an enquiry 'after the flesh'.[1]

---

[1] For a liberation perspective, see especially Gottwald, 1983.

I shall be approaching the issue differently: theologically rather than exegetically. As LaCugna (1991: 214) notes of work in this area over the last few years: ' ... christology for the most part has been driven by exegetical concerns; only rarely are pneumatology and trinitarian theology integrated into christology in an essential way'. Here the approach is theological, suggesting a particular understanding of the presence of God in the flesh 'within' social relations. What may we learn from a Christian perspective about these social relations, and the social structures that they embody, given an interpretation of the life of Jesus of Nazareth? By this I mean particularly an interpretation of this life in terms of its culmination: cross and resurrection. To this end, the following chapters explore an interpretation of cross and resurrection that might meet the depth of the Marxist charge: Christianity functions to mediate falsely, and this function in part at least may be attributed to its seeming incapacity to offer a theological place for social forms. (It follows that if this place cannot be 'found', the identification of the idolatry of social forms remains problematic.)

I am proposing this way forward in the light of the Marxist critique of ideology which invites the construction of a more liberating theology, not the development of a quasi-sociology. The aim of political theology is not knowledge of capitalism, but rather knowledge of its determined position and status within capitalist social relations. A liberative theology cannot do the work of other disciplines. Instead, the truth of theology lies elsewhere: in the truthfulness of its knowledge of God. Theology is, I suggest, not being invited to abandon its task but to do it differently. This difference/change is forced upon theology if it, against the Marxist critique of ideology, wishes to be liberative, neither too close nor too distant.

But we need to be careful how we interpret a phrase like Christianity's 'truthfulness of its knowledge of God'. The intention here is to offer what might be called practical truthfulness. The kind of theological discourse being attempted here is intended as a contribution to redemption understood in a materialist sense. It is the attempt to construct a theology against the sorts of materialist pressures to which a full account of redemption should refer us. This is why what follows in this chapter will attempt to explore an interpretation of incarnation and resurrection in relation to an account of society. A theological contribution to the transformation of society is the intended outcome – an outcome to be enacted, and not a transformation in consciousness only. It is an attempt not to refer to redemption in general terms, but to the specific character of redemption in relation to social forms.

I am suggesting that the transformation in the embodiment of Jesus of Nazareth must, for the Christian, be the primary reference point for an engagement with society. A Christian account of redemption must take as its focus an interpretation of the life, death and resurrection of Jesus of Nazareth. If this account of redemption is persuasive, then this will be a properly theological engagement, but may also be one in which the capacities of human beings are not falsely mediated. Such an engagement, if it can be defended, may thereby stand as a Christian contribution to liberation.

We may trace here the interrelation between the presence and absence of God, between the latency and actuality of God's relationship to the world (and especially to human society). In the previous part, I argued that the correct response to the 'proper creation perspective' arising out of the attempt to construct our theological discourse in a manner appropriate to its 'object', is conversion: a fresh manner of relation to 'all that is'. I suggested also, following an argument by Nicholas Lash, that such conversion is a material affair. There can be no turning away from idolatries of the social through the will alone, or through a change in consciousness. Practical conversion has material dimensions. In this perspective we may grasp the presence and absence of God. In the transformation of human community, away from distorted forms of social relations, the eclipse of God may be countered. But this is not semi-Pelagianism. God too, we might say, seeks the transformation of irrelation, a turning away from forms of idolatry. The sinful structures and practices in which human beings are enmired are not to be denied, and these prevent conversion. But, at least for the Christian, God also seeks the transformation of such circumstances.

In a sense, this enables a 'second' engagement with Marxism. Not only is the decentred God of Christianity the criticism of Feuerbach's idolatrous 'competitor-God' (Lash), and not only is the presence of the Christian God a call to (material) conversion. We may say, in a second engagement, that if the Logos is indeed the orderer of sociality – an affirmation of the social being of humanity and an affirmation of the nurturing qualities of human society – then we also have, in the presence of the Logos in crucified and resurrected flesh, some indication of God's initiative for the transformation of social relations. This is the redemption of humanity in its social, material being: the reconstruction of anthropological matters through a reconstitution of sociality.

God, we might say, is decisively present to us 'in' Jesus of Nazareth. This presence, as personal, is respectful. And yet, as I contend in the next section, it is decisive. The question here is: how might this decisive and yet hidden presence be understood as informing us about God's activity in material creation and material redemption toward the transformation of social relations? The issue here is not only that Christianity is not the interruption of attempts to transform social relations. It is to enquire, in addition, as to the meaning of the wisdom of God given in cross and resurrection, so that we might gain some insight into the practice of resurrection and the nature of the (created) social world, and into God's presence to distorted social relations. In short, God's presence and absence to social forms need to be understood Christologically.

II   THE CENTRALITY OF CROSS AND RESURRECTION

In the previous chapter I stressed the ordering activity of the Logos in creation. I suggested in the previous section that the incarnation invites us to see God as present 'in' these social relations. But we also need to add a further emphasis: the redemption of sociality.

The social relations of the time of Jesus of Nazareth are not ours; the forms of production, and the relations governed by such production are different. In this chapter I shall therefore be suggesting a quite general way in which we may interpret resurrection as offering insight into the practice of liberation, and as revealing the character of the social world. It is in the next chapter that I shall engage more directly with the sorts of distortion in our social relations, and how God may be present to these. Under the God-initiated dynamic of created to redeemed sociality, the crucial insight into the liberation of humanity into new, less restrictive forms of social relation will be found in a consideration of the cross and resurrection of Jesus of Nazareth.

In suggesting this way of proceeding I am consciously aligning myself with a tradition that goes back certainly as far as the Reformation. For this tradition, it is the resurrection that informs us of the potentials of the world. And it is the cross that informs us of God. God's nature is hidden and revealed in the cross; yet it is in resurrection that the possibilities for humanity are revealed – not least possibilities for social organisation. As James Alison (1993: 20) has argued: ' ... the raising of Jesus was the gratuitous giving back of the whole life and death that had ended on Good Friday ... ' Yet there remains the need to attempt to determine the significance of this 'giving back' for social organisation.

An interpretation of resurrection offers us an insight into the nature of the 'social' world – this is what I intend to explore here in relation to political liberation. 'The crucifixion and resurrection of Jesus Christ are the main Christian criteria of what knowing the world means for God. They are the wisdom of God in its greatest concentration' (Hardy and Ford, 1984: 108). I take it that this wisdom is not restricted to particular events or experiences that are interpreted as 'religious'. If the argument of chapter 3 is persuasive, nothing falls outside God's creativity. Therefore, it is quite legitimate to enquire as to what this wisdom might authorise Christians to say and do in relation to society. I agree with Hardy and Ford that 'The resurrection is God's way of referring back Jesus to the world' (Hardy and Ford, 1984:

126). The question here is: what might we learn of the world from this 'reference back'?

In making this suggestion, I am accepting what I take to be the *constitutive* nature of the event of cross and resurrection.[2] I am suggesting, as will become clear in section IV, that cross and resurrection do not simply illustrate the pattern of the Christian life, but that the 'revolutionary' implications of resurrection are constitutive of it. Whatever liberating practice is 'nerved' by the event of resurrection, this liberation is connected to an account of 'salvation (including its reconciling effects) [which] is constituted primarily by divine action, not by human knowledge of that action' (White, 1991: 20). For Vernon White it is important to make this case to secure the universal salvific nature of the Christ-event. My concern here is somewhat different. I am seeking to interpret how this 'event of divine self-giving' (White, 1991: 21) might be understood in relation to political practice. Put negatively, I am trying to avoid an account of resurrection, with its attendant eschatological implications, that fails to generate a Christian praxis, or generates too general a praxis.[3] So, in the next few sections I seek to show how resurrection might be the nerve of Christian practice in a constitutive sense, and to draw out in section VI some of the implications of this constitutive account in relation to an interpretation of society.

Resurrection is more than an illustration of the life of the Christian believer (although it may indeed be that). Resurrection is more than a 'pattern' to be imitated, more than the suggestion that suffering for others is the profoundest love. A political practice in the perspective of resurrection will depend upon a constitutive sense that enables an interpretation of the 'reality' of the social world in Christian perspective, and thereby guides 'the practice of resurrection'. Indeed, my account of 'the practice of resurrection' will only be persuasive

---

[2] It is important to note this as I offer no sustained defence of this acceptance.
[3] As I hope will become clear as this chapter unfolds, I do not intend here an account of resurrection which is simply the projection of desiring subjects, as the recompense for 'the unanswerable resistance of the Real' (Jameson, 1989: 183).

if there are ontological, and not solely epistemological, 'consequences' of the Christ-event.

But, having said this, my argument is also somewhat restricted. The full range of the constitutive claim for the Christ-event includes salvation for humanity and the redemption of nature: 'real evil of the real world is faced and healed *ontologically* in the life, death and resurrection of Jesus' (Gunton, 1988: 165). My argument here does not embrace the range, but merely tries to suggest some ways of understanding resurrection as the nerve of Christian practice, and as a way of beginning to think theologically about the social world.

Perhaps one way to interpret my argument is to adapt some words of Colin Gunton. Gunton argues that one aspect of the problem in showing the universal significance of Jesus is that of 'empty rhetoric': 'What prevents the claim of universality from being mere empty rhetoric, unrelated to the way things actually are with the world?' (Gunton, 1988: 168). (This, we might say, is Lash's concern (1981: 147–8) that the world is too often only *interpreted* in redemptive terms by Christians.) The final step in Gunton's response to his own question is ecclesiological. But in a preliminary step he insists that 'the reordered relationship has to be realised, to take concrete form in time and space. The *ontological* relationship of the creator and created, grounded in the Word and reordered in the enhypostatic humanity of Jesus, must become *ontic*' (Gunton, 1988: 170). Whereas Gunton develops his argument in the direction of ecclesiology, the rest of this chapter lingers a little longer with the issue of 'concrete form in time and space'. How might Christians enact this reordered relationship? How might Christians act against the eclipse of God? And what might this reordered relationship tell us about society and Christian social practices of liberation?

All this might seem strange. For instance, is it not likely that Marxists would simply rule out the very possibility of a constitutive account of resurrection? Perhaps. But the interpretation of Marxism that I have been offering in this book is not much concerned with what Denys Turner, in a discussion of this issue, has rather quaintly described in the following terms:

'Christians believe that the universe is peopled with agencies and entities and activities and events – a God, an act of creation, an act of redemption ... ' (Turner, 1983: 175).[4] On my interpretation, Marxism is not much concerned with these 'ultimate' considerations, although some Marxisms, notably Engelsian dialectical materialism, have ruled out the possibility of the existence of these 'entities'.

But this does not really concern my argument. My argument here is to attempt to show that Christian theism is not ideological, does not *inherently* misdescribe. Put another way, it is an attempt to suggest how theological discourse might be non-ideological, might not be an intermediary. We are referring here, to employ an argument by Nicholas Lash, to the correctness and not the truthfulness of Christianity. I am persuaded by Lash's argument that 'The "truthfulness" of Christianity ... is primarily a practical matter: it is to be "shown" in the transformation both of individuals and of social relationships' (Lash, 1986a: 138). But there is no hope in this truthfulness being 'shown' if truth-conditions are not met. How an interpretation of the death and resurrection of Jesus of Nazareth might meet these truth-conditions (that is, the Marxist critique of ideology) is the concern of this chapter.

So whether theological discourse 'refers', so to speak, is a rather different point. Here we are concerned with correctness: if there can be no non-ideological discourse of God, then I do not see how the issue of the falsity or otherwise of Christianity might be raised because we could not be sure we were genuinely referring to God. In the meeting of such truth-conditions lies the possibility that the speaker's intentions might be genuine: this is ' ... the claim that an interaction partner deceives neither himself nor the other but rather truthfully presents his intentions' (Peukert, 1986: 185). There can be no knowledge of a liberating God if, in the very discourse on that God, the speakers of such discourse are systematically articulating reactionary, specialising or

---

[4] I consider that this is not really adequate: I do not see how God might be contained by the universe; nor would I argue that there is an act of creation, an act of redemption: creation and redemption need to be held together more closely.

alternative positions. Such discourse may indeed employ the terminology of liberation but this is, in itself, no guarantee of the liberative status of such theological proclamation. An oppositional theology does rather turn upon a particular construal of its own epistemological status. Neither too close to nor too distant from determining limits and pressures, it speaks from its place of practical decentredness, calling attention to those limits and pressures as these inscribe its own discursive embodiment.

III   THE PRACTICE OF RESURRECTION

Putting aside the issue of how resurrection might inform our understanding of social forms until section VI, I enquire here as to how an account of resurrection might be understood as the nerve of Christian action in the world. Of resurrection, Hardy and Ford have suggested: ' ... the character of God lets us imagine him creating an event through which people are offered, without coercion, possibilities that meet their deepest desires – for affirmation, a fresh start, purpose, community, life beyond death and much else' (Hardy and Ford, 1984: 131). Are there political implications to be drawn from such a suggestion: what possibilities regarding *political* liberation might Jesus' resurrection enable Christians to see and act upon? From a different perspective, Rebecca Chopp speaks also of 'new possibilities', arguing that 'crucifixion and resurrection' are among those grace-filled 'words full of Word' (Chopp, 1989: 12). What might the implications of a non-ideological account of resurrection be for an understanding of liberation? What fresh possibilities does it envision, nerve and demand? Resurrection is, after all, the eschatological transformation of the Logos made flesh – it is thereby the revelation of the 'true (eschatological) nature' of the ordering work of the Word.

We might approach this issue by noting that the importance of death has been raised by some liberation theologians. Commenting on the question of death in the context of ascertaining the nature of a specific *Christian* contribution to liberation,

Assmann points to: ' ... a whole series of radical questions to which Marxism has not paid sufficient attention, of which perhaps the most significant is the Christian affirmation of victory over death, that final alienation to which Marxism can find no satisfactory answer' (Assmann, 1975: 144). He concludes that Marxism, although it carries an expectation that Marxists must be prepared to be killed, cannot really respond to this problem which is 'so deeply relevant to revolutionary practice' (Assmann, 1975: 144). Assmann does not develop this insight but he correctly identifies a way forward: the possibility that theology can make a contribution not at the edges, so to speak, of the liberation process, filling in the gaps with which Marxism cannot deal, but rather in its understanding of the revolutionary process based on its account of resurrection.

We need here an interpretation of resurrection that enables us to see more clearly the sort of political practice made possible by the 'revolution' in mortality given in resurrection. What does resurrection tell us concretely about the 'transcendence' of current circumstances? This problem has been explored by Leonardo Boff:

> The resurrection of the crucified Jesus shows that it is not meaningless to die for other human beings and God. In Jesus' resurrection, light is shed on the anonymous death of all those who have lost out in history while fighting for the cause of justice and ultimate human meaningfulness. (Boff, 1980: 291)

The issue not addressed by Boff (nor by Assmann) is the effect that such an understanding can have on our practice *now*.[5] It may be quite correct to argue, as Terry Eagleton does, that 'the opaqueness of our present bodies will be transfigured into pure transparency by the power of God' (Eagleton, 1970: 55). But what does the resurrection of the body say about revolutionary praxis now? How might these strongly visual images be interpreted in relation to society?

[5] It is interesting to note the consequences for the 'actuality' of resurrection in more 'immanentist' attempts to rethink the relation between God and the world: see McFague, 1984: 45–57; Carter Heyward, 1982: 57–9; Ruth Page, 1991: 81–6.

IV   RESURRECTION AND SOCIALITY: A REVOLUTION IN
EMBODIMENT

For the Christian the fact of death remains: we shall all perish, certainly as individuals, and, perhaps, as a race. But the significance of death, on account of the resurrection of Jesus, has been altered. Christians see the limit of death differently: still in the context of oppression in many parts of the world, real, brutal and terrifying, but – to echo Lash (1981: 193) – in' principle overcome. Not only therefore, as Boff suggests, are past deaths in the pursuit of justice placed in a new light, but the future deaths of Christians (and others) are similarly placed in a new light. This is what I meant by the claim that the resurrection might have heuristic and practical consequences for Christian praxis *now*.

I do not wish to overstate my claim about resurrection here. Christians do not have some blueprint as to what the future might look like. The form of the future is both a practical issue, and a matter that escapes the competence of theology alone. Yet a theological enquiry insists that this matter is governed by the transformation of human limits given in the resurrection, of 'working within the present for its surpassment' (Eagleton, 1970: 70). But how is this a specifically Christian contribution to political practice? What does resurrection tell us here? I think that understanding history as 'gift' allows a particular Christian engagement with society in a fashion that both affirms the nurturing aspects of society (the activity of the Logos in creation) but also demands its discriminating surpassment (the resurrection of the Logos enfleshed, Jesus of Nazareth) – I discuss this in section VI. Here, in connection with Christian political practice, I concentrate upon the resurrection as the revolutionising of a limit in sociality, and the intimate connection between resurrection and human *society*: a concern with the possibilities for social action given in the resurrection as eschatological harbinger.

In the consideration of the resurrection as a transformation in sociality (that is, in the transformation of a limit to human embodiment), there emerges the shape of what resurrection might tell us about Christian political practice. Such an argument turns upon the claim that Christian theology can allow for more radical discontinuities and continuities than can Marxism. Death remains a severe discontinuity, but not an ultimate one. The Christian understanding of death, in the context of the resurrection of the body, calls for the grasping of the limit of our mortality, and of revolutionary praxis in the face of it precisely because the Christian can trust in and hope for continuity in that severe discontinuity.

Terry Eagleton has eloquently argued for this position:

The Jesus who confronted and conquered tragedy in the world-historical action of the cross was also the Jesus who wept over the death of an historically insignificant friend; it is only in the kingdom of heaven, where 'death shall be no more, neither shall there be mourning nor crying nor pain', that the redemptive power of that first tragic action will penetrate the darkness of the second with its own victory. (Eagleton, 1970: 113)

In this way, what are discontinuities at one level are continuities at another, deeper level: 'the christian revolutionary perspective reaches to a depth within and beyond the projects of revolutionary socialism' (Eagleton, 1970: 113). Across tragedy, across death, for the Christian there is the hope of continuity. The depth of the Christian position is to be secured, as we shall see in the next section, by a trinitarian interpretation of resurrection. Here I wish to emphasise that resurrection invites a new way of thinking about death. Writing of the complexities involved in interpreting the resurrection, Helmut Peukert has argued that we 'require an adequately developed conception of existing unto death' (Peukert, 1986: 226). Such a conception I am sketching here: resurrection is a revolution in one of the 'marks' of the sociality of humanity and is thereby the reconstruction (of the social fact) of death.[6]

---

[6] Death then is not, as Peukert reports of some existentialist interpretations, 'the farthest horizon of authentic self existence' nor 'the cause of the radical individualization of subjects' (Peukert, 1986: 233). However, my argument differs from Peukert in that I am not seeking to disclose the object domain of theology. See McCarthy 1990: 200–15 for the suggestion that Peukert's argument formally corresponds to Kant's attempt to disclose such a domain (the immortality of the soul and the existence of God) as postulates of practical reason.

Death, in the perspective of resurrection, is not to be interpreted individualistically. Death as the boundary which undermines the solidarity of efforts by social agents to transform the conditions of social organisation is ruled out by resurrection. Resurrection as a revolution in embodiment is precisely the 'returning' of the individual to their social being: it is the recreation of a limit of human sociality. This, of course, may be learned from the accounts of the resurrected Jesus, as James Alison has pointed out: in these scenes Jesus always 'appears' as the one who was *crucified*, his resurrected body bearing the marks of his subjection to the particular social forces of 'state' execution. The resurrection, as the overturning of a limit of embodiment and so as a transformation in sociality, insists on the reconstitution of the horizon of human being as social being. Death here is not the denial of sociality; instead, sociality is here reconstructed.

The resurrection returns Christians to the revolutionary process in order to seek the transcendence of history or, better, the transcendence of social structures and relations, in the knowledge that Christian revolutionary praxis is enabled by the 'revolution' of the resurrection of Jesus of Nazareth, which in turn prefigures the general resurrection of the Kingdom. This knowledge insists that even in death human being is social being. As Denys Turner has argued, for the Christian 'on account of the resurrection of the body, what can be risked in revolution is greater than for the Marxist, because death is *part* of the Christian understanding of revolution, rather than its *end*'. If it is true that 'the Marxist conception of revolution has to put death on one side, as absurd – having no place' (Denys Turner) and is thereby unable to engage with death as the most extreme limit of humanity, then the same is not the case for Christianity. As Turner makes clear: 'Because of the *resurrection of the body*, for the Christian, death becomes part of the revolutionary process: it *is* the discontinuity which the Kingdom overcomes; so the Kingdom is *the* revolution.'[7] This yields, of course, a more radical conception of revolution, as

---

[7] In private correspondence.

Eagleton has already suggested, in which the revolution of resurrection encompasses death, rather than being 'restricted' by it. (Having said this, it is important to acknowledge that although the revolution that Christians call the Kingdom, given proleptically in the resurrection of Jesus of Nazareth, may be more radical than the Marxist understanding of revolution, the Christian also recognises that it is only in faith and trust, in the loneliness of suffering, the strenuousness of prayer, the communal event of the Eucharist, that death is not to be regarded as an ultimate boundary.) Yet the basic point remains: Christians are promised that the most radical of discontinuities – the restriction of sociality by death – will be overcome; Christians are called to enact in hope its overcoming.

This returns us to the conception of death as a social action. Resurrection insists that death is not the victory of 'the individual' over the social. Rather, it insists upon the revolutionising or transformation of a particular limit, death, of the sociality of humanity. Death is a boundary of the sociality of humanity. And humanity, if we are to follow the argument of the previous chapter, is precisely social, and as such consists of work, embodiment and language. Thus if resurrection is a transformation of a limit of human being, then this is a 'social' limit and such a transformation reconstructs the social basis of human life against its closure in death.

Resurrection is the transcendence of the limit of death, a limit that is a general characteristic of social humanity. As a transformation in one of the 'marks' – embodiment – of sociality, resurrection invites the reshaping of the other two marks. If a crucial limit of embodiment is death, then resurrection reconstitutes this limit. As such, it reconstitutes work and language in that it enters into a new relation with these. In other words, what is required is the reshaping of language to grasp this event: the language of resurrection is eschatological language. Further, work is placed into a new, eschatological horizon: persons, products and relations are reconfigured within a new eschatological horizon in the move from created to redeemed sociality; the practices of work are thereby thrust into their own future. Thus resurrection invites a 'new mode of living together' (Eagleton, 1970: 47) in the face of death. It is a returning of human beings to their social history – the latter now to be understood differently. Death, then, in the perspective of the resurrection, is not to be interpreted as the denial of the social basis of human life, as that which only has reference to the individual. This implication of the event of resurrection connects with a development that we arrived at it by a rather different route: sociality is the (transcendental) condition of human activity, and not even death – at least for the Christian – is the denial of sociality.

V   RESURRECTION: A TRINITARIAN PERSPECTIVE

I am suggesting that resurrection secures the Christian conception of 'revolution' as perhaps more fundamental than the Marxist's. This fundamental nature of resurrection is not a reference solely, or even primarily, to the individual, but rather to human life understood more widely: precisely, human life as social. Such a revolutionising of a human limit is both the reconstruction of sociality and thereby admits of a more radical conception of social revolution. How might this be understood more concretely? If resurrection is 'revolution' for the Christian, then how does this 'revolution' engage with social life? This question can only be answered by an account of the 'focus' of resurrection, an interpretation of the one who is resurrected: Jesus of Nazareth. It is here we must begin if we are to gain a fuller understanding of resurrection. If the Christian God is the sort of God who may create an event that enables the possibility of Christian political practice, how might this event be understood?

To begin, we may note that the character of the resurrection event cannot be understood too simply. In a number of recent studies (Peukert, Rowan Williams, Alison, Hardy and Ford), the emphasis has been placed on a trinitarian interpretation as the only satisfactory way of drawing out the dimensions of this event. The resurrection of Jesus can only be grasped through a focus on the person of Jesus himself, by reference to the One

Jesus called Father and by attention to the experience of new life in the community of the first followers of Jesus. Only these dimensions provide an adequate context for grasping the complexities and sheer God-given abundance of resurrection. The first dimension we have met already: the continuity of Jesus' identity through death is the 'revolution' in mortality referred to in the previous section. We may also begin to explore what it means to say that the resurrection is God's way of referring Jesus back to the world. This reference back is first understood in terms of the community that asserts its identity in relation to him. And there is more: if the proper *context* for the affirmation of Jesus' resurrection is the Christian community, then the proper *perspective* is the God who recreates life out of death. This may be understood as the 'proper creation perspective' of chapter 3, here interpreted Christologically. In short, to enter into fellowship with Jesus is already – implicitly – to be drawn into thinking in trinitarian terms (and to be drawn into fellowship by and with a trinitarian God). In the interrelation of these dimensions, as we shall see, lies an adequate theological context for interpreting resurrection.

In this account, attention is to be paid to the human person, crucified and resurrected; to the God to whom such an event is to be attributed; and to the experience of a community instituted by Jesus and sent out as apostles in the power of the Spirit. The structure, and thereby the form of our appropriation, of the event is trinitarian. Yet in beginning here the argument inevitably engages with a difficult problem: that of finding and fashioning, encounter and response, authority and appropriation. In beginning with the person of Jesus of Nazareth, I am suggesting that it is here that God encounters us: the trinitarian engagement with the resurrection event is, we might say, 'authorised'. But what precisely is *given*? And what is *invited* and *enabled* in response? If the argument of this section is right, an adequate response to this question is to be found in the interrelation of the trinitarian dimensions. I plan to consider this interrelation, following closely the structure of an argument by Rowan Williams (1986), but paying rather more attention to resurrection. In delineating the matter in this way, I wish to stress that resurrection generates a conceptuality of abundance, creativity and liberty for grasping the triune God.

Briefly, Williams suggests that the sort of 'effect' that Jesus' resurrected presence had on the earliest 'Christian' communities was an utterly radical reconstitution of limits: 'the claim that Jesus of Nazareth "reveals" God (more specifically, the God of Israel) is a statement affirming that what is thought to be characteristic of God alone – radical "generative power", global creativity, the capacity to constitute the limits of human existence, and so forth – has been experienced in connection with the life and death of a human being ... ' (Rowan Williams, 1986: 203). We have here then the capacity ascribed to this person to liberate adherents into a new form of community – furthermore, a community without 'limits'. This gives some indication of the creativity to be ascribed to God the Creator, and of the creativity of God the Word as dependent. The creativity of the Spirit may be understood as present to the Christian communities: a creativity such that it too may be described as divine 'yet which is not straightforwardly identical either with the absolute creativity which is the source and context of all things, or with the historical event generating the reconstruction of the human world' (Rowan Williams, 1986: 204). We are returned to the point made above: the event of the resurrection has three dimensions: the perspective provided by the God who can transform death into life, the context provided by a community that recognises no boundaries, and a focus on an historical person.

In this perspective, it is perhaps not surprising that Jesus should come to be understood as Godlike. More than this, Jesus comes to be understood as Godlike in the form of *response* to the One he called Father. In what we might call a practice of obedience, Jesus referred everything to God (and was, also, for others) – so graced, we might add, by the Spirit. We have here then a particular form of 'Godlikeness': a 'Godlikeness' that turns upon an acknowledgement of dependence and obedience; in shorthand, from Gethsemane to Calvary. This has two consequences: first, it allows some account to be given of Jesus as divine; second, it privileges an account of divinity in terms of response and obedience: a relation of freedom (and not a relation of competition). It is precisely in this relationship of free obedience that Jesus is the exalted one.[8]

Here is perhaps the core of authority that Christians claim in speaking of Jesus as God incarnate: it is the givenness of his capacity to reconstitute humanity that is at issue here. His resurrected presence (in the Spirit) is the liberation of human beings: from old religious, social and personal ties into a new cruciform community. But we may also say that this liberatory capacity is Godlike in and through obedience. Freedom is secured and enacted in a relationship of obedience.

Such a stress on the creativity of the presence of the risen Jesus in the Spirit on account not of a claim to 'ungenerated' status but due to his status as obedient son (cf. Philippians 2. 8–9) allows for a more variegated account of creativity. Indeed, Williams suggests an account of creativity which turns upon the practice of response and obedience (in the sense that Jesus refused to acknowledge limits to his being for others). So Jesus 'acknowledges as his "limit" only the will of the God he calls Father: his liberty is itself a function of his obedience. So Jesus shares the creativity of God, yet not as a "second God", a separate *individual*: he is God *as* dependent – for whom the metaphors of Word, Image, Son are appropriate' (Rowan Williams, 1986: 204). This suggests a mutuality in the economy of redemption: a mutuality of obedience, but a form of obedience in which Jesus enters freely into his destiny: the one who is resurrected. There is therefore a relationship of dialogue, of will and response acknowledged and enacted in cross and resurrection, at the heart of the divine economy. This is a

---

[8] This way of putting the matter is an attempt to insist on the entire economy of Jesus' actions. Jesus does not simply declare a message, but rather in his actions discloses and bears witness to the 'reality' Jesus himself called 'Father'. The resurrection is to be understood as the vindication by God of this entire action. It follows that I regard Ruether's suggestion of a 'message Christology' (1981: 45–56; 1983: 116–38) to be insufficient. (For the designation of Ruether's position as a 'message Christology', I am indebted to Daphne Hampson, 1990: 64–6.)

glimpse into God's being, as we shall see in more detail in chapter 8.

The important point to note here, and we shall meet it again in a moment, is that it is precisely into such a relationship of obedience, which is freedom, that the Christian community is invited to enter into, in the Spirit. Not because this freedom is a form of security, but because this freedom in obedience is an entering into the creative liberty of God, that is both to be joined with and enacted. Indeed this process is marked by a double movement: a reconstitution of humanity that is universal in scope, and an affirmation that the head of this reconstituted humanity is Jesus of Nazareth present to Christian communities. There is then both a narrow focus and yet the universalising of limits. The person whose identity persists in resurrection through death is the revolution in mortality, and is the surpassment of limits of gender, race, cult, territory, nation, and so on. Here we discover that the language of new creation is not simply appropriate, it is required to make sense of this life. There is a thorough revolution in the nature of relationships as transformed by the presence of the risen Christ (Gal. 3.28). Rowan Williams puts it this way:

So to come to be 'in Christ', to belong with Jesus, involves a far-reaching reconstruction of one's humanity: a liberation from servile, distorted patterns in the past, a liberation from anxious dread of God's judgement, a new identity in a community of reciprocal love and complementary service, whose potential horizons are universal. (Rowan Williams, 1986: 202)

What does this mean? James Alison suggests that here 'the intelligence of the victim is the discovery of the sort of human beings we are, and how we tend to build our personal and social identities on a series of exclusions' (Alison, 1993: 45). And the reconstitution of humanity is the demand for the practical overcoming of these inclusions toward a greater liberty. In other words, awareness of this series of exclusions is not the obliteration of the differences secured by these exclusions. Instead, the Christian community enjoys its form of responsible solidarity in the attempt to consider the significance of these exclusions in their material dimensions, and their significance for the restriction (or otherwise) of freedom toward a new future. This is the 'mark' of the presence of the Spirit. We have only to recall the argument of the previous chapter to note that such restrictions often take the form of mistakes as to the character of our 'being with others', and thus to the restriction of our freedom to be social beings.

Finally, what of the identity of the God who is revealed as the author of the event of resurrection? We have a God who is not restricted by space-time or matter: indeed, in the resurrection of materiality this God transforms all three. We have here what Rebecca Chopp calls 'kairotic time', which 'calls into question all that is presupposed' (Chopp, 1989: 49). All may well be called into question, but it remains a calling into question that is directed to a particular revolution in embodiment: Jesus of Nazareth. We may be called into God's time, a time of liberty: but it is liberty of proportion, and not indeterminacy; it is a liberty which reconstructs the Logos-created sociality of human beings. This God acts to restore the one who claimed, in free obedience, that it is not foolish to give up your life for your friends. Such a God declines to allow death to mark a boundary in sociality and thereby affirms the social character of human life.

Yet, in the context of my argument, we must all the time seek to draw out the political resonance of such abundance. First, we are authorised to speak of a God whose divinity is to be understood as a creativity which restores to Jesus his world and his freedom; this creativity is of course to be connected with the abundance of God in creation. Second, the freedom of Jesus is to be understood as his being for others: in this freedom, on account of resurrection, Jesus secures his own destiny and thereby discloses the creative freedom of a God who saves those who die for others; the appropriate response is to enter into new patterns of emancipatory solidarity as the shaping of this freedom. Third, as outlined in the previous section, fresh possibilities for new patterns of practice in community – a revolution! – are enabled; we are returned to the present in order to imagine, desire and enact its surpassment.

I began this section by asking, given that the revolution enter-
tained by the Christian may be understood as more radical
than that acknowledged by the Marxist, what might resurrection tell us about Christian political practice? We are now in a
position to note the first stage of a response to this question.
(The next section offers the second stage.)

First, resurrection is to be grasped within a trinitarian structure: there can be no entering into the dynamic of resurrection
without attention being paid to the level of universal questioning that the resurrection of Jesus initiates. Here is the question
of Christian community: a community that on the one hand
acknowledges no limits apart from its Lord, and yet on the
other is thrown into confusion by this acknowledgement. In
other words, if there are no 'limits', then how are we to live?
We are back again to the issue of conversion: the revolution in
the flesh of Jesus of Nazareth is the invitation to the community
(which has no limits) to acknowledge, in such a resurrection,
the referring of all matters to the boundless creativity of the
Father, and the creativity in dependence and obedience of the
Son. 'God invites us into his "world" . . . the primary order of
all things, the creative liberty of God' (Rowan Williams, 1986:
208). It is, above all, an invitation in the Spirit to enter into
this liberative creativity: a 'following after' in response to the
call of Christ. In short, an invitation is made to live a life for
others in response to the 'creativity' of Gethsemane, Calvary
and the road to Emmaus.

Second, we may note the historical character of the
engagement. Even if we admit that the level of disorder initiated by Christ is perhaps most evident in the early Church, the
structure of appropriating the resurrection does not change.
To enter into the resurrection is still to ascribe 'normative
focus' to the testimony to Jesus; it is to refer this focus to the
creative liberty of the Creator; it is to ask as to the form of
community in the Spirit that is 'ruled' by the creative liberty of
the Son from the Creator. If resurrection is a form of grace and
a referring of Jesus back to the world, it is an invitation to enter
this liberty, and enact (or share) it. This then is the historical
character of the enquiry: given the invitation, how shall we

live? Given the call, how shall we undertake the difficult task of conversion (of ourselves and of others)? We are justified, but what is the form of this sanctification that can only take the narrow way from Gethsemane to Calvary? And, because it is an historical and practical enquiry, it is of course open to many forms of ideological distortion, domination and bad faith.

VI   A SOCIAL ONTOLOGY OF SACRIFICE?

A trinitarian interpretation of resurrection – an event which might be understood as God's gracious invitation to human beings to share in and share God's liberty – suggests that the resurrection is about the conversion of a 'community without limits', and its conversion away from idolatrous practices and toward the liberty of God. An account of Christian liberation will *wish* to begin with the resurrection as, with the cross, it is the culmination and focus of God's action for Christians, and *needs* to begin here as God's action to resurrect tells us of the social world.

At one level this may be interpreted as indicating that the resurrection is the transformation of *Jesus'* relations – that is, in terms of immediate social relations. Jürgen Moltmann has argued thus: ' ... Jesus lived in mutual relationships with the poor and the sick, sinners, and the men and women who had been thrust out of society. It was in these relationships that he spread his gospel' (Moltmann, 1990: 145–6). Here social relations refers in the first instance to Jesus' relationships with other people, such as his immediate group of followers.

I am seeking to say more than that the trinitarian appropriation of resurrection tells us about Christian practice. I also wish to say that in the perspective of resurrection (and the conception of God that arises from this – more on this in the next chapter), Christians learn to think theologically about the *social* world; more specifically yet, theological thinking makes a contribution to our understanding of how the social world is, and might be. In the light of the work of the Logos, society has its place in creation and redemption, and this claim informs Christian political practice.

One way of beginning to explore this issue is to note a premise of Rowan Williams' argument: the account of the work of Christ is implicitly constitutive. The radical creativity experienced by the Christian communities in Christ is such that it can only be referred to 'the *arché* of the Father, the ultimate source' (Rowan Williams, 1986: 208). The sorts of creativity experienced are universal: we must 'say of Jesus that the "generative" character of his story is as radical as the generative significance of our language about the world's source and context, God' (Rowan Williams, 1986: 202). The event of incarnation is decisive in that the disconcerting – because immediate – presence of God enfleshed, although perhaps generating a whole range of problems for how the 'community without limits' might organise itself and enact its hope, is the criticism of our idols, both conceptual and practical. It is the criticism of attempts to domesticate God (for God does a new thing), to remove God from the world (for 'God' is present in social relations), to treat God as a possession (for 'God' is crucified), and to claim God as one's own (for the revelation of God in Jesus is of a universal God whose only 'limit' is the acknowledgement of Jesus of Nazareth as risen Lord – it is this response that is the 'form' of the Christian community).

In short, the incarnation is to do with the raising of questions – how shall we live? what is the nature of conversion? from what shall we turn away? – rather than the provision of conceptually neat or practically repressive answers. 'Jesus is God's "revelation" in a decisive sense not because he makes a dimly apprehended God clear to us ... but because he makes things darker ... Jesus represents the *immediacy* of divine presence and creativity in the world, and thus the overthrow of our conceptual idols' (Rowan Williams, 1986: 202–3). In such immediacy, we learn that if we have to do here with a restoration of creation this event is not to be surpassed. If it is creation that is recreated, the agent of recreation must be on a par with the original creative agency.

Williams' argument is not explicitly constitutive, in the terms I suggested in section II of this chapter. But its form, and the substantial conclusion to which it comes – the normative focus on Jesus of Nazareth – is, implicitly at least, constitutive. By the same token, the weakness of the account is the same weakness that Hardy traces in Bonhoeffer and Forsyth (see chapter 5, section III): the demand for a new 'form' of social relations, for the enactment of the creative liberty of God, is, in Williams' argument, the gift of God in redemption: Christ in the Spirit. Williams writes: 'The Spirit is Jesus' Spirit and therefore God's Spirit: it is what God gives in Jesus, and that gift is always and invariably the breaking of bondage and the dawn of hope' (Rowan Williams, 1986: 205). Here the matter is quite explicit: the gift is Jesus, and this gift has redeeming power (through the invitation into the creative liberty of God).

The difficulty with this position we have already seen: the undue narrowing of God's work in creation. If it is appropriate to understand the social character of humanity as the work of the Logos in creation, redemptive community, given in the gift of the Son in the Spirit, it must be understood more widely than the community of the Church (even if this Church is a 'community without limits'). This is to privilege too sharply the place of the Church in creation and redemption (and generates an account of the Church over against society – a problem discussed further in chapter 8, section III). Yet, if the argument of chapter 5 is persuasive, then society also has its place in creation and redemption. It, too, is God's gift. It also, on the constitutive account outlined at the beginning of this chapter, needs to be understood as reordered in the ontological reordering in the relationship between God and the world that occurs in the cross of Christ.

I am suggesting that we are driven not only to a constitutive account, but to a consideration of the implications of such an account in the light of the previous argument. It is an account, as White (1991: 20) notes, that turns upon God's act, not knowledge of that act; an act that is an ontological reordering, whether or not such reordering is ontically manifest. Therefore, we need to understand the resurrection of Jesus of Nazareth not simply as trinitarian in the structure of its appropriation in an historical process, but as having reference to the trinitarian action of God in creation, incarnation and redemption. And this means, of course, that we are concerned with the place of society in the 'order of redemption'. The action of God in the death of Jesus is constitutive of Christian liberation in that it is an 'objective' act. It has wider reference than to the Christian community. It is a reordering of universal scope that encompasses all creation. Such a conclusion is suggested by the trinitarian structure of this interpretation of the event of cross and resurrection: there is a reordering of creation in the cross and resurrection as both creation and redemption are through the Logos (made flesh).

Indeed, we are now in a position to think a little further about the work of the Logos in redemption. We have already seen that the sociality of human being is best ascribed to the proportioning activity of the Logos in creation. Therefore, in the redemptive activity of Christ we might suggest an ontological reordering of sociality, which might be tested in the ontic acknowledgement and enactment of the practice of social transformation. (A discussion of this practical affirmation is reserved for chapter 7.) One way of grasping this acknowledgement is to return to the issue of the transcendental character of society, and its transformation. I have already suggested, following the rather different arguments of Roy Bhaskar and Daniel Hardy, that sociality might be understood as transcendental, and that the affirmation of the creative and enabling possibilities of enacted sociality or social relations, in theory and in practice, is a matter of social transformation 'through' social contradictions.

This is all very well, but we shall not get very far if we do not have some sense of the reordering that has occurred in cross and resurrection in relation to the transcendental character of sociality, itself in its turn due to the activity of the Logos in creation. It is quite appropriate to reflect on the trinitarian structure of the witness to the resurrection, and to insist on its invitation to conversion. But, from the perspective of a God of abundance active in creation, incarnation and redemption, what are we authorised to say about the reordering of sociality within the 'order of redemption'?

A full response to this question would require (at least) a sustained engagement with the atonement metaphors of victory, justice and sacrifice. Such a response cannot be attempted here. However, we may note one consideration before entering a brief discussion of this matter. I have already contended that the social character of human being might best be ascribed to the work of the Logos in creation. The redeeming work of the Logos must therefore be seen as in some form of continuity with this ordering work. If this is not the case, then the incarnation looks as though it is some kind of 'intervention' from a God who is usually 'absent'. Such a view would hardly fit with the 'proper creation perspective' advanced in chapter 3. Or, if the incarnation is not seen as an intervention, it can be seen as stopping history dead, thereby undermining the way in which Christians learn their language, and indeed learn to be Christians: this is an example of what Buber, according to Lash, termed 'automessianism' – the tendency of the churches to regard themselves as having Christ for their possession and, thereby and more dangerously, claiming 'definitive messianic status' for themselves (Lash, 1988: 209). Another way of viewing this matter is to suggest that the incarnation is not really a *divine* engagement (other than perhaps in the rather restricted terms of the 'quality' of Jesus' 'religious experience'). The difficulty with this view is that although it may avoid docetism, it is not really a constitutive account of the incarnation, and it is not really clear to what extent – decisively? unsurpassably? – God is present. And if this is not clear, the nature of the redemptive reordering, and its practical implications, are also not clear.

The central point here is to note both continuity and discontinuity in God's redeeming activity in incarnation. Yet in this all too brief discussion, I shall develop such a suggestion only in relation to the metaphor of sacrifice as it fits best with the creation perspective developed in the previous part. And yet I shall be seeking to interpret it in a particular direction: if the event of atonement is a reconstitution, a recreation, a resurrection of embodiment, then how might it interpret an account of society? But before we get to this question, a short note on the notion of sacrifice is required.

The metaphor of sacrifice allows us to say that it is God's self-giving that is crucial, and in this self-giving there is a reordering of that which is already ordered, through the Son – the mediator in creation and redemption. A detailed discussion of the metaphor of sacrifice is not possible here, but I think that it remains a crucial metaphor for Christianity and retains its resonance on account of the fact that expressed in this metaphor is God's commitment to Jesus of Nazareth, and in that commitment – if it is understood in trinitarian terms – is some indication that God's purposes for creation cannot be set aside: the disorder of sin is counteracted. To this may be added a further sense: the character of God's creation is sacrificial in that it is the expression of God's grace.

It is the conclusion to the logic of the metaphor that interests me here: the world is to be understood as gracious gift; and the gift of the Son is given to restore that first precious gift. Herein lies the nature of God's abundant generosity: gift follows gift. Colin Gunton argues that this restoration of relationship has wide-ranging practical consequences: 'Sacrifice has to do with the rightful ordering of life in the world, and that involves us in taking seriously notions of pollution and uncleanness which extend beyond the merely moralistic ... [the] anthropocentric and individualistic' (Gunton, 1988: 136–7), and which indeed extend beyond the human.

We may say that to understand the social world as 'gift' is to enter into a discussion of the central metaphors of atonement (together with creation worked out in a trinitarian fashion), especially the metaphor of 'sacrifice'. I have concentrated upon sacrifice as it seems best to express the sheer creative gracefulness of God; it brings into focus the dynamism of God's abundance. In this context I wish to refer to a 'social ontology of sacrifice' (the terminology is adapted from Gunton, 1991a: 173–5): if the commitment to a revolutionary practice by Christians is one form of sacrificial life, made most explicit perhaps by the possibility of death and martyrdom that such practice may entail, then it is caught up in the wider logic of sacrifice that turns upon the life, death and resurrection of Jesus of Nazareth. This is not to say that 'sacrificial' political practice in some way anticipates or echoes the trinitarian life of God. But rather that such practice is comprehended, although perhaps not made intelligible, in that this social world is also sacrificial in terms of its relation to God. It is God's gift in its creation, and in its recreation. So, we may give ourselves in response to and in dialogue with that which is already given: grace begets the freedom of obedience. (I do not intend 'obedience' here narrowly. Obedience is not solely assent to a proposition, a theory about the world. Obedience is a practical matter, engaging the will, memory and the imagination, as well as the intellect. It is a joyful assent to the graceful ordering of God, not a form of grudging acknowledgement. But neither is it a sentimental matter: the notion of obedience encompasses the responsibility of solidarity and the cost of discipleship.)

That is, Christian political practice is invited to enact Christian hope in the context of the social world as gift, as sacrificial. Not only does this nerve Christian practice and suggest the nature and extent of what may be risked by the Christian, as I argued in sections III and IV. It also invites Christians to understand the social world in particular ways. A 'social ontology of sacrifice' allows a particular interpretation of the social world in relation to political practice such that Christian practice is governed by this sacrificial logic, but in perhaps rather surprising ways. By this I mean that something more must be said than is suggested by the following quotation from Paul Fiddes (taken from a discussion of political engagement): 'To engage in the historical adventure of liberating humanity is to enter into the mystery of atonement' (Fiddes, 1989: 196). This may be right; but atonement has a double focus: God's actions, and a creation 'on its way' to eschatological redemption. Atonement has reference both to God's action, and to a setting free of the world which was bound. The condition of humanity is not one that may be changed simply through a fresh decision, a change of mind. It is of such depth that God commits Godself in a redemptive move that reorients creation towards its eschatological goal. It is thereby a move that has a double reference: God and humanity (in creation).

We might then ask: if 'part' of the action is directed toward the 'human world', how does this alter our understanding of our social world? If society has its place in creation and redemption, how is this reordering to be understood as it impinges upon society? In other words, we are licensed, by an engagement with God's work in Christ, to do more than to enquire as to the 'form' of God's triune presence to society (an affirmation of the transformation of society – Hardy's social dynamic – toward the 'given' and yet unrealised social character of humanity).

The possibility of fresh forms of social organisation is given again in the eschatological reordering activity of the Son, and this stress on *eschatological* reordering is to insist that it is not to be understood conservatively in terms of a *return* to origins, but rather that redemption is to be understood in terms of the eschatological horizon of God's future rule.

Yet, to avoid idealist misreadings, it must be insisted upon with equal vigour that resurrection encompasses embodiment: 'The resurrection life includes the human death of Jesus' (Alison, 1993: 20). But Jesus is not simply returned revivified to the world; rather his existence is both in and not in continuity with his earthly life. As Alison writes: 'He is always present after the resurrection simultaneously as crucified and as risen Lord ... It is as crucified Lord that Jesus is risen' (Alison, 1993: 20, 21). In arguing thus, I am not seeking to minimise the task of human beings but to place it in its proper context: Jesus' abiding work. Or, to put it differently: the reality of the social character of humanity can only be understood by reference to the social being of God as trinitarian presence. Not in the sense that we know what this form of society is to be like on account of the presence of the God whose being is social, but rather that the possibility of social change is reaffirmed in the reordering work of the Son in the Spirit. That is, the reconstitution of a 'mark' of sociality is the reordering of sociality toward its future.

This is not to argue that the Christian community must 'correspond' to God's action in the divine economy of incarnation, cross and resurrection. It is to enquire into God's presence to social forms in the 'order of redemption'. God not only invites conversion; God is also the orderer and reorderer (through trinitarian presence) of the social being of humanity. How this might be understood is the subject of the next chapter.

VII CONCLUSION

Before moving to the discussion of God's trinitarian presence to social forms in the next chapter, a summary of the argument of this chapter might be helpful. We have to do here with the gracious action of the trinitarian God *and* the transcendence of the present toward the future in human praxis. The matter is precisely the interrelation of these two: the double focus on God and the world. The event of resurrection is an invitation into the practical wisdom of God. But what does this wisdom teach? How might Christians be politically and theologically wise?

The path to this point has perhaps been an arduous one. My argument has been to propose resurrection as the nerve of Christian practice and as a basis of Christian liberation.[9] In other words, here lies the interrelation of human praxis and God's gracious initiative. I made a number of moves that have all turned upon the 'reality' of God's actions. First, it is important to recall the context given by the argument of the previous chapter. I suggested that it was important to understand society (as the configuration of sociality) as transcendental, and that the 'marks' of sociality might be traced to the ordering work of the Logos in creation. But, and here we move into this chapter, Christianity refers not only to an ordering, but also to a liberating reordering in the cross and resurrection of Jesus of Nazareth.

I began by arguing that resurrection is a revolution in embodiment, one of the 'marks' of sociality. As such I suggested that resurrection is the reconstitution of social life through death, and this must be understood as the nerve of

---

[9] In arguing that resurrection is *a* basis, I am acknowledging that for a fuller presentation of Christian liberation more attention would need to be paid to the cross.

Christian liberation. The practice enabled by the revolutionary implications of the resurrection of the body might be more radical than that suggested by the Marxist. An insistence on the actuality of the event of resurrection indicates a reordering in one of the 'marks' of sociality, and a consequent reshaping of the others. Only interpreted in this way might resurrection be trusted, and thus nerve Christian praxes. But what is resurrection, that it may be trusted? Only a trinitarian interpretation, I argued, will grasp all its dimensions. Important conclusions emerged from the trinitarian engagement with resurrection: the actuality of this event, its generation of a conceptuality of liberty, creativity and abundance for grasping the triune God, and the insistence that in this trinitarian process Christians are enabled to learn and relearn about their God.

Two arguments come together at this point. Resurrection not only invites a certain way of learning about God, and authorises a certain conceptuality for interpreting God's economic actions. It also points to a reordering in the embodiment of the Word enfleshed of that which is already proportioned in the operations of the Logos. From this position the connection between the substantial matter of the liberation of creation in cross and resurrection and the ordering work of the Logos in creation is easily made. The issue then becomes: what is the nature of this reordering? How is God present in triunity to social forms? If the resurrection of Jesus of Nazareth is constitutive of Christian liberation, then the ontological implications of such a claim have some significance for our understanding of society.

God's relation to the world is specified here in particular terms: a 'social ontology of sacrifice', marked by a dynamic of abundance. But here we reach important matters that move us into the argument of the next chapter. How are we to interpret this relation between God and the world despite its lack of actual testimony and ontic enactment? The creation perspective offered in part II and the account of sociality traced back to the work of the Logos suggest that this relation persists, and is 'real'. The resurrection in embodiment and the brief excursus into the constitutive nature of atonement make the same point (but from the perspective of redemption): in Jesus, there is a liberation away from forms of idolatry made pervasively and permanently possible – whether or not this is acknowledged. Indeed, if the Christ-event is constitutive and 'objective' then there persists an ontological reordering, whether there is human acknowledgement or not.

Of course, there also persists the *eclipse* of God in anthropological practices which include forms of irrelation and idolatry. We may also note the actual practice of churches (and other groups and movements) that seek to enact the creative liberty of God, and counter such an eclipse. Yet what is fundamentally real is the reordered relationship between God and the world. What is encountered is not necessarily that which really 'is' and which really persists; the actions of God persist despite the eclipse that darkens our vision and restricts our movement. We have to do with a world of idolatry and irrelation in which there are also practices which bear witness to, and may be graced by, the abundance of God. Such practices include those which acknowledge that God's 'openness' to the world invites human responsibility for human affairs, enables new forms of emancipatory solidarity, and envisions a new future.

So I am committed to the view that in God's action there is a reorientation of creation toward its eschatological goal. Here is the double focus again, generating a tension that will inform the next chapter. The connection of God to the world – God's 'openness' – in its concentration in resurrection (and the cross) invites attention not only to Christian practice, to how Christians learn about the triune God, and to emancipatory movements in wider society, but also to a reordering. In this ontological reordering, Christian theology must pay attention not only to the intentions of human agents and the outcomes of their actions. Instead, attention must also be paid to the 'essential' practices of modern society.

This attention is invited partly on account of the transformational interpretation of society suggested in chapter 5. I have already suggested that sociality resists incursions into social freedom, and is to be construed in terms of a transformational (not voluntarist or reified) account of society. Such potentials may, I suggested (following Hardy), be attributed to the operations of the Logos in creation. There is already a certain dynamism within creation, a form of structured abundance. (In this way, Christian theology may acknowledge secular movements of emancipation.) But attention must also be paid to the ontological recreation of sociality: the affirmation and surpassment of the social character of human being toward richer, more complex forms of human living – Eagleton's 'new mode of living together'. To do this, Christian theology must pay attention to the social *conditions* (and not only outcomes) of human agency in order to test them for emancipatory possibilities. We again encounter the practical decentring of experience: what remains crucial, in the acknowledgement of the abundance of God, is patterns of practice nerved by the revolution of resurrection, but directed to the structural conditions of social life. Such is the radical character of the political commitment of an oppositional theology: to act toward society as if a resurrection in embodiment has occurred, and as if such interventions will receive eschatological justification.

The relation between the triune God and an ontology of the social suggested here is not necessarily one in which the former immediately and directly *clarifies* the latter. (There will always be social structures, but which particular structures?) Yet this relation is marked by a sacrificial abundance, a reconstruction of embodiment in which Christians are invited to trust and which nerves particular praxes. God is revealed for who God is: the sacrificial God who seeks to establish and re-establish relation in the cross and resurrection of the Son; the world is understood as open to (that is, constituted by and sustained through) God's action, and to be revealed as on its way to the final transformation of the general resurrection. This points to God's active involvement 'with' the world. But God's active involvement 'with' the world is not such that we might move from God's being to practical recommendations. Rather, God's involvement 'with' the world – as creative, embodied in incarnation and redemptive – is an invitation to human beings to risk conversion in a critical assessment of the anthropological

practices and ontological principles in their situation. Fundamentally, to ask in the context of a social ontology of sacrifice:
How are we to live? What are the 'limits' of human community? What might we trust?

Plainly, a dark knowledge of resurrection and of God's
atoning work is suggested here. Our knowledge of the 'reality'
of resurrection, and in turn the 'reality' of the trinitarian God,
is not such that there can be any unidirectional move from the
being of God to the being of the world (see also chapter 5). The
trinitarian character of our knowledge of resurrection is a
learning about learning: that we do not know who God is, but
whoever God is, this God is creative and engaged with creation
in Word and Spirit. Such a *docta ignorantia* cannot easily be used
to underpin a movement from the being of God to social
matters. It is also to insist that God's abundance is not
exhausted within such a unidirectional move.

How are we to understand this dark knowledge? And how
are we to be guided by it? The danger here lies in that it may
come across as a form of special pleading. God, I am claiming,
is intimately involved with social forms as the reorderer of
sociality. Yet I have already suggested that the 'relation of
resurrection' between God and the world does not require
ontic enactment for its 'ontological depth' to be 'real'. But then
how are we to understand 'ontological depth'? As a way of
responding to this question, the argument of the next chapter
offers one way of understanding how God's triune presence
may be understood as informing the possibility of transformative practice in society: that Christian theology, on account of
careful attention paid to resurrection, is able to hold to the
dynamic presence of the Spirit to the structural activities of
society.

But perhaps we are now in a position to think of God's
involvement in a fresh way, in terms of a 'social ontology of
sacrifice'. This discloses a God who is not to be understood as in
competition with human beings, and who sanctifies no part of
our social world (chapter 3); whose presence-as-'openness' is
the call to conversion (chapter 4); which tells us much about
the enacting in the world of the liberty of God (chapter 6), but

much less about the pattern and the goal of political practice (certainly not deducible from the social being of God) or the 'relational' character of the world (chapter 5); and whose gift to human beings is the ordering and reordering of social life understood in terms of a 'social ontology of sacrifice'.

Yet an important difficulty remains: if Christian thinking about God turns upon the cross and resurrection of Christ, what might this tell us about the presence of the Christian God to social forms? The next chapter contains some hints towards a response to this question.

CHAPTER 7

Society and God's trinitarian presence

I INTRODUCTION

In the previous chapter I argued that resurrection refers to a reconstitution in the sociality of human being. As such, it insists on a radical conception of revolution: death is not the boundary of social being. This offers a new horizon for Christian thinking about liberation. In the reconstitution of embodiment as social, social matters are taken up into the eschatological horizon of resurrection. Such an horizon may be understood as the nerve of Christian practice.

Yet, how is this a feature of an oppositional theology? How does this allow the determination of theology as neither too close nor too distant? Resurrection as the transformation of a limit of sociality restores human being to its character as social being. It thereby insists that praxes of emancipation are not to be interpreted as bounded by death. Work, embodiment and language of course have their social horizon: they are all relations of production. Now, embodiment has its social, yet also eschatological, horizon. In this way, work and language are thereby reconstituted, in the attempt to render intelligible such a revolution in embodiment. The attempt to reconstruct work and language in a particular society is also to be understood as placed within this eschatological horizon. Christians may work for the surpassment of the present in that it has already, as embodied, been affirmed and surpassed in the resurrection of a body. Here the fresh possibilities for political practice may be nerved. Further, resurrection may be understood as securing a social ontology of sacrifice in which society is to be understood as placed.

Such a theology is neither too close nor too distant. It does not argue for utopian revolutionary schemes; it insists that the only way forward will be through the transformative potentials of society. Even emancipatory transformation is a 'working over'. Neither is it too close: it insists that Christianity is concerned with a revolution in embodiment that nerves particular praxes. It insists, further, that the 'marks' of sociality, although necessary, are enacted in the 'freedom' of society: that is, the marks of sociality are enacted in relations of production, which are governed by substantive social activities. Christian theology is thereby directed to these social relations as the locus of human agency in order to reconstruct the social structures reproduced in and through such relations. Such a theology is oppositional in the sense that a commitment to resurrection ensures its commitment to an extended account of sociality: even through death, God invites humanity into its social future. Yet, this sociality is always enacted in specific relations. So the way to the new future is in and through specific social relations.

As such, an oppositional theology is invited to pay attention to its own relations of production and so to the substantive activities that may be reproduced through its intellectual practice. Such an oppositional theology is thereby concerned to consider the recording on its own 'body' of the pressures and limits of the dominant hegemony. It asserts that through attention to sociality as the work of the Logos, and the invitation to revolution in resurrection, it is invited to consider such pressures. An oppositional theology seeks neither merely to articulate the language of liberation, nor to secure its own relevance in the academy; nor does it refer resurrection solely to the Church as part of that community's self-understanding or to the escape of Jesus from the world: it is not to be limited to alternative or specialising modes. Rather, holding to its commitment to read the actions of God as inscribed in the materiality of the world (in creation and resurrection), it maintains that this commitment issues in the practice of resurrection.

Yet, one further substantial issue remains. In the epistemological perspective sketched here, the Spirit must be interpreted as holding Christianity to this materialist perspective. To such a difficult matter, I now turn.

II   ONE GOD: CREATOR, LIBERATOR, REDEEMER

Trinitarian thinking is founded upon the action of God in Jesus of Nazareth. The 'identity' of the Trinity is given here. As we saw in the last chapter: an interpretation of resurrection itself requires a trinitarian structure. Moreover, a trinitarian engagement suggests an account of social ontology that is 'sacrificial': as ordered by the Logos and reoriented in the Spirit toward its eschatological goal in and through cross and resurrection.

A trinitarian specification of the motif of conversion introduced in part II is now possible. The answer to the 'creation question' has the form 'God', and in giving this answer persons are invited to reconsider their attitude to 'all that is'. Above all, they are invited to reconsider their attitude toward false forms of relating, i.e. of relation to 'things in the world'. Here idolatries of the social, with their misconstruals of work and embodiment, and their deformation of language, are central. The conviction that the Christian God is the One who creates *ex nihilo* is the form of the invitation to turn away from forms of social idolatry.

But if this proposal is not to be seen as naive, such a conversion must be a 'material' conversion. Social idolatries are saturated by the constitutive determinants of the dominant hegemonic in which material interests are invested. No one can 'turn away' from forms of social and economic organisation as if that turning in itself deprived those forms of their power. If such forms are idolatrous in that they demand from us loyalties that they do not merit, then such forms will need to be transformed, not simply (in some too literal sense) be turned away from. Thus, against Marx's suggestion that the Christian religion must be an intermediary, falsely mediating human capacities to the detriment of revolutionary change, we may say that reflection on protocols of theological discourse offers a different conclusion.

The trinitarian expansion of the argument suggests that God is not simply the One who creates, but also the One who engages redemptively in creation through the Word made flesh, and who seeks to bring creation to its eschatological goal. So this God acts to liberate; the 'form' of liberation is personal. God meets us as a person and thereby respectfully encounters human beings. But the manner is not restricted to the personal. In this crucial stage of the argument, two important points come together. The first is to stress that Christianity does not deny the social nature of human being; instead such a nature may be seen as central to Christianity in that sociality may be attributed to the Logos' creative work.

Such an affirmation of sociality may be joined, through an affirmation of incarnation, to the second point: the liberating work of God in Jesus of Nazareth. God meets us in the flesh of Jesus of Nazareth, a person constituted by a particular set of social relations. In this narrative, embodiment is not, in the perspective of resurrection, to be interpreted as 'closed' by death. The resurrection of Jesus of Nazareth is an eschatological glimpse of what is to come, and that glimpse includes – on account of the resurrection of the *body* – our materiality, our embeddedness in social relations. The transformation of resurrection is not a denial of our social being, but rather its reaffirmation. The social being of humanity, as 'extended' in resurrection, is thrust into its future; God's actions disclose the 'character' of social being. In resurrection, we have the returning of Jesus to the social history of humanity: the incarnate Christ is the living Christ who is present to all of such history as its liberator. Christian political practice is enabled by and patterned after this claim.

These points then may count as a theological response to a second objection implicit in the account of Christianity as intermediary. Not only may we say that Christianity is not about false mediation; it is the embracing of our status as constituted as social beings, and as reconstituted in the redemptive work of the Word. Christianity is not necessarily the buttress of varieties of individualism. It is rather to be interpreted as the response of prayer and praise to the God who reorders created sociality. The best that Christianity can arrive at is not intersubjectivity; Christianity affirms the priority of social relations – a genuine appreciation and appropriation of sociality – and the determined place of theological discourse 'in relation to' society. Christian theology thereby not only affirms the primacy of social relations, but accepts the epistemological consequences of this for theological thinking.

For the Christian, liberation comes only through the mediation of the Word in cross and resurrection. Liberation is thereby cruciform and eschatological. Liberating practices are only possible through the liberating mediatorship of the Son, and so in active recognition of the sacrificial character of social forms. But what is this sacrificial character? We might approach this issue through some words of Colin Gunton:

> Christology universalizes: but the universal salvation must then take concrete shape in particular parts of the creation. We are accordingly concerned . . . with a process of recreation which respects the createdness and freedom of that which is reshaped. It is the function of God the Spirit, the Lord and giver of life, to *particularize* the universal redemption in anticipations of the eschatological redemption. (Gunton, 1988: 170)

I noted in the previous chapter that the metaphors of atonement may be said to have a double focus: God and the world which, I suggested, would create a tension that would run throughout this chapter. It is evident here: the universal character of the reordering work of the Word redirects creation to the Father. But the particular 'concretion' of this reordering in the world is the work of the Spirit. This point can be made in reference to the life of Jesus: 'Jesus was free in the midst of the pressures towards enslavement to the demonic because his life was maintained in freedom by the action of the liberating Spirit.' And this concretion marks the economic actions of the Spirit: 'So it is in general: the Spirit is God enabling the world to be itself, to realise its eschatological perfection' (Gunton, 1988: 167).

We may now begin to trace a tentative account of the presence of the triune God to social forms that this argument in theological materialism must hold to. Our enquiry will be a double one: the universalising work of the Word and the particularising presence of the Spirit. But, as we shall see, the presence of the Spirit will not be such as to secure *anticipations* of the eschatological redemption. Rather, it will be the presence of God to and against particular restrictions of the reordering work of the Logos. The surpassment of present circumstances towards more abundant and less restrictive forms of social organisation may be understood as the presence of the Spirit of God. But this is to anticipate. The argument of the remainder of this chapter covers much ground in somewhat summary and sketchy fashion. In brief, I argue for some conclusions as to how the reordering work of the Son and the particularising work of the Spirit might be understood in relation to social forms. I suggest that one of the implications of this is a hint of 'contingencies' in God's being, analogously to the way that God, in some circumstances, may be understood to relate contingently to certain social forms.

I am seeking to develop a 'positive' account of the Trinity as part of a liberative theology. The 'negative' function of course remains important. The Trinity not only enables the negotiation of God's presence as transcendent and immanent, it also denies a single way of construing God's relation to the world. God is neither entirely transcendent, nor to be identified solely with a particular person, nor to be understood solely in immanentist terms. Indeed, this difficulty with the categories of transcendence and immanence led me to suggest a preferable term: God's 'openness'.

But trinitarian thinking may be employed as part of a liberative theology to explore the nature of God's actions toward the world. In a sense, the way that trinitarian thinking is employed in this chapter is still negative: it is a guard against attempts to deny or restrict God's presence to social forms, or attempts to affirm too strongly God's presence to a particular set of social forms. But God, as we shall see, may be understood as present to social forms. In effect, this is the Christological control of incarnation: God is engaged in the most personal way possible with human beings. Indeed, engaged even to the point of dwelling within social relations – this is the unreserved

character of the risk God takes. In incarnation God does not
spare Godself from the contingencies of human life. The
actions of the Spirit of Jesus likewise are not the sparing of
Godself from the contingencies of human life. And these contingencies need not be interpreted narrowly: we are, as the
liberation theologians insist, always in the realm of power and
politics. Such a claim is true both of the relations that governed
Jesus' crucified body, and the interests that govern contemporary theological construction.

At first sight this discussion of God's presence to social forms
may appear odd. Perhaps a more usual way for Christian
theology to proceed is through a discussion of the Church.[1]
Although the direction of my argument is toward the Church
(as becomes clearer in chapter 8), the route is a little more
circuitous. Tracing the sociality of human being back to the
work of the Logos in creation, and not the gift of Christ in the
order of redemption, means that God is present as the orderer
of sociality. Before we come to the community of 'redeemed
sociality' we must first consider redeemed sociality in the
'wider' context of social relations. The imperative is for the
churches to join this dynamic of reordering and to be a witness
to this reordering – a dynamic in which society is placed. The
difficulty is: how are we to understand this 'placing'? How are
we to understand the trinitarian dimensions of this dynamic?
To offer one, rather brief, response to this question is the
subject of the rest of the chapter.

III   THE PRESENCE OF THE SPIRIT

To argue that the redeeming work of the Word is concerned
with the reordering of human social life into richer and more
abundant forms is open to an obvious objection: the lack of
evidence for the proposition. Part of this problem may also be
understood in terms of the accusation that Christians understand current forms of 'abundance' to be the most extensive

---

[1] This is the route taken by Gunton (1988). The final part of Fiddes (1989) concen-
trates upon the Christian and Christian communities. The refrain throughout Lash
(1988) is *community*, and often Christian community.

possible – a sort of 'Christian stoicism'. (It was once said to me by a Christian that capitalism was the best form of social organisation possible given the sinfulness of human beings.) Here then a new issue must be addressed: not only is the social character of humanity to be understood as traceable to the work of the Logos in creation and redemption, and so as God's gift. Attention to the practical overcoming of restrictions to this gift may be understood as traceable to the activity of God's Spirit. In other words, the 'transcendence' of alienation on which Marxism insists and which, on a Christian interpretation, might be understood as the presence of the triune God (given in the affirmation and 'expansion' of the social character of humanity) is not to be left hanging in the air. Consideration of this matter is consideration on the presence of the Spirit of God.

Way back in chapter 4 I quoted Herbert McCabe's suggestion that the very transcendence of God is the condition for human liberation. The contradictions of modern society cannot be traced to the 'mystificatory' presence of the gods; human beings are responsible for their own circumstances, under the judgement of God. This is fine as far as it goes, but we are now in a position to understand the presence of this God more specifically: in trinitarian terms. We have already seen that the form of God's immanence in the world is the Logos enfleshed. The form of God's transcendence is the Spirit. Colin Gunton, following John Zizioulas, has forcefully made this point: 'talk of the Spirit is not a way of speaking of God's immanence, but of his transcendence. (The Spirit may be active *within* the world, but he does not become *part of* the world)' (Gunton, 1991b: 123). It is only on the grounds of the transcendence or otherness of the Spirit that she may be present to particulars; it is only as 'other', and so as unrestricted to and by 'parts' of the world, that the Spirit may be present.

We are now in a position to connect McCabe's observations on the liberating consequences of God's transcendence with an understanding of the Spirit: the 'function' of the Spirit in the economy of redemption is that of 'demystification', in theory and practice. The notion of judgement should not be understood abstractly, but rather as the presence of God to deny that which restricts human forms of life, at the theoretical level (ideology) and at the practical level. It is therefore much too general to say that the Spirit is present in terms of analogies, outlines, anticipations. Rather, she is present as the critique, in theory and practice, of the 'mystifications' of modern society that restrict more creative forms of human life. And this is precisely an eschatological point: liberation takes its reference from the work of the Spirit.

The Spirit is the power of demystification. Indeed, Jürgen Moltmann has suggested just this but in connection with the task of political theology: 'The political theology of the cross must liberate the state from the political service of idols and must liberate men from political alienation and loss of rights. It must seek to demythologize state and society' (Moltmann, 1974: 327). And political theology may do this, we may say, as a response to and as enabled by the presence of the triune God, whose being is social, in the Spirit.

To argue, first, that the work of the Spirit is to particularise the universal redemption wrought in Christ and, second, that the presence of the Spirit is the power of demystification is easily said. But if liberation is given eschatologically in the Spirit, how are we to understand this? If such a claim is not itself to be open to charges of generality, what might it mean? I propose to approach this question through a consideration of social contradictions and their denial. (How the Spirit might be understood in relation to the practice of the Church is a matter for the next chapter.)

Here, I want to explore a response to the charge that whatever is, is God-given; that the present forms of social life are as abundant as they will be; that God is present in the form of the guarantor of the present state of relations.[2] What positive

---

[2] Of course, it can be pointed out that – as it avoids the matter of historical change or development – such an objection is somewhat unhistorical. But this sort of objection often fastens upon some aspect of 'human nature' that, it claims, is available for 'nonhistorical' interpretation: the fear of death, or the sinfulness of human nature (often connected with sexuality).

case might be made to those Christians who do think that
Christianity is about preservation, or not about public matters;
and against those who see claims to God's presence in terms of
buttress rather than criticism?

One way of approaching these questions is to recall my
contention that the Spirit is the Spirit of demystification: she is
the presence of God that seeks to display that which contradicts
God's abundance, reoriented toward the 'final abundance' of
the Father in the work of the Son. We may make the matter a
little more concrete, and more difficult to respond to, if we
consider what Marx may have meant by contradiction. In
chapter 4 I quoted Claus Offe drawing attention to the difference in application in certain socio-economic matters: contrast
military planning and urban planning. But, for Marx at least,
the notion of contradiction had a particular reference. Let us
somewhat briskly review Marx's position.

For Marx, as is well known, a crucial contradiction in
capitalist society refers to the constriction of the forces of
production by the relations of production. Indeed, this dialectic of constriction and surpassment is the movement of history,
as is suggested by some of the earlier work of Marx and Engels
(1970). This dialectical interpretation reaches classic
expression in the '1859 Preface', and there employs the terminology of forces and relations. And yet, while such language
might refer us to issues of ownership and the class division of
society, Marx's more technical, economic analyses do also, I
think, turn upon the notion of contradiction.

We might begin here by noting that Marx began *Capital*
with an extended discussion of the commodity form, and the
contradiction inherent within this form: the contradiction
between use value and exchange value.[3] In the contrast
between the values of exchange and use, and its mediation in
the form of the secret of money, Marx thought he had dis-
covered the 'essence' of the capitalist process. How was it that a

---

[3] There is of course some debate whether there can be a use of the term 'contradiction'
in a sense other than the logical. Marx plainly thought that there could – I do not
plan to enter this debate here, except to note that Marx employed contradiction in a
logical as well as a dialectical sense.

qualitative matter – the use-value of a product – might be exchanged in purely quantitative terms?

We need not go into the complex answer to this question. But we must note here that Marx connects this process to the fetishism of commodities (see Marx, 1954: 76–87). In the dialectical, contradictory mediation between these two forms of value is the practice of fetishism. Hence Marx could write: 'A commodity is therefore a mysterious thing, simply because in it the social character of men's labour appears to them as an objective character stamped upon the product of that labour; because the relation of the producers to the sum total of their own labour is presented to them as a social relation, existing not between themselves, but between the products of their labour' (Marx, 1954: 77). We may immediately recognise here the motif of alienation that ran through Marx's early writing, without necessarily deciding upon the extent, form and importance of the continuity. What is more to the point for our purposes here is that the contradiction in the commodity form is not simply a narrow economic matter, but rather has direct implications for the organisation of economic work, in that what characterises products – human purposive action – appears not as the work of human eye, hand and brain (precisely as social attributes and skills) but as inhering in the products themselves. A social relation thereby transmutes into a 'natural' one. Precisely what human beings should be asserting control over (as their own) appears not to be their own product. In a Marxian perspective, this is the denial precisely of the social relations between producers, and divorces the producer from his or her product. And as we have seen, this production needs to be understood widely, as encompassing all levels of production, including the intellectual. It is this contradiction that Marxism is committed to understand and transform.

We begin to see the difficulty concerning God's presence to such restrictive forms of social relations in which people, through their alienated work practices, reproduce capitalist society. Thus, whatever they intend at a conscious level, all social actions (or nearly all) by personal agents contribute to the reproduction of a system of economic and social organisation that is enslaving and alienating. How then might we understand God as present to these contradictions? Or, rather, as present to those 'contradictory' relations of production in which are found persons, their products, and their forms of irrelation? God of course is required to be really present as the graceful power of demystification: as the power that seeks, through human hearts and hands, the transformation of such restrictive forms into emancipatory and abundant ones toward the glorious abundance of the Kingdom. And yet the Spirit may not be present to them in the sense that God's presence constitutes and sustains them: God's presence *qua* presence does not make the irrational rational, or turn irrelation into relation. We need, in other words, some critical and trinitarian specification of the creation perspective properly set out in chapter 3.

Nor, we may add, will it do to say that the Spirit is only present to 'individuals' in social relations. This would be either to backtrack on the claim that God is the giver of the social character of humanity, or it would be tacitly to acknowledge that persons are individuals first, and then only after such self-constitution are they qualified by 'accidental' social relationships. If we wish to say, as the trinitarian perspective of this book invites us to, that we are relational beings whose very relationality is God's gift of our freedom and that 'the supposition of universal human solidarity provides a fundamental consolation for human social life' (Hardy, 1989: 35), then we need some account of God's relationship to those social forms which restrict relationality. When actual human relations appear to contradict the claim that the social character of humanity may be understood as due to the presence of the triune God (whose being is social), then grasping how God might be understood as really present even to such relations of unfreedom is important. A theological theodicy, as we noted already in the work of Peukert, must engage with the issue of (the absence of) human freedom. In other words, we need some theological specification of the presence of God's Spirit as the epistemological telos which guides thought and action toward the surpassment of current social organisation.

I suggest that we might grasp something of the 'second difference' if we see the activity of the Spirit as making reference to the eschatological abundance that originates in the *arché* of the Creator, as re-presenting Jesus, and as the freedom of God in relation to the world. Such an interpretation of the activity of the Spirit does of course need particular development in relation to the Church – an issue discussed in the next chapter. Here I am concerned with the activity of the Spirit in relation to the social order.

IV   THE SPIRIT AND THE CROSS

In the argument of this section and the two following sections, I seek to make three points: that the cross is the critique of idolatry, that the presence of the Spirit is here governed by the cross, and that the work of the Spirit is eschatological.

Perhaps we might begin our enquiry with the cross of Christ, in the first instance to identify a Christological 'control' to the activity of the Spirit (who is, at least in part, the gift of the Son). In chapter 6 I made the claim (which I did not defend there, and I shall not do so now) that resurrection is a way of grasping what the world means for God. In the dialectic between cross and resurrection, it is the cross that reveals something of God. The cross identifies the way that God is towards the world: a revelation of God in the economy of redemption. The difficulty here is that this can be understood in a variety of ways. For example, some theologians argue that the cross suggests the suffering of God. I have already noted that the doctrine of simplicity rules out a conception of a suffering God. It will here stand us in good stead.

What then may we say about the cross as a control for the activity of the Spirit? Perhaps we might begin with Luther who, in this matter, is 'the mountain that there is no way round' (Hardy and Ford, 1984: 63). The cross of Christ is, for Luther, the central event in which the identity of God is given. We may look for 'evidence' of God elsewhere but for Luther the cross is the key place, in humiliation and weakness, where Godself is revealed. So Luther could write in thesis 20 of the 'Heidelberg Disputation':

He deserves to be called a theologian, however, who comprehends the visible and manifest things of God seen through suffering and the cross . . . Now it is not sufficient for anyone, and it does him no good to recognize God in his glory and his majesty, unless he recognizes him in the humility and shame of the cross. Thus God destroys the wisdom of the wise . . . (Luther, cited Lull, 1989: 43–4)

Such a view suggests more than 'a deep participation of God in the human life of Jesus' (Fiddes, 1989: 26) – an observation which (as Fiddes notes) requires no commitment to a particular account of Christology or atonement; nor is this observation only to be regarded as a principle governing our thinking on the atonement, as Tillich suggests – 'God's atoning activity must be understood as his participation in existential estrangement and its self-destructive consequences' (Tillich, 1978: 174). Rather, it is to insist that 'God will be Godlike above all in the cross, and so all doctrine of the nature of God must begin from the cross as the revelation of God' (Fiddes, 1989: 30). Whether accepting this point means entertaining the notion of a God who suffers, as Moltmann and Fiddes contend, is a rather different point. Luther did not, I think, reckon it was necessary to go so far:

Now if . . . Reason . . . should say that the Deity surely cannot suffer and die, then you must answer and say: That is true, but since the divinity and humanity are one person in Christ, the Scriptures ascribe to the divinity, because of this personal union, all that happens to humanity, and vice versa. And in reality it is so. Indeed, you must say that the person (pointing to Christ) suffers, and dies. But this person is truly God, and therefore it is correct to say: the Son of God suffers. Although, so to speak, the one part (namely, the divinity) does not suffer, nevertheless the person, who is God, suffers in the other part (namely, in the humanity). (Luther, 'Confession concerning Christ's Supper', cited Lull, 1989: 379)

The argument here may not be very carefully worked out, but I think that it is clear that Luther is not entertaining the idea that in the cross *God* suffers (in God's *immanence*). And yet, sustained attention to the cross is the guide to God's nature.

This position, and its subsequent development, has been criticised for not taking seriously the commitment of God in

Jesus Christ. Moltmann has criticised the Christologies of Barth and Rahner for remaining within a soteriological framework in their interpretations of Christ's death and thereby failing to ask what Christ's death means 'in itself', for God (Moltmann, 1979: 62–4). Paul Fiddes has criticised Barth and Moltmann (among others) for failing to construe adequately the relation between the 'death in God' in the economic Trinity and the immanent being of God (Fiddes, 1988: 112–23, 135–43).

I do not want to enter this important debate. I merely want to register what seems to me to be the guiding thread of the theology of the cross (as Luther articulates it): the affirmation that God reveals Godself decisively and irrevocably on the cross, and yet remains hidden. God's revelation here, I wish to suggest, is complete and yet contingent, given and yet hidden. (Perhaps the variety of interpretations given in the 'Pauline' epistles and the four gospels hints at the early Church's wisdom in acknowledging the 'indeterminacy of meaning' (Milbank) here. Our knowledge of God must be governed by the cross, and yet the cross tells us little. It precisely defeats our attempts to 'grasp' God.)

What is the effect of this? Moltmann argues, in a discussion of Paul and Luther on the significance of the cross, that the cross is, through the destruction of human self-aggrandisement, the return of human beings to their humanity:

The theology of the cross leads to the criticism of the self-glorification of dehumanized man and to his liberation ... The knowledge of the cross is the knowledge of the God in the suffering caused to him by dehumanized man, that is, in the contrary of everything which dehumanized man seeks and tries to attain as the deity in him. Consequently, this knowledge does not confirm him as what he is, but destroys him. It destroys the god, miserable in his pride, which we would like to be, and restores to us our abandoned and despised humanity. The knowledge of the cross brings a conflict of interest between God who has become man and man who wishes to become God. It destroys the destruction of man. It alienates alienated man. And in this way it restores the humanity of the dehumanized man. (Moltmann, 1974: 70, 71)

This powerful rhetoric does not perhaps quite convince. (Can 'knowledge' of the cross restore to us our humanity? Is not such a restoration, as Moltmann acknowledges elsewhere, a practical matter?) But the underlying point is sound: the 'lack of knowledge' of God given in the cross denies human pretensions to construct an account of God: a God of the big battalions on *our* side (over against *them*), a God whose actions overwhelm social contingencies. In other words we are returned to our circumstances: to ask the theoretical and practical questions as to what is to be human in the perspective of the revelation of God in the cross.[4]

I suggested above that one aspect of the work of the Spirit is the re-presentation of Christ, crucified and risen. If the previous chapter was concerned with the Christological control of resurrection, here we are concerned with the Christological control of the cross. In the revelation of Christ crucified, we are reminded that there is not in Christian revelation any straightforward answer to the question: what is it to be human? Even less is there information about forms of social organisation. Christians may not consistently have grasped this, and the tendency to regard the Word incarnate as a sort of answer has led to the characteristically Christian 'contribution to the eclipse of God': 'Christians persuade themselves that now, in the doctrine of the Word incarnate, they have laid hold of the *nature* of God, and made of God's truth their possession' (Lash, 1988: 271). This of course is to fail to attend to the rigours of a theology of the cross, to the re-presentation of the crucified Christ in the Spirit in such a way that our idolatrous claims are denied. In the cross there is an unveiling and a veiling; God is fully and contingently present.

V   THE SPIRIT AND SOCIAL CONTINGENCIES

This leads to a second point concerning the activity of the Spirit, and is a matter still concerned with the control of the cross of Christ. Both Hardy and Ford (1984: 64) and Molt-

---

[4] On these grounds perhaps we should avoid the notion of salvation being concerned with the deification of human beings, even if such language is given strong eschatological qualification (see Milbank, 1986: 227; McCabe, 1987: 20–2). Indeed, such language should be avoided lest we too easily give inappropriate content to

mann (1974: 72) criticise Luther for failing to extend the theology of cross into the heart of trinitarian thinking. (Perhaps Luther's failure here may be connected with his polemic against Münzer's theological rationale for the 'preferential option' for the German peasantry.) In considering the relation of the Spirit to social forms I think that we may heed this warning. I have already stressed that the Spirit may be understood in terms of transcendence. Here this emphasis secures the point that particular restrictions caused by social relations cannot be traced to the work of the Spirit: the Spirit precisely transcends them. To breach (always selectively!) the otherness of God from the world in order to secure a divine buttress is to fail to attend to the mode of the Spirit's presence: her transcendence. To claim the presence of the Spirit as possession is immediately denied by the presence of the Spirit in the form of transcendence. Attempts to confound particular groups or forms of organisation with the will of God are denied precisely by God's presence as transcendent and free.

The work of the Spirit may therefore be understood as the electing God who chooses people for new life in two ways. First, as we have seen, in the re-presentation, in word and sacrament, of the crucified Christ, human beings encounter the denial of their fashioning of 'knowledge' of God and of their attempts at self-deification. This may be understood pneumatologically as the denial of the Spirit to restrictive forms of social organisation. But this is to grasp the matter too simply. We must note that the 'knowledge' mediated is that of a revelation, complete and yet contingent. Thus the presence of the Spirit needs to be understood in terms of the same 'control': as fully present and yet contingently so. This is the form of God's presence: fully and effectively so, and yet free. The fullness of the presence of God in transcendent particularity is no denial of the contingency of that relation.

The Spirit, we might say, mediates 'the reality of historical "absence" – an absence which, as indeterminacy of meaning,

---

Moltmann's claim that in 'knowledge' of the cross our humanity is restored to us or construe the matter in terms of non-material redemption.

was already an aspect even of Christ's presence on earth' (Milbank, 1986: 229). But it is a double mediation: the representation of the 'actuality' of God's revelation in the denial of human pride, arrogance and attempts at idolatrous self-deification (the criticism of the cross) and a second affirmation and denial of the presence of the Spirit to social forms (the transcendence of the Spirit). God's Spirit relates freely to the contingencies of freedom of human social life. God's Spirit thereby relates to the contradictions of modern society. (All social contradictions are necessarily social contingencies, but contingencies are not necessarily contradictions.) But the form of the relation is that of contingency, that is, freedom. The Spirit is thereby present in a relation of freedom, particular and universal, to the contingencies of social life.

If at this point we recall my suggestion that society is both the condition and the outcome of social life and is thereby both necessary and contingent, then these social contingencies are of course the enactment of human freedom. But this is not to be interpreted as meaning that all contingencies are an embodiment of human freedom. Forms of social organisation are an enactment of human freedom, but this is not to say that they embody or enable freedom. The 'result' of freedom may be unfreedom.[5]

Here then we encounter the full reach of the Christological control: the Spirit is present decisively and yet contingently to human contingencies. God's Spirit relates freely to forms of human freedom and unfreedom, forms of relation and irrelation, as both particular and universal presence. If this is persuasive, then it suggests that all created forms fall within the action of the Spirit without drawing the conclusion that the Spirit is present to forms of irrelation and mystification as the power that secures such forms. The Spirit is present in a relation of freedom decisively and contingently to the social

---

[5] This is in effect Bhaskar's distinction between the reproduction and the transformation of society. Indeed, such contradictions may be understood as the actions of people in the past impinging upon the present in the form of unfreedom. This is the labour of the dead persisting into the present: 'In the social production of their life, men enter into definite relations that are indispensable and independent of their will' (Marx, 1977: 389).

contingencies of human life. As the expression of human agency then these are the products of human freedom. But it does not follow that because these are the products of human freedom that they enable human freedom: even social contradictions are the enactment of human freedom.[6]

VI   THE SPIRIT AND SOCIAL FREEDOM

I am not suggesting here that God is present decisively and contingently solely to individuals in social relations and structures. (That is, I think, the weakness of the account by McCabe, 1987: 11–15.) Rather, I am suggesting that the Spirit is freely present to the freedom (and unfreedom) of structures and relations. Institutions, states, markets, economies have their own form of contingency and of 'freedom': they change and develop (often along lines that can be predicted). Social forms are the product of human action, although they are not reducible to such action. (As we have seen, society is not to be understood as the straightforward result of human agency, although it persists only through human agency. This, we may recall, is the distinction between condition and outcome first broached in chapter 5.)

In so arguing, I am aware that it cuts across our sensibilities regarding human agency and the 'position' of agents in society. Our very language resists the theorising of social forms. And it is very much a matter of conceptuality: social forms as the condition of society cannot be shown, and certainly cannot be experienced. Indeed, even when we recognise structures we still tend to regard them as aggregates of individuals. Even theologians such as McCabe and Gunton, whose epistemologies are decisively anti-empiricist, have difficulty in articulating an anthropology that escapes the individual and the individual-in-community. This is the pressure of the dominant forms which acts to secure the 'naturalness' of our privileging of the individual. Perhaps I may add here that my rehearsal of

---

[6] Of course, if this were not so, such contradictions could not be changed: we are back to the transformational character of society.

Bhaskar's transformational, relational account of society (which could, I think, easily be traced back to Marx) is an attempt both to find a proper place for human agency in freedom and also to find a conceptual way of showing that human intentions cannot on their own form an adequate basis for an account of society.

If God is present to social contingencies as contingencies (and not solely as a gathering of human agents), an important question remains: what is the 'direction' of the Spirit's actions? The presence of the Spirit is the opening up, the raising up, the freeing up of social forms toward richer forms of social organisation. The Spirit is decisively present to emancipatory change and contingently so to social contradictions – understood as social forms. Is this unwarranted 'economic speculation'? No, because it is governed by the trinitarian outlook that social life is from the Creator (whose 'mark' is creative liberty) in the ordering and reordering work of the Word (in creation and redemption) and is to be brought to its eschatological futures in the action of the Spirit. If this last claim is not to be abused, is not to be transmuted into ideology, it requires specification. It requires an insistence on the very openness-in-freedom of the Spirit, and the control of the cross (where Christians 'learn' about God, hidden and revealed).

In the argument of the previous paragraph, some of the material of the third point has been rehearsed (perichoresis indeed!): the eschatological reference of the work of the Spirit. Emphasis here is important for three reasons: to stress the 'reality' of the reordering toward the abundant Kingdom of the Father, in terms of the criticism of idolatry; to underscore the claim that God is not indifferent to structures (as the remarks on the transcendence of the Spirit might imply); and finally, to underline that the third hypostasis is not solely a matter of our understanding the trinitarian relations better (although this is not unimportant), but is also concerned with the eschatological end of creation.

The Spirit's transcendent freedom in relation to the world must not be understood as aimless. She seeks to extend and deepen the redeeming work of the Logos. If the work of the

Logos is to be understood in terms of a reordering, a redirection of social forms toward the unoriginate creativity of the Creator, then the work of the Spirit is concerned with the 'securing' of this reordering. The action of the Spirit may be understood as 'as freeing, opening out' (Gunton, 1991b: 128). But to what, we might ask, is the work of the Spirit directed? The Christological control introduced earlier may help us here. The cross of Christ is the criticism of our attempt to idolise ourselves (which does not mean only ourselves as persons, but also our form of living together). The work of the Spirit is directed toward the re-presentation of this dynamic: as the power of demystification, she is the criticism of idols. The presence of the Spirit is the invitation to human beings to consider the humanity (or otherwise) of their forms of life.

Here we encounter the second emphasis. We saw in chapter 5 that the work of the Logos needs to be understood in terms of creation and not simply in terms of gift to the community of the Church. Holding to this creation perspective here allows us to say that the eschatological work of the Spirit is directed, precisely as the Spirit of the Word, to the redemption of creation. This does not mean, for instance, that all institutions are enabling. But it is to say that institutionality is important. Specific forms of social organisation may not appeal for their legitimation to the Spirit, but rather that social organisation as such, given through the Logos, is important to the Spirit. The activity of the Spirit gives hope: not only for the individual and the Church, but for society also.

This stress on the freeing or opening out in the work of the Spirit and its eschatological reference allows us to make a final, technical, point. There has perhaps been a tendency (Augustine springs to mind) to consider the relations governing the *one* God as being 'accidental' rather than 'actual'. This has then led to the suspicion that such modalist 'logical' forays are attempts simply to say something about the relations, rather than saying nothing. The eschatological reference points to the 'reality' of the hypostasis of the Spirit: the presence of the Spirit is not simply an attempt better to understand God (a matter of sorting out the 'grammar' of revelation) but is rather the insistence on the 'actuality' of the work of the Spirit. (This of course is not to deny that the activity of human beings tends toward the eclipse of this presence.)

Yet it is a strange 'actuality': free and yet present; transcendent universal and yet transcendent particular. (This is the pneumatological specification of God's 'openness'.) Just as human beings may, and sometimes do, enjoy relations of freedom (a contingent social 'fact'), thus also the Spirit relates contingently, that is freely, to the social world. The action of the Spirit is the making 'real' of the reordering work of the Son, an action directed toward the freedom of human beings. Just as human beings express their freedom in and through social contingencies, so God also acts through the contingent form of God's relation to the world: freedom. The free presence of the Spirit is both unreserved and contingent. (Similarly, social contingencies are 'real' – as the enactment of social freedom – and yet are open to amendment.)

From this we may draw a surprising conclusion: have we not secured here the basis of the 'second difference'? The actions of the Spirit encompass the creative directing of creation toward its eschatological goal, a direction toward the creative liberty of the Father through the Word. Perhaps we are not able to say what this means: the Kingdom has no content other than given to it by its 'first-born', Jesus Christ. The Kingdom then, as given in cross and resurrection, suggests a creative reordering, a 'resurrection'. And the persistence of God towards its reordering is the presence in freedom of the Spirit.

If we revisit the argument of the previous chapter, and join it with the argument of the last few pages, we are now able to see that the mark of the Trinity in the divine economy is freedom: the unoriginate, unsurpassable, inconceivable creative freedom of the Creator; the freedom in dependence and obedience of the Word; the free relating to social contingencies, or to human freedom in social forms, of the Spirit. The economy of God is thereby given in relations of freedom. This is a matter that we shall consider again in the final chapter.

VII AGAINST IDEOLOGY: TRINITARIAN THEOLOGY

For now, let us keep to the main narrative. I began this part of the argument by enquiring how the Spirit might be understood as present in ways that deny Christian attempts to confuse the will or presence of God with a particular form of social organisation. We now see the shape of the answer that might be given. The Spirit is the presence of God drawing creation to its eschatological goal. As transcendent universal presence, she cannot be understood as providing the legitimation of certain forms of social organisation. As transcendent particular presence, she is the 'form' of the re-presentation of the cross: the criticism of human attempts to idolatrous self-deification. The Spirit here frees us to be who we are: human creatures, elected into our humanity. But there is no fixed answer given as to what this humanity might be. Here again is the motif of conversion: given that we are 'free' to be human, what is it to be human? And whatever the answer, it is 'shaped' by the Spirit's activity as eschatological activity: we surpass this present, enabled by the Spirit, into a hopeful future.

The resolution of social contradictions cannot thereby be secured by reference to the Spirit. The presence of the Spirit is not the provision of fresh information as to how to solve our social problems. But the presence of the Spirit is such as to deny that God is on the side of the big battalions: there is no 'side' that God could possibly be on. The activity of the Spirit is toward the eschatological goal of abundant life; the Spirit may be present when we ask: how are we to live? But there is an ontological point, as well as an epistemological one. The Spirit may be understood as present, fully and contingently, to social forms, which are themselves the products of – although not reducible to – human freedom. (Indeed, 'free' human activity does not necessarily issue in 'relations of freedom'.) The freedom of the Spirit is engaged with the contingencies of social forms toward their dynamic 'expansion' into freer, more emancipatory forms of organisation.

In order to raise such questions about human living with proper material depth, and in order to engage in fully emanci-

patory practices, a crucial aspect of a theology for enlightenment will be the distinction between social condition and social
outcome on which the transformative account of society turns.
This will necessitate attention to those activities which are
reproduced in social relations. It is to the reconstruction of
these activities that the Spirit is present as the criticism of
mystification, as contingently present to contradictions, and
yet fully present to the emancipatory actions of social agents.
The direction of the Spirit in affirmation and surpassment
directs Christian theological attention to what might be affirmed, and what surpassed. Neither relations, nor the activities which they reproduce, may be traced in univocal fashion to
the actions of the Spirit in redemption; rather the 'expansion'
of human society is to be traced to the dynamic of affirmation.
The presence of the Spirit is neither the overcoming of our
sociality, nor the buttress for particular forms of social organisation. Rather, the presence of the Spirit invites proper
consideration to the transcendentality of society, and to the
surpassment of particular, contingent practices of such
transcendentality.

In closing, let me note that the sort of trinitarian thinking
possible here was circumscribed by my criticisms of the trinitarian critique of society in chapter 5. There, and in more detail
in this chapter, I have sought a way forward that respected the
strengths but avoided the weaknesses of the trinitarian critique
of society. The constructive trinitarian development of this
chapter was perhaps prepared in the last. There I argued for a
revolutionary account of the practice of resurrection, and from
this non-ideological position developed a trinitarian appropriation of the resurrection event, in form and in substance.
This yielded a social ontology of sacrifice: an interpretation of
social forms as God's gift. I argued that the social character of
humanity as God's gift of the freedom and comfort of human
solidarity is to be understood as reordered in the atoning work
of the Logos.

In the present chapter, some detail of the continuation of
this reordering work toward the eschatological goal of the
Kingdom has been offered: the Spirit is God's presence to the

contingencies of social forms. In this way it was hoped to show the immediate relevance of an account of the Trinity along realist lines. Quite how far a non-ideological theology has been developed is an important matter, discussed in the next and final chapter.

CHAPTER 8

Unfinished business

I REVIEW AND PROSPECT

I have sought to give due weight to the Marxist insistence on the social location of all intellectual production – the materiality of ideas; and on the Marxist insistence that Christianity functions as a false intermediary. I have sought to offer some thoughts on the nature of a liberative theology and on the contribution of Christianity towards political liberation that is mindful of Marxist strictures. Theology here must look to its own resources: I hope that I have developed resources available in mainstream Christianity in order to provide the materials for an engagement with Marxism. But although Christianity may have its own resources, this is a rather different issue from the matter of its social location. Here, if I am right, it is Marxism that gives the grounds for the securing of cognitive credentials – it is these credentials that theology must secure if it is to be liberative.

My concern has been to articulate a conception of Christian liberation and of the status of theological discourse that are not open to Marxist rebuttals. I have been seeking to offer the outline of a theology that is not open to the Marxist retort that theological proposals lack self-critical sense of their own social location (and so have a tendency to be ideological).

It may be of some concern that central Christian themes are being read so closely together with Marxist thinking. Indeed, Marxism appears to be specifying the grounds of the development of a theological position. Of course, it is a perennial problem for the Christian theologian as to where the balance might lie in the relation between the articulation of Christian identity and the grounds for and articulation of Christian relevance. Hans Frei has, for instance, offered an interesting five point typology which suggests the variety of ways in which theologians 'give priority to either Christian self-description or Christian theology as member of a class of disciplines' (Frei, 1992: 27). I have tried to avoid a static opposition between what Moltmann has termed Christian identity and relevance. Instead, I have taken seriously the comment that 'the development of a concept of God demands the development of categories of freedom' (Peukert, 1986: 229). This quotation captures the double reference of the current theological task: to speak of God and freedom; to speak of God and humanity in terms of freedom. There can be no falling behind this insight, as Peukert notes, and I have suggested that Marxism specifies the epistemological rules for this theological task.

Theological thinking may function as ideology, and thereby have a particular social function; it may not simply be 'a pure intellectual act' but rather 'a practical affirmation, an embryonic activity' (Kolakowski, in Bottomore (ed.), 1988: 296). The Marxist critique of ideology, and the critique of capitalist society that informs it, is, throughout my argument, attempting to specify the conditions of the 'correct' production of theological knowledge so that such knowledge might be the practical affirmation of liberation. And I am suggesting in this part, and in part II, ways in which theology might meet this specification of conditions. But far from being constraining, this is what allows theology to be liberative. An oppositional theology must pay attention to the epistemological dynamic of closeness and distance. The task of Christian theology becomes the specifying of these conditions that Marxism insists Christianity must meet (part I) and the attempt to think theologically against these strictures (parts II and III) in such fashion that precisely the ambivalence between theological discourse and social reality is excluded, and that this relationship is incorporated into theology in a self-reflexive, critical moment (part II) and more constructively (part III). Such is the nature of a liberative theology, I am arguing. Other types of theology must simply hope that their theology is liberative – by accident, so to speak. But concrete Christian praxes cannot be developed from a conception of liberation governed by a theology whose claim to be liberative is grounded in so haphazard a way. It is poor theological theory and practice, although it may well be recognisable as theology, and perhaps, through luck, as good theology.

My aim has been to explore the character of the Christian hope, its constitutive nature, and the sort of practice it enables. I have been concerned with the suggestion that 'our lives depend on our capacity to speak hope, to entrust to if-clauses and futures our active dreams of change, of progress, of deliverance. To such dreams, the concept of resurrection, as it is central to both myth and religion, is a natural grammatical augment' (Steiner, 1991: 56). I have been seeking to suggest that if this grammar is to be 'trusted', important implications follow for our thinking about matters social and political. Indeed, it may function as a Christian basis for liberation if society is understood in terms of a 'social ontology of sacrifice' constituted and encompassed by God's actions in creation and redemption.

The theological decision taken here points to a fundamental difficulty or tension within Christianity. If one begins from the particularity of the Christ-event, it may then be difficult to reach out into wider anthropological concerns. And yet, if one begins from wider anthropological concerns, then it may be difficult to arrive at the particularity of the Christ-event. It must be clear by now that I have sought to refuse the antithesis. It seems to me, and I have learned this from liberation theology, that it is the very question of what it is to be human, of the possibility of articulating some account of human capacities against the dominant hegemony, both theoretically and practically, that is an important starting point. Yet, in seeking to articulate this, I have been driven to that seemingly most impractical aspect of Christianity, the resurrection of Jesus Christ. Here lies, I have argued, the possibility of theological insight into the trustworthiness (or otherwise) of theological engagement with social forms.

Above all, in approaching resurrection in this way, I have sought to stress the eschatological nature of the Christian conception of liberation. The practice of resurrection, and the constitution of liberation in resurrection, is embodied in an eschatology of hope. The world as gift is a reference to its eschatological redemption in the 'return' of creation from the Spirit through the Word to the Creator; the practice of resurrection contains within it a reference to a general resurrection and the eschatological justification of such practice.[1]

However much Christianity may have acted as a myth of stability in the past, and perhaps does so still today, this is not a necessary part of Christianity. I have suggested that certain protocols, and attention to resurrection, may provide the shape of an oppositional theology. If it is Marxism or, more precisely, the Marxist critique of ideology which specifies the conditions for an intellectual practice, then perhaps Christianity may meet these conditions. It does this not to develop a 'post-Marxist' position – if the argument of this book is right, there is no such position. Rather, it does so in order to have inscribed into its own practice some awareness of its position, neither too close to nor too distant from determining pressures and limits. Indeed, whether or not the proposal contained in parts II and III is persuasive, I hope that something of the complexity, importance and practical nature of the development of an oppositional theology has emerged. I am claiming, perhaps too boldly, that such an exercise in ideology critique – the identification and reconstruction of ideological strategies of containment in theology – is *the* primary task for a theology whose construction takes place in the powerful 'centre'.

The purpose of the remainder of this chapter is two-fold. There is the matter of the assessment of the argument: is it the case that a constructive theological proposal has been made (against a certain construal of the Marxist account of ideology)? If the proposal is even thought, to a greater or lesser extent, to be persuasive, what is the way forward from here?

---

[1] An emphasis upon the beauty, and not simply the moral order, of the 'final' creation might be included here.

What theological agenda emerges from this study? But before we get to the consideration of these questions, there are two matters that need discussion in order to complete the argument. I shall comment on each only briefly. Section II addresses the issue of the relation between the economic trinity and the immanent trinity. I broach the issue only in so far as it touches upon the presence of the social God to social forms. It could well be developed much further. The issue addressed in section III is the glaring lack in the previous chapter: a few comments as to how, in this perspective, the Church might be understood. The remainder of the chapter is taken up with the review and assessment referred to earlier.

II   ECONOMY AND IMMANENCE

In the preceding chapters, and particularly in the previous two, I have concentrated upon the actions of God in the economy: enquiring after the divine actions in the economy controlled by the 'concentration' of divine action in the life, death and resurrection of Jesus of Nazareth. Here, and particularly in cross and resurrection, we encounter the self-identification of God in fleshly social relations. More precisely, I spoke at the end of chapter 7 of the relations of freedom that govern the triune actions of God in the economy.

The difficult matter here is whether the actions of God and the characterisation of God therefrom in the economy may be taken as a reliable guide to God's 'inner' being, to Godself in itself. Put another way, that 'what God has spoken to us is not just some particular message (behind which he might have rather different messages up his sleeve), but is his *self*-statement in the flesh and texture of our history' (Lash, 1988: 274). My concern here is not an act of hubris in the attempt to know something about the unknowable God: to articulate a speculative knowledge. I am instead concerned with the attribution of the social character of humanity to the triune sociality of God, and how this social character has been reconstituted in the actions of the triune God in cross and resurrection. Further, I have sought to show that this 'resurrection perspective' nerves Christian praxis. If this approach is to be persuasive then it is important to determine whether this triune sociality, constituted by relations of freedom, may, in however attenuated a fashion, be understood to be who God really 'is'. A faithful confidence that the revealed God is *God* is important not only for theoretical reasons – although this is not an inconsiderable matter. It goes to the heart of Christian *practice*. It may well be that the character of the political practice nerved by the resurrection is more radical than that of the Marxist (see chapter 6, sections III and IV). And yet, in committing oneself (even unto death) to the 'revolution' in and against restrictive social relations, it becomes imperative to know that this social character, this 'being-with' (Hardy) given in work, embodiment and language, is genuinely the image of *God*. In other words, that sociality or 'freedom with others' marks – in however apophatic a manner – the inner being of God and not only God in 'outward' manifestation.

I am not persuaded that an account of trinitarian being needs to be secured to underpin an account of personhood or persons-in-relation (although, as we saw in chapter 5, this position has undoubted strengths). Nor am I sure that it is helpful to construe a direct 'correspondence' between God and humanity. (And *if* there is, such an image is too often eclipsed in and by forms of social organisation.) Rather, we must carefully consider how to frame an account of the relation between the social character of human life and the sociality of the triune God. Such a relation is important as, without it, it becomes difficult to see how society (although contingent) should be understood as *God*'s gift. And without this relation as safeguard the tendency will be for Christianity to develop along individualistic lines (with the resulting dualisms: religious experience/other experience; mind/body; individual/society; salvation/political process; Jesus/God; the elect/the world). In order to avoid the charge that the Christian account of sociality turns upon the presence of the social being of God and yet, in the final instance, this social being cannot be known – to avoid this sort of charge, it seems worthwhile considering (briefly and without conclusion) the relation between the economic trinity and the immanent trinity.

I find Lash's account of the relation insightful, and yet insufficient. Nonetheless his interpretation raises (sometimes implicitly) some important issues which we must consider. Lash insists that the drawing together of the immanent and economic trinities is not so much an issue about our knowledge of God (or lack of it) but about our capacities to accept the trustworthiness of our experience. The litmus test here is death (again). On what grounds is experience of the Christian God to be trusted? Indeed, how is it trustworthy so that we might even give our lives – an act of ultimate trust? So Lash writes: '. . . we are able to trust God's trustworthiness . . . because what God has given us is not just some particular gift (which he might withdraw or we might exhaust), but is his imperishable *self-*gift, his joy, his Spirit' (Lash, 1988: 274). In this manner, Lash avoids being drawn into the disputes about the relation, from sharp difference to identification, between the immanent and the economic trinity. Nevertheless, Lash affirms the central point about the relation: we have here to do with *God*. (Or, perhaps better, *God* here has to do with us.)

I am not sure that this is sufficient. Lash persistently and persuasively construes these matters in terms of human practice. Yet I sought to suggest in the previous chapter ways in which we might understand God as present to social forms in order to get beyond accusations that Christianity lacks the conceptuality to specify the actuality of social relations. I think the Marxist charge against Christianity, as I am construing it, is not simply that Christianity often fails to think in terms of and generate an adequate praxis. (This is Lash's interpretation of the matter.) The problem is also the charge that Christianity has no resources to handle the conceptual matters. Therefore, whatever praxis issues from Christian interpretation will always be deficient as Christianity (often, although not constitutively) lacks the means even of approaching social matters. Indeed, this is precisely its ideological function: it inhibits and misconstrues knowledge of the social realm. In limiting such access, it effectively protects the realm, rendering it impervious to criticism as it cannot be thought. This in turn transposes the social realm into an (unacknowledged) idol: it has, in effect, to be 'respected' because although it cannot be engaged with directly it does not cease its operations. The social realm persists, uncriticised because unconceptualised. It demands our allegiance – otherwise we shall not eat! – but we cannot identify the object of our allegiance. The claim is allegiance to the one God, the practice a blind following after social idols, everywhere unrecognised.

Even so, Lash's account has implicit strengths. His interpretation of the relation between economy and immanence does not require a discussion as to the precise nature of the relation, because he is concerned rather with our capacities for trust rather than what the death of Jesus 'means' for God. And yet the danger of Lash's account is that it remains at the level of a restatement of the intention behind the distinction: both to insist that God is really present in the economy, and that the reality of God is not exhausted by the identification of such actions. In other words, Lash continues to develop his argument in terms of pedagogy: may the Christian trust the pedagogical practices of Christianity, or does she have reasons to be sceptical?

But there remains another side to the issue, which the distinction between immanence and economy is intended to highlight: in the light of the discussion of cross and resurrection, what difference does God make? (That Lash does not concentrate on this can, I have already suggested, following Jones (1990), be traced to a certain lack of attention to the particularity of the Christ event.) In asking this question we are also enquiring after the identity of the agent. This is the case because God 'acts' (to make a 'difference') in concentrated fashion in the cross and resurrection, and *this* is the self-identification of God. Straightaway the issue of the relation between *this* self-identification and the being of God is raised. (And to argue thus is not to argue that God's actions make a *particular* difference.)

The difficulty with moving beyond Lash's position and so beyond the regulative guidance of Christian pedagogy, is that we enter the discussion as to the precise manner of the relation between economic and immanent trinities. Yet the moment that we note the intention of the distinction, but then enquire 'Well, how is this distinction secured? How are we to think of it?' then we immediately encounter a particular difficulty: the contemporary articulation of the distinction is caught up in a discussion of the suffering of God. Much of the discussion of the relation between economic and immanent trinities is taking place in the context of a theology of the cross, precisely interpreted in terms not only of redemption but also in terms of a 'death in God'. Put crudely, the debate encompasses not only what the cross means for the world but also what it means for God.

We may note that the logic of the development is impeccable. If the event of the cross is decisive and constitutive, it must be such for God economically *and* immanently. To deny the conjunction is to deny that the cross really is an event for God in Godself, and such a denial would put in question how the event is constitutive and redemptive. If the link is granted, then the next question is: what does it mean for the 'inner' being of God? If it cannot be specified, however inadequately and cautiously, how cross (and resurrection) are to be understood as really an event for God and so as God's self-revelation, are we then driven to the conclusion that God may, as Lash notes, have other messages up His sleeve?

To resist the argument to drive the suffering of Jesus into the heart of the immanent Trinity is to make the theological decision to separate the immanent and divine trinities. The protocol of divine simplicity is already a guard against attempts to understand God as suffering. But there are other reasons for wishing to keep them separate. John Milbank has noted what he calls the tendency of the 'strong' version of the identity between economic and immanent trinities (which reaches its nadir, he suggests, in the theology of Jüngel) toward a kind of 'atheism' and an affirmation of the autonomy of the world. The 'strong' version underpins an account of God becoming God in the cross and may thereby be interpreted in terms of a theodicy and – in strongly immanentist terms – as the overcoming of death (Milbank, 1986: 224–5). But, for Milbank, such a development marks a departure from the traditional interpretation of theodicy which sees the key issue as sin, not death. Hence, the strong version drifts toward a form of developmental gnosis in which the world is to be *interpreted* in terms of the reconciliation of the alienation of death. And this, of course, is not a theology governed by a 'strong' creation perspective. The collapse into atheism (or is it pantheism?) obscures the distinction of God from the world. And, as we have seen, the 'openness' of God toward the world is crucial for a liberative theology.

Obscuring the distinction of God from the world leads to an epistemological point concerning knowledge of God. The 'strong' version of the identity creates a particular problem: the obligation to claim knowledge of the 'inner room' (Moltmann) of God's being. Perhaps we should not shy away from claiming some knowledge of God in Godself, but neither should we set up a theological compulsion to do so. The difficulty here is that we are obliged to consider God's immanent being in the terms of an interpretation of God's economic relations. We repeat here in the order of knowing the mistake discussed in the previous paragraph concerning the order of being. There we noted that the being of God is construed in terms of the development of the world, here our knowledge of God is construed 'tightly' in the terms of the 'givenness' of our knowledge of God in the economy. This creates the tendency, first, to claim too much for our knowledge of God's inner being. Second, it grounds the inflated claim to knowledge in the 'form' of God's redemptive acts. This issues in the confusion that to commit oneself to the 'reality' of God's redemptive activity is also to commit oneself to an overextended knowledge of God in Godself. We end up in the position of a tension between defending an overpresumptuous claim to familiarity with God or denying God's redemptive activity. Theology thus has its own form of 'economism'! Just as some forms of Marxism reduce intellectual and cultural matters to their economic determinants, likewise a theology which assumes the identity of economic and immanent trinities tends to 'reduce' knowledge of God to the economic relations – in effect, a form of 'economic immanentism'.

For the reasons given above it seems theologically more appropriate at least to separate the economic and the immanent trinities. Failure to do so infringes the creation perspective set out in part II and thereby infringes the distinction of God from the world. And we have seen that the infringement of this distinction tends toward non-liberative forms of theology. And the reasoning behind the distinction is that of seeking to secure a protocol against idolatry. The grounds on which we specify the *connection* (because distinction is not separation) is a rather different matter. Whether we may be confident that recent efforts in theology properly secure the grounds is not a matter I wish to discuss here. Perhaps all that needs to be insisted upon for the sake of my argument is to note the counter-idolatry grounds for the distinction.

Yet, that we might be able to specify the connection remains important if we are to be able to trace – in however attenuated a fashion – the presence of God in the economy to the inner nature of God. The presence of the triune God to social forms, as the giver of the 'consolation' of social life, as the orderer of social forms, and as the powerful pressure that seeks the 'expansion' of such social forms, is a genuine glimpse of God. If a method might be found for specifying the connection, then perhaps we might understand the inner being of God in the terms already introduced in this part. The inner being of God might be understood in terms of triune relations of freedom: relations of abundance, proportion and solidarity. In other words, the triune God is to be characterised by an inexhaustible and overflowing liberty. But this 'quality' of overflowing is not to be understood in terms of sentimentality or the overwhelming of structure: it is a 'formed' liberty that enables response. Finally, the 'substance' and 'form' of liberty is secured in the dynamic and creative character of the divine unity, which enables the triune God to *be* Godself: not simply the enabling but the securing of the triune relations. Put briefly, we may tentatively say that in the immanent Trinity, love, power and justice are not absent.

Here is the heart of the practical point I have been making. The social character of humanity may be attributed to a God whose being is social, and is marked by relations of freedom. The resurrection is not, as we have seen, the denial of this position. It is rather, in part at least, an invitation to human beings to commit all of themselves to the liberating process that seeks the extension of human freedom. And the God who acts in this event is in turn a social God who *really* has to do with us in our social relations. This is the dialectic of the affirmation of our sociality and the surpassment of restrictive forms of social relations.

It will be clear that in a full account two matters would require extended treatment: the triune *persons* and the issue of the filioque. As regards the former, I have some sympathy with Lash (1988: 275–80) and Fiddes (1989: 139–43) as to whether it is appropriate any longer to talk about the Trinity in terms of *persons*, as distinct from 'personal'. This is implicit in the argument of chapter 5. There I raised some difficulties in moving from an account of the Trinity to social and political matters; furthermore, it was not clear that an interpretation of the Trinity that foregrounded the 'persons' was necessarily that informative nor was in fact required as part of a theoretical and practical task of securing human personhood. There is, in other words, the tendency within the position I called the trinitarian critique of society to run a number of concerns together.

On the issue of the filioque, I do not want to enter into an extended discussion. I simply want to note here that the difficult interpretative issue here is the force of the filioque. I note with interest John Milbank's comment that:

Historians of theology have now followed Pusey in showing that the *per Filium* was widely affirmed in the patristic east (not least by Cyril of Alexandria in connection with his anti-Nestorianism), and that the *Filioque* in the west was mostly not intended to convey a drastically different content. Cyril in the east and Marius Victorinus in the west illustrate how theologians taking seriously the New Testament texts could emphasise both the agency of the Spirit in the life of Christ and the eschatological giving of the Spirit by Christ. (Milbank, 1986: 214)

The difficulties might perhaps lie elsewhere, as Milbank proceeds to argue. What is important is that redemption is secured only and all through Christ, and yet not Christ 'independent'; and the presence of the Spirit is governed by the cross and ressurection. This, of course, is no more than an attempt to conceive the trinitarian relations perichoretically. And perichoresis is not 'linear'.

III CHURCH IN SOCIETY

In section III of the previous chapter, I said that we would return to the matter of the Church. This is the second issue that needs briefly to be raised. For much of this part of the book I have been stressing the actions of God in creation and redemption. This stress on the 'breadth', so to speak, of God's activity has allowed me to emphasise the place of sociality, and its reordering and reorientation toward the Kingdom in Word and Spirit. But then what of the Church?

We may offer some brief reflections on the Church through a consideration of how the Spirit is present to it. If a trinitarian approach frees the Church to be itself, as instituted by Christ and constituted by the Spirit (Gunton, 1991b: 127; 1989: 58–65, following Zizioulas), then how is the Spirit present to it in the 'economy of demystification'? I am tempted to say that the presence of the Spirit needs to be understood rather differently from that outlined in chapter 7, section III: should not the stress, in this context of a discussion of the Church, be placed upon the *un*reserved nature of the presence? But that would perhaps be a mistake. It would suggest that the Church has the Spirit for its possession – a position that I have consistently sought to deny (through reference to a theology of creation). In addition, we must note the following claim: 'do we not often have to give thanks to God for the human progress in society beyond the church, which often seems to be what saves the church from its own worst side?' (Marshall, 1992: 17). I suggest then that the same dialectic of presence and absence, of particular presence in universal transcendence, characterises the presence of the Spirit to the Church. What differentiates the

Church, of course, is a point already noted in chapter 6: the Church is explicitly in dialogue with its 'founder'. The actions of the trinitarian God persist in their latency whether or not such actions are explicitly acknowledged. Yet their ontic manifestation and enactment is the 'function' of the Church in its dialogue with its founder.

I have called this section 'Church *in* Society'. This, it seems to me, is the right emphasis. 'And' has the emphasis quite wrong. The Church is not separate from the world. Its persons, relations and products are located within existing social relations. (Indeed, confirmation of this may be found in the fact that the Church's 'wisdom' is sometimes the wisdom of the less creative practices of the world.) Its distinguishing characteristic is its active and practical acknowledgement of the Lordship of Christ. This is the matter of its dialogue with its 'founder', in word and sacrament in the Spirit. (The rest of society is not in this explicit dialogue – and thereby dialogues 'anonymously'?)

May we say then that the Church thereby witnesses to the redemptive activity of God in terms of an 'ontology of sacrificial community' within a 'social ontology of sacrifice'? But what in this context does 'witness' mean? To argue that the Church is best understood as an ontology of sacrificial community is another way of saying 'Church in Society'. It is to 'locate' this community within social relations. Such witness turns upon the dialogue with its 'founder': with the range and urgency of the questions engendered by and encountered in the re-telling of the narrative of the life, death and resurrection of Jesus of Nazareth. It is, above all, to bear witness in the sense of enacting the reordered relationship secured in the Word enfleshed, in the power of the Spirit. If the re-presentation of the crucified Jesus in the Spirit frees us to be creatures, to be human, then this is not an abstract matter. (We are back at the practical nature and the material dimension of conversion.) The freedom of the Spirit works through the freedom of 'converted' Christians toward the enactment, through the Son, of the creative liberty of God.

We return to the matter of the enactment of the discontinuity and revolution of the resurrection of the body discussed in chapter 6. Such a practice of resurrection is secured by entering into the processes of atonement given in the cross through the presence of the Spirit. John Milbank puts it along these lines but in rather different terminology:

Through Christ, God is already able to offer to himself an undistorted image of his glory in humanity; at the same time it is not a matter of indifference to the divine being that this glory is not yet restored in its concrete entirety. For this reason, one may tentatively suggest that Christ's outpouring of the Spirit is not simply equivalent to the restoration of our capacity for deification lost since the fall (as for Cyril of Alexandria). Instead, because of the continuing contradiction of the loss of divine glory, the infinite response of the Spirit to the Son is now *eschatologically identical* with the setting of all human beings on the path of deification, itself a work of inter-human participation and exchange. (Milbank, 1986: 227)

The witness of the churches is then to be understood as a practical matter: 'a work of inter-human participation and exchange'. It is the enacting of the memory of the crucified one, in word and sacrament and other forms of witness, that is the testimony of the churches in society. The witness of the churches is to the demystificatory presence of the Spirit and against the pressures and forces of mystification. And this witness is Christocentric. It is Christocentric in the sense that the cross is the criticism of human attempts to be gods and so lapse into idolatry. It is Christocentric in the sense that the resurrection insists on a certain context for political practice: sociality as the gift of God, (re)ordered through the Word and encompassed in the response of the Spirit.

That is not to say that such Christocentric witness gives the Church 'answers'. For instance, Jones (1990: 402–4) has queried whether Lash's interpretation of the trinitarian structure of Christian pedagogy offers sufficient guidance in the making of particular decisions (the issue of violence is cited). I am not persuaded that an account of God should necessarily offer us such guidance. It is interesting to note that Jones cites a determinedly *ethical* issue which perhaps ought not to be raised outside particular political practices. But a further point that

Jones makes is very pertinent: what are the practices that Christians may identify as those of the world and as those of the Kingdom? I think the contrast is not perhaps helpful. It is rather the orientation that Christians should be seeking, in terms of the affirmation of the telos of the 'expansion' of the social character of humanity, that is important here. The trinitarian doctrine of God is not to be restricted to pedagogies nor to specifications of *Christian* practice, in that the doctrine of God also marks the presence of God and specifies the manner of God's engagement with the world. Yet an important question remains: how might this presence and engagement be interpreted in terms of actual, concrete practice?

We might develop this a little further by noting that this new perspective creates a number of difficulties. I shall rehearse two here. First, we may say that in one sense, the rôle of the Church can now be understood more carefully: it has its place within a society which in turn has its place within the divine economy. But in another sense this fresh 'positioning' is problematic. On the one hand we have the extraordinary, indeed universal, claims made by the Church; on the other, we have what in the 'developed' world can only be described as its 'residual' status. To speak of the 'residual' status of the Church is not to say that it is unimportant, but that its practices no longer have the 'pressure' of the past. But this creates a difficulty, as Charles Davis has forcefully noted:

The confused hesitancy of political theology about the Christian contribution to political policy and action is the reflection, in my opinion, of the lack of any real and effective functional relationship between Christian institutions and society as at present organised. Christian talk on politics has become unreal, stripped of both theory and programme, because it is the free-ranging speech of the disengaged. (Davis, 1980: 64)

Davis further suggests that many individual members of the churches may be committed to working for change, but this is not equivalent to the commitment of the churches themselves. The reason for this lack of commitment, suggests Davis, is that the churches 'are no longer a functioning part of political society' (Davis, 1980: 64). And where the churches do in fact remain a functioning part of political society, Davis goes on, they tend to interpret their interests in political society narrowly and ecclesiastically. (An example of narrow, churchly interest might be the churches' involvement in the education provided by the state.)

As a matter of empirical record, perhaps the argument may have to be granted to Davis. But this is not all that might be said. To argue that the churches are not members of political society may be right, but the impulse for transformation need not come from 'established' political society. (Indeed, it may not come from within 'Western' society.) We need at this point to consider the possibilities of the emergent, and its capacities for engendering change.

Now I would accept that the emergent is not necessarily oppositional in character. The emergent may be only specialising or alternative – this much can be seen in the area of cultural initiatives. But the advantage of these three terms is to suggest that new movements are not necessarily 'given' as one or the other; they may be *transformed* from one into another through argument, through solidarity, through the encounter of resistances. (The fragmentation of the punk movement in Britain in the late '70s into oppositional and alternative elements would be a good example here.) Of course, it is difficult to identify the emergent. Moreover, it is difficult to identify whether the emergent is oppositional, or is susceptible to rapid appropriation by dominant forms. But it seems to me that the only way of enacting Christianity's universal claim is through the connection of the residual status of the Christian churches with genuinely emergent movements. This practical realignment may be the only way of overcoming the 'free-ranging speech of the disengaged'. Apparently, Bonhoeffer said that the challenge of Nazism to the German Protestant churches in the 1930s was that 'we become converted, rather than Hitler'. And such a conversion, as we know, is a practical matter, with costly consequences. Overcoming the 'free-ranging speech of the disengaged' now will be, as perhaps it always has been (for idealist talk is cheap), a matter of costly conversion.

The theological rationale for this is clear. Less restrictive, more creative forms of social reorganisation will only be possible through the reordering of social organisation across a range of 'sites of production' – economic work, institutions, cultural work. The enactment of the 'difference' given in the ontological reordering of God in Christ can only be won through the connection of residual status with emergent movements. This would be one form of Christian witness (and would probably be for many churches a matter of conversion?). The rationale therefore is theological, and is not at all concerned with being 'modern' or 'up to date'. The practical alignment of the churches with the oppositional emergent is not the attempt to be relevant. The emergent *qua* emergent is not of immediate *theological* interest. The matter here is not the emergent and the churches' alignment with the same (with the accompanying suspicion of Pelagianism), but rather a matter of the conversion of the churches. *This* is the importance of the emergent. The emergent marks the commitment of the churches to be a witness to the trinitarian action of God. The emergent marks the commitment of the churches to discover the face of Christ in the breaching of the series of exclusions on which human societies are often founded; the Church travels to the land of the Other to encounter Christ. In so far as they fail in such witness, they contribute to the eclipse of God; they are salt without savour. In so far as they so enact such an alignment, this may be seen as eschatologically identical with the response of the Spirit to the Son (the realisation of justice-in-power).

Second, we encounter the issue of human agency. In insisting that the praxis of the Church must be through the connection between residual status and emergent forms, then the emphasis on praxis raises the issue of human agency. An ontology of sacrificial community must be understood as placed within a social ontology of sacrifice. This means that the work of the churches is governed by the same dynamic as other work. This refers us to the transformational account of society which sees the social structures as, in part at least, the unintended outcome of human activity; as *re*produced in productive activity.

This does, I think, enable a particular Christian and theological engagement with society in that it allows for the suggestion of a correction to the insistence on the revolutionising of social limits given above. (And one aspect of a conception of sin could be grounded here – although such a development lies outside the scope of this book.) This is because human purposive activity is 'taken up' in various ways: recall that in chapter 5 I argued that social activity is both production and *re*production/transformation. This may be understood as resistance to the process of transformation.

One way of understanding such resistance has been a constant refrain throughout this book. An affirmation of intentional activity in relations of production includes the centrality of interaction between new thought and an understanding of social forms. Even here, ideas, arguments, intentions are not articulated in a vacuum, but within the dominant hegemonic. The danger here is that theologians collude in the tendency of intellectual production by considering that their articulation of a discourse of liberation is politically efficacious. The materiality of ideas directs us not simply to new states of affairs but to the social relations in and through which human intentionality is expressed, and to those structures that are both condition and (unintended) outcome of such intentionality.

This suggests that an account of Christian liberation demands engagement not solely with the criticism of what is empirically given, but also with the transient, concept-dependent, intention-governed but real, structures that govern human activity: real structures, and the social relations in which people find themselves with regard to these structures (Bhaskar). For the Marxist, the empirical is not all that is. Rather, the empirical needs to be referred to the practice of social labour. So Marxists insist that there can be no radical amelioration in social life, without reference to the social structures that govern it, and the social relations that organise it. This suggests that there will be *un*intended outcomes to human activity – what we might call resistances to the revolutionary process. If Christianity affirms the opaqueness of our material life, precisely its materiality, while demanding its surpassment, then we grasp something of the opaque character of social life (of sin as social). Sin as social resides in the 'reality' of social structures.

Above all, Christians will recall the 'route' of human agency is the narrow one from Gethsemane to Calvary. In the insertion of Christian communities into the asymmetries which predominate in contemporary society, there is genuine risk. Thus whatever is given (and I do not intend here a 'causal' account of grace) in the eschatological activity of the Spirit, is not to suggest, despite the importance of new practices, that change is ever without the limiting effects of ideology and idolatry, and without cost.

IV   A FINAL LOOK AROUND

We are now in a position to consider the argument. I do not plan to do this by rehearsing each step but rather to draw out what I regard as some of the important, sometimes implicit, issues and consequences.

We may begin by noting the interpretation of the theological task given in the argument: self-criticism, critique and construction. As presented here, these are not separate themes. But they are analytically distinct. The self-critical task begins from the insistence and the acknowledgement that theological thinking does not take place in a vacuum. But this means more than the obvious point that all our thinking is contextual. It means that all thinking needs to be understood as a material practice among other material practices. In other words, the human person is bound up in and through embodiment, language and other forms of work in a range of practices I have termed (following Bhaskar) relations of production. A central feature of the Marxist case is that some intellectual relations of production are to be understood as ideological. That is, certain ideological forms of thought may be understood as traceable back to other relations of production, and yet as precisely obscuring that connection. Certain arguments, interpretations, concepts may appear as coherent, persuasive, etc., but are only so if their *appearance* as free-floating is accepted. The task of materialist self-criticism is to enquire whether such thought forms are indeed ideological. Such self-criticism embraces the range of conceptual enquiry (although some disciplines are perhaps more susceptible than others to hegemonic pressure). So theology is not excluded from this task: self-criticism is crucial,

The dynamic of self-criticism generates critique. Are there theological arguments that lack this sense of self-criticism (even while articulating a discourse of liberation)? In some chapters of this book I have highlighted a theological argument that is not self-critical (in relation to the materiality of discourse). In other words, I sought to move beyond the articulation of the principle that attention needs to be paid to the materiality of discourse if the 'lapse' into ideology is to be avoided. I have also sought to demonstrate, so to speak, what a critique based on the materiality of discourse and its corruption in ideological discourse, might enable us to recognise about certain theological proposals. There is, if you like, only limited interest in the Marxist account of ideology itself. What is more interesting is that such an account offers us the structure of ideology so that we might be able to grasp how theology functions as ideology.

The constructive part of the theological task has perhaps occupied only part III. (Indeed, it may be a matter of complaint that it is not very constructive!) But I have tried to offer an outline of a theology, systematic in outline if not in execution, that meets the strictures regarding theological self-criticism. It is, I hope, a 'materialist theology'. This does not mean of course that the entire subject matter of theology is to be understood as political practice. Rather, it is to insist that theology is *already* a material practice and so is open to the distortion toward ideology that is a possibility for all intellectual practices.[2]

A theology which carries through this three-fold task may be understood as liberative. I have sought to carry through this

---

[2] In arguing this, I am also aware of another difficult matter: the relation between the theoretical practice of the churches, and the practices of worship, organisation, etc. I do not plan to pursue this difficulty here.

programme across a number of theological issues in order to attempt to show that the full range of non-ideological theological construction may be possible. The Marxist critique of ideology does not rule out theological construction, but insists that such construction be carried out somewhat differently.

In seeking to carry out this construction, we must bear in mind the main charge against Christianity. Not only does Christianity fail to generate adequate praxes, but it finds the full rigours of the task of a transformational interpretation of society too demanding. Even a Christianity which is 'materialist' in form is closer to Feuerbach than Marx. It cannot escape the corrosive individualism and the obscuring of the social which is its ideological function. Further, the range of categories that Christianity employs for this mediation is restricted or organised in unhelpful ways. This is the real heart of its ideological function. Thus Christians argue over whether Christianity does or does not falsely mediate. And yet, paradoxically, the argument takes shape precisely within the conceptuality of Christianity itself. We saw a particular outworking of this in chapter 5 in Hardy's critique that even when Christianity seeks to address social matters, it does so within a conceptuality restricted to *community*. Also in chapter 5, I explored the strengths and weaknesses of a trinitarian critique of society, a development that seeks also to grasp human relations. And yet, even here, the full implications of what it is to integrate a counter ideological epistemology into theological construction are not grasped, and unfortunate ontological formulations are the result.

The central theological task of attentiveness to theological language in response to the actions of God remains in place. But to it is added a new concern: the denial of the autonomy of theology as a discourse. Rather, theology must be understood as part of the development of a social history. Theology is a material intellectual practice and so is affected by, and may also affect, the development of that history. Attentiveness to theological language as part of the relations of production of modern society is the crucial recognition demanded here. Theology is, with all other disciplines, a determined discourse. The issue is then: in what manner is it determined? Is it too close or too distant? This book has been concerned with developing protocols that might enable theology to be neither too close nor too distant. The attempt has also been made to highlight some theologies which are too close to determining pressures. Finally, a little has been done to construct the outline of a theology that might be neither too close nor too distant.

None of this rules out theologies of spirituality or critical enquiry into the theologies of the New Testament – to offer just two examples. But it is to insist that all theological thinking is done within and in relation to the pressures of the dominant hegemonic forms. What we are concerned with here is, if you will, the permanent Christian task of seeking to guard against idolatry. This is not new. What is new is the manner of the attentiveness suggested here. Unless theology has protocols against inattention inscribed into its very epistemology, it may well end up as some form of apologia for a society divided by class (and much else).

The persuasiveness (if any) of the above argument thereby operates on a number of levels. It is possible to accept the need for 'material' protocols against the idolatry of ideology without accepting the precise formulation given here. Further, my attempts at theological construction may be deemed insufficient. But perhaps the more important point is the urgency of these issues: Christian theology – if it does not choose this way – must at least come to terms with the issue of ideology. And this is not Pelagianism or intellectual hubris. It is rather an attempt to specify how the practice of Christianity, both theoretically and practically, is the criticism – and not the deepening – of the eclipse of God.

V   THEOLOGY IN THE NEXT EPOCH?

The difficulty for the Christian theologian is to persuade the Marxist that Christian theological discourse is possible at all. Of course, the Marxist does not deny that theological texts will go on being written, that theological conversations will take place. But the Marxist is unpersuaded that this can have any relevance, because the Marxist doubts whether such talk can ever be 'correct', let alone affirm something of the 'truthfulness' of Christianity. The Marxist is persuaded that Christian theology necessarily turns upon a disjunction between divine and human freedom. Indeed, Christian theologians do seem to be preoccupied with this difficulty: Gunton (1991a: chapter 2) suggests that Kasper, Moltmann and Cupitt are united by the problem of the tendency of theology to construe the relation between God and human beings in terms of competition.

Marxism, as we saw in chapter 3, is the criticism of such idolatry. The issue that animates this book is not, at first glance, an ontological one. The issue of this book is the idolatry of ideology: the tendency of Christian theology, even in discussions of liberation and cognate areas, to be ideological, and thereby to misrepresent human beings to themselves and to misrepresent the Christian God. So the task of the Christian theologian becomes the work of trying to offer an account of theological discourse that does not operate in a systematically ambiguous fashion between social pressures and claims to its own autonomy.

But the result, in another sense, is a positive one in that it seeks to specify an ontology that encompasses the 'actuality' of God's commitment to the world and especially to social forms (and of freedom in one sense), but which leaves an ontology premised upon a competition between God and human beings behind. Theology is not, on this account of the lessons to be learned from the Marxist critique of ideology, condemned to silence, or, perhaps worse, the whispered speech of a theological liberalism. This, it seems to me, is the result of the argument in Kee (1990), where Marxism is employed to restrict theological knowledge, but with no sustained argument as to why the restriction proposed secures a liberative theology. Kee's final chapter is called 'Religion in the Next Epoch'. Whether there will be religion in the next epoch (whatever this is and whenever it comes), I have no idea. If the argument from Tillich rehearsed in chapter 1 is sound, it seems that there will be tendencies for human beings in times of crisis or uncertainty to appeal to religion.

But I think it is possible for there to be *theology* in the next epoch. It must travel by the narrowest of ways, the Marxist critique of ideology, but then perhaps we are familiar with the dangers of the broad way. And adherence to the narrow way in the forms of protocols and theological proposals suggested above may allow Christians to have some confidence in their theological insights into social forms. In other words, Christianity does have the resources to engage with social matters: it is not necessarily a false intermediary. Insistence on God's 'openness' to the world, an affirmation of social praxis, and an interpretation of society in trinitarian perspective does perhaps allow the Christian theologian to approach the issue of the trustworthiness (or otherwise) of social forms.

If some of what I have argued is persuasive, then perhaps, if theology adhered to the 'shape' of a systematic theology that is implicit in these pages, it might be possible to move to a more 'positive' account of a liberative theology. I hope to have hinted at the shape of some of the issues that would feature in such a book.

I am not claiming that Christianity has a great many insights into forms of social organisation. Nor am I suggesting that there is some being called 'God', whom we may objectify, and thereby learn much from concerning a range of issues (including social matters). Nor am I suggesting that the primary reference of Christianity is to its own pedagogy in which persons are referred to their own forms of life in order to establish, in practice, what it is to be human. I am concerned with none of the above – although the motif of conversion is important to my argument (and I have taken it from the argument regarding Christian pedagogy).

Rather, I am suggesting that Christian practices are not concerned – necessarily at least – with false mediation; Christianity does not necessarily function as ideology and thereby deny Christians clear 'vision'. Rather, the God who is the source of all things, who is distinct from the world, and who cannot be identified with any part of the world (not even Jesus because the dead do not speak) and who is 'available' to the world in a decentred discourse, is the 'cause' of the call to conversion. Acknowledgment (in grace) that 'all that is' depends upon God is the central claim here. And the enactment of this acknowledgement is not narrowly a spiritual or a theoretical matter. Conversion, I repeat, is a practical matter with material dimensions.

Christianity is thereby not concerned with turning any part of the world into a possession, with the baptism of any part of the world (and certainly not with the attempt to possess the 'nature' of God through Jesus). Christianity is the invitation of a graceful God to human beings to assess what is really important, what is true and trustworthy. (And we may well be presented with the insistence to decide what is important and what will secure forms of relation against forms of irrelation through attention to and participation in the practices of the emergent, which may presage the surpassment of this present into truer, richer forms of social life.) Conversion is above all a question: given that this is from God, how shall we live? Given that we seek to cling to things that are untrue and untrustworthy, we lapse into idolatry. That it is our Christian practices that disable us from seeing this as idolatry is precisely the Christian contribution to ideology.

The motif of conversion needs to be secured in a trinitarian account of God's grace. (Such an expression might stand as the description of the argument of part III.) It is not that accounts of personhood are secured by reference to the 'three person'd God'. It is rather that we are invited into the practice(s) of conversion, of turning away from forms of the idolatry of the social, through God's engagement with us. God's trinitarian engagement takes the form of relations of freedom or, in Rowan Williams' words, 'creative liberty' in which we are invited to participate *afresh*: a participation in this liberty, and an enactment of this liberty through the sharing of it. (I say 'afresh' because of course as creatures we already participate in these relations of freedom through our 'created sociality'.)

We participate in God's freedom through our constitution as social beings – the ordering work of the Logos in creation. We are invited to participate in and invite others to participate in this liberty through the reordering of our sociality through the

Word in the Spirit. Thus we acknowledge that the eschatological goal of even the forms of our social being is the glorious and unsurpassable creative liberty of the Creator. We do not know this for ourselves. Yet we may learn it through attention to the act of God's self-identification in the cross and resurrection of Jesus Christ. We participate in God's freedom through our social freedom (or not, in the case of forms of social unfreedom). And we acknowledge this fact, and the redirection of these forms to the Creator in the life, death and resurrection of Jesus Christ.

I am not persuaded that this tells us much about our social relations. Or, if it does, it will only be at the end of an extensive sociological enquiry. (This is part of the agenda that is set by my argument.) But it does tell us that Christianity is not necessarily a false intermediary. Theology is centrally concerned with the articulation of an understanding of God whose being is social, who relates to human beings through the contingencies of social forms and social freedom, whose presence in creation is the call to conversion and whose presence in redemption is toward more creative forms of human life. The self-presentation of the Christian God is the denial of human attempts to be gods, and is thereby the election of human beings into their freedom to be creatures. That is, to seek to work out, theoretically and practically, a properly human form of what the 'being-with' given in work, embodiment and language might be.

Could the triune God be more involved with human beings as social, and yet more respectful of human freedom? And is not the rest the practice of freedom?

References

Adams, James L. (1985) 'The Storms of Our Times and *Starry Night*' in *The Thought of Paul Tillich*, ed. J. L. Adams, W. Pauck and R. L. Shinn, San Francisco: Harper and Row, pp. 1–28

Adams, William (1991) 'Aesthetics: Liberating the Senses' in *Marx*, ed. T. Carver, Cambridge: Cambridge University Press, pp. 246–74

Adorno, Theodor and Horkheimer, Max (1979) *Dialectic of Enlightenment*, London: Verso

Alison, James (1993) *Knowing Jesus*, London: SPCK

Althusser, Louis (1979) *For Marx*, London: Verso
(1984) *Essays on Ideology*, London: Verso

Althusser, L. and Balibar, E. (1979) *Reading Capital*, London: Verso

Alves, Rubem (1975) *A Theology of Human Hope*, Wheathamstead: Anthony Clarke

Aronson, Ronald (1977) 'The Individualist Social Theory of Jean-Paul Sartre', in *Western Marxism: A Critical Reader*, ed. New Left Review, London: New Left Books, pp. 201–31

Assmann, Hugo (1975) *A Practical Theology of Liberation*, London: Search Press

Ball, Terence (1991) 'History: Critique and Irony', in *Marx*, ed. T. Carver, Cambridge: Cambridge University Press, pp. 124–42

Best, Steven and Kellner, Douglas (1991) *Postmodern Theory: Critical Interrogations*, Houndmills: Macmillan

Bhaskar, Roy (1979) *The Possibility of Naturalism*, Brighton: Harvester
(1989) *Reclaiming Reality: A Critical Introduction to Contemporary Philosophy*, London: Verso

Boff, Clodovis (1987) *Theology and Praxis: Epistemological Foundations*, Maryknoll, NY: Orbis

Boff, Leonardo (1980) *Jesus Christ Liberator: A Critical Christology of our Time*, London: SPCK
(1988) *Trinity and Society*, London: Burns and Oates

Bottomore, Tom (ed.) (1988) *Interpretations of Marx*, Oxford: Basil Blackwell

Browning, Don S. and Fiorenza, Francis F. (eds.) (1992) *Habermas, Modernity and Public Theology*, New York: Crossroad

Buber, Martin (1957) *The Eclipse of God*, New York: Harper Torchbooks

Burrell, David (1986) *Knowing the Unknowable God*, Notre Dame: University of Notre Dame Press

(1987) 'Distinguishing God from the World' in *Language, Meaning and God*, ed. B. Davies, London: Geoffrey Chapman, pp. 75–91

Callinicos, Alex (1985) *Marxism and Philosophy*, Oxford: Oxford University Press

Carr, Anne E. (1988) *Transforming Grace: Christian Tradition and Women's Experience*, San Francisco: Harper and Row

Carver, Terrell (1982) *Marx's Social Theory*, Oxford: Oxford University Press

Chopp, Rebecca (1987) 'Feminism's Theological Pragmatics: A Social Naturalism of Women's Experience', *Journal of Religion*, 67, pp. 239–56

(1989) *The Power to Speak: Language, Feminism, God*, New York: Crossroad

Christ, Carol and Plaskow, Judith (eds.) (1979) *Womanspirit Rising: A Feminist Reader in Religion*, San Francisco: Harper and Row

Cohen, G. A. (1978) *Karl Marx's Theory of History: A Defence*, Oxford: Clarendon Press

Copleston, Frederick (1955) *Aquinas*, London: Penguin

Dalferth, Ingolf (1989) 'Karl Barth's Eschatological Realism', in *Karl Barth: Centenary Essays*, ed. S. W. Sykes, Cambridge: Cambridge University Press, pp. 24–45

Davies, Brian (1987) 'The Doctrine of Divine Simplicity' in *Language, Meaning and God*, ed. B. Davies, London: Geoffrey Chapman, pp. 51–74

Davis, Charles (1980) *Theology and Political Society*, Cambridge: Cambridge University Press

Deleuze, Gilles and Guattari, Félix (1984) *Anti-Oedipus. Capitalism and Schizophrenia*, London: Athlone Press

Dowling, William (1984) *Jameson, Althusser, Marx: An Introduction to the Political Unconscious*, London: Methuen

Dussel, Enrique (1985) *Philosophy of Liberation*, Maryknoll, New York: Orbis

Eagleton, Terry (1970) *The Body as Language: Outline of a 'New Left' Theology*, London: Sheed and Ward

(1978) *Criticism and Ideology: A Study in Marxist Literary Theory*, London: Verso

(1991) *Ideology: An Introduction*, London: Verso

Edgley, Roy (1983) 'Philosophy' in *Marx: the First 100 Years*, ed. D. McLellan, London: Fontana

Fiddes, Paul S. (1988) *The Creative Suffering of God*, Oxford: Clarendon Press

(1989) *Past Event and Present Salvation: The Christian Idea of Atonement*, London: Darton, Longman and Todd

Fleischer, Helmut (1973) *Marxism and History*, London: Allen Lane

Frei, Hans (1992) *Types of Christian Theology*, London and New Haven: Yale University Press

Geras, Norman (1990) 'Marxism and Moral Advocacy', in *Socialism and Morality*, ed. D. McLellan and S. Sayers, London: Macmillan, pp. 5–20

Geuss, Raymond (1981) *The Idea of a Critical Theory*, Cambridge: Cambridge University Press

Gottwald, Norman (ed.) (1983) *The Bible and Liberation. Political and Social Hermeneutics*, Maryknoll, NY: Orbis

Grey, Mary (1989) *Redeeming the Dream*, London: SPCK

Gunton, Colin (1988) *The Actuality of Atonement*, Edinburgh: T. and T. Clark

(1989) 'The Church on Earth: The Roots of Community' in *On Being the Church*, ed. C. Gunton and D. W. Hardy, Edinburgh: T. and T. Clark, pp. 48–80

(1991a) *The Promise of Trinitarian Theology*, Edinburgh: T. and T. Clark

(1991b) 'The Spirit in the Trinity' in *The Forgotten Trinity*, ed. A. Heron, III, London: BCC/CCBI, pp. 123–35

Gutiérrez, Gustavo (1974) *A Theology of Liberation*, London: SCM Press

(1983) *The Power of the Poor in History*, London: SCM Press

Habermas, Jürgen (1983) *Philosophical-Political Profiles*, London: Heinemann

(1987) *Toward a Rational Society*, Cambridge: Polity

Hall, Stuart (1981) 'Cultural Studies: Two Paradigms', in *Culture, Ideology and Social Process*, ed. Tony Bennett *et al.*, Open University, pp. 19–37

Hampson, Daphne (1990) *Theology and Feminism*, Oxford: Blackwell

Hardy, Daniel W. (1989) 'Created and Redeemed Sociality' in *On Being the Church*, ed. C. Gunton and D. W. Hardy, Edinburgh: T. and T. Clark, pp. 21–47

Hardy, Daniel and Ford, David (1984) *Jubilate: Theology in Praise*, London: Darton, Longman and Todd

Harvey, David (1984 pbk edn) *The Limits to Capital*, Oxford: Basil Blackwell

(1989) *The Condition of Postmodernity*, Oxford: Basil Blackwell

Heyward, Carter (1982) *The Redemption of God. A Theology of Mutual Relation*, Lanham, MD: University Press of America

Jameson, Fredric (1989) *The Political Unconscious. Narrative as a Socially Symbolic Act*, London: Routledge (orig. 1981)

(1991) *Postmodernism, or the Cultural Logic of Late Capitalism*, London: Verso

Jenson, Robert W. (1989) 'The Christian Doctrine of God' in *Keeping the Faith*, ed. G. Wainwright, London: SPCK, pp. 25–53

Jones, Gregory L. (1990) 'Living in Holy Insecurity: Nicholas Lash's *Easter in Ordinary*', *Modern Theology*, 6: 4, pp. 385–404

Kee, Alistair (1990) *Marx and the Failure of Liberation Theology*, London: SCM Press/Trinity Press International

Kolakowski, Leszek (1978) *Main Currents of Marxism*, Volume 1 *The Founders*, Oxford: Oxford University Press

LaCugna, Catherine M. (1991) *God For Us. The Trinity and Christian Life*, New York: HarperCollins

Larrain, Jorge (1983) *Marxism and Ideology*, London: Macmillan

(1986) *A Reconstruction of Historical Materialism*, London: Allen and Unwin

Lash, Nicholas (1981) *A Matter of Hope. A Theologian's Reflections on the Thought of Karl Marx*, London: Darton, Longman and Todd

(1986a) *Theology on the Way to Emmaus*, London: SCM Press

(1986b) 'Considering the Trinity', *Modern Theology*, 2: 3, pp. 183–96

(1988) *Easter in Ordinary: Reflections on Human Experience and Knowledge of God*, London: SCM Press

Lull, Timothy (ed.) (1989) *Martin Luther's Basic Theological Writings*, Minneapolis: Fortress Press

McCabe, Herbert (1987) *God Matters*, London: Geoffrey Chapman

McCarthy, Thomas (1991) *Ideals and Illusions: On Reconstruction and Deconstruction in Contemporary Social Theory*, Cambridge, MA: MIT Press

McFague, Sallie (1987) *Models of God: Theology for an Ecological, Nuclear Age*, London: SCM Press

MacIntyre, Alisdair (1968) *Marxism and Christianity*, London: Duckworth

Mackey, James (1983) *The Christian Experience of God as Trinity*, London: SCM Press

McLellan, David (1986) *Ideology*, London: Macmillan

(1987) *Marxism and Religion*, Basingstoke: Macmillan

McLellan, David (ed.) (1983) *Marx: the First 100 Years*, London: Fontana

Marshall, Brian (1992) 'New Departures in Systematic Theology: The Doctrine of the Trinity and Social, Political and Economic Questions', unpublished paper, 22 folios

Marx, Karl (1954) *Capital*, I, London: Lawrence and Wishart

(1959) *Capital*, III, London: Lawrence and Wishart

(1973) *Grundrisse*, Harmondsworth: Penguin

(1974) *The First International and After*, Harmondsworth: Penguin

(1975) *Early Writings*, Harmondsworth: Penguin

(1977) *Karl Marx: Selected Writings*, ed. D. McLellan, Oxford: Oxford University Press

(1990) 'Value, Price and Profit' in *The Essential Left*, ed. D. McLellan, Boston: Unwin Hyman, pp. 51–105

Marx, Karl and Engels, F. (1974) *The German Ideology*, London: Lawrence and Wishart, 2nd edn

(1975) *On Religion*, Moscow: Progress Publishers

Meeks, M. Douglas (1989) *God the Economist*, Minneapolis: Fortress

Mepham, John (1972) 'The Theory of Ideology in *Capital*', *Radical Philosophy*, no. 2, Summer, pp. 12–19

Mészáros, Istvan (1979) *Marx's Theory of Alienation*, London: Merlin Press

Metz, Johann Baptist (1980) *Faith in History and Society: Toward a Practical Fundamental Theology*, London: Burns and Oates

Míguez Bonino, José (1975) *Doing Theology in a Revolutionary Situation*, Philadelphia: Fortress Press

(1983) *Towards a Christian Political Ethics*, London: SCM Press

Milbank, John (1986) 'The Second Difference. For a Trinitarianism Without Reserve', *Modern Theology*, 2: 3, pp. 213–34

Moltmann, Jürgen (1967) *Theology of Hope*, London: SCM Press

(1974) *The Crucified God*, London: SCM Press

(1981) *The Trinity and the Kingdom of God*, London: SCM Press

(1984) *Humanity in God*, London: SCM Press

(1988) *Theology Today*, London: SCM Press

(1989) *Creating a Just Future*, London: SCM and Trinity Press International

(1990) *The Way of Jesus Christ*, London: SCM Press

Page, Ruth (1991) *The Incarnation of Freedom and Love*, London: SPCK

Pannenberg, Wolfhart (1991) *An Introduction to Systematic Theology*, Edinburgh: T. and T. Clark

Peukert, Helmut (1986 pbk edn) *Science, Action and Fundamental Theology: Toward a Theology of Communicative Action*, Cambridge, MA: MIT Press (orig. edn 1984)

Plaskow, Judith (1980) *Sex, Sin and Grace: Women's Experience and the*

Theologies of Reinhold Niebuhr and Paul Tillich, Washington, DC: University Press of America

Ruether, R. R. (1981) *To Change the World: Christology and Cultural Criticism*, London: SCM Press

(1983) *Sexism and God-Talk. Toward a Feminist Theology*, London: SCM Press

Sartre, Jean-Paul (1968) *Search for a Method*, New York: Vintage Books

Scott, Peter (1993) 'Theology after Gorbachev?', *Theology*, March/April, pp. 117–27

(1994) 'Prophetic Expectation', *Theology*, (forthcoming)

Segundo, Juan Luis (1976) *The Liberation of Theology*, New York: Orbis

(1980) 'Capitalism versus Socialism: Crux Theologica' in *Frontiers of Theology in Latin America*, ed. Rosino Gibellini, London: SCM Press, pp. 240–59

(1984) *Faith and Ideologies*, London: Sheed and Ward

Smart, Ninian *et al.* (eds.) (1988 pbk edn) *Nineteenth Century Religious Thought*, I, Cambridge: Cambridge University Press (orig. edn 1985)

Sobrino, Jon (1978) *Christology at the Crossroads*, London: SCM Press

Steiner, George (1991 pbk edn) *Real Presences*, London: Faber (orig. edn 1989)

Surin, Kenneth (1989) 'Process Theology' in *The Modern Theologians*, ed. D. F. Ford, Oxford: Blackwell, pp. 103–14

Thistlethwaite, Susan (1989) *Sex, Race and God. Christian Feminism in Black and White*, London: Geoffrey Chapman

Thompson, John B. (1984) *Studies in the Theory of Ideology*, Cambridge: Cambridge University Press

(1990) *Ideology and Modern Culture*, Cambridge: Polity

Tillich, Paul (1977) *The Socialist Decision*, New York: Harper and Row

(1978) *Systematic Theology*, II, London: SCM Press

Timpanaro, Sebastiano (1980) *On Materialism*, London: Verso

Turner, Denys (1983) *Marxism and Christianity*, Oxford: Basil Blackwell

(1984) 'Marx, Matter and Christianity: Turner Responds to Lash', *New Blackfriars*, 65: 764, pp. 69–77

(1986) 'De-centring Theology', *Modern Theology*, 2: 2, pp. 125–43

(1987) 'Feuerbach, Marx and Reductivism', in *Language, Meaning and God*, ed. B. Davies, London: Geoffrey Chapman, pp. 92–103

Weedon, Chris (1987) *Feminist Practice and Poststructuralist Theory*, Oxford: Blackwell

White, Vernon (1991) *Atonement and Incarnation*, Cambridge: Cambridge University Press

Williams, Raymond (1977 pbk edn) *Marxism and Literature*, Oxford: Oxford University Press

(1980) *Problems in Materialism and Culture*, London: Verso

(1981) *Culture*, London: Fontana

(1983) 'Culture' in *Marx: the First 100 Years*, ed. D. McLellan, London: Fontana, pp. 15–55

(1985) *The Country and the City*, London: Hogarth Press

(1989a) *The Politics of Modernism: Against the New Conformists*, London: Verso

(1989b) *Resources of Hope*, London: Verso

Williams, Rowan (1986) 'Trinity and Revelation', *Modern Theology*, 2: 3, pp. 195–212

Young, Frances and Ford, David F. (1987) *Meaning and Truth in Two Corinthians*, London: SPCK

Young, Pamela Dickey (1990) *Feminist Theology/Christian Theology: In Search of Method*, Minneapolis: Fortress

Index

CAMBRIDGE STUDIES IN IDEOLOGY AND RELIGION

Books in the series

A Theology of Reconstruction: Nation-Building
and Human Rights
CHARLES VILLA-VICENCIO

Christianity and Politics in Doe's Liberia
PAUL GIFFORD

Protestantism in Contemporary China
ALAN HUNTER AND KIM-KWONG CHAN

Politics, Theology, and History
RAYMOND PLANT

Christianity and Democracy: A Theology for a Just World Order
JOHN W. DE GRUCHY

Pastoral Care and Liberation Theology
STEPHEN PATTISON

Religion and the Making of Society: Essays in Social Theology
CHARLES DAVIS

Theology, Ideology and Liberation: Towards a Liberative Theology
PETER SCOTT